Women, Social Science and Public Policy

edited by

JACQUELINE GOODNOW
&
CAROLE PATEMAN

for the
Academy of the Social Sciences in Australia

Sydney
George Allen & Unwin
London Boston

First published in 1985
George Allen & Unwin Australia Pty Ltd
8 Napier Street, North Sydney, NSW 2060, Australia

George Allen & Unwin (Publishers) Ltd
Park Lane, Hemel Hempstead, Herts HP2 4TE, England

Allen & Unwin Inc.
Fifty Cross Street, Winchester, Mass 01890, USA

National Library of Australia
Cataloguing in Publication entry:

Women, social science and public policy.

  ISBN 0 86861 693 1.
  ISBN 0 86861 685 0 (pbk.).

  1. Women—Addresses, essays, lectures.
  I. Goodnow, Jacqueline, 1924– . II. Pateman,
  Carole. III. Academy of the Social Sciences
  in Australia.

305.4

Typeset in Times by Asco Trade Typesetting Limited, Hong Kong
Printed by Bright Sun (Shenzhen) Printing Co. Ltd., China

Contents

Preface

This book grew out of a symposium held in 1983 by the Academy of Social Sciences in Australia on the topic 'Women and the Social Sciences: New Modes of Thought'. The Academy presents an annual lecture and symposium in Canberra each year, usually on unrelated topics; in 1983, the annual lecture, delivered by Jacqueline Goodnow, opened the way for the papers and discussion in the day-long symposium. All the contributors were speakers at the symposium.

The Academy took an interest in the social position of women before it became fashionable (even though, as in other similar bodies, the Fellows of the Academy are almost all men). In 1958, the Academy—then the Social Science Research Council of Australia—sponsored a research project under Norman MacKenzie on women's role in Australian society, and *Women in Australia* was published in 1962. In 1974, a second edition appeared, entitled *Women and Society: an Australian Study* by Sol Encel, Norman MacKenzie and Margaret Tebbutt. It was written, as Sol Encel notes in the preface, in the context of the revived organised feminist movement.

By 1983 the impact of feminist arguments, questions and challenges had been felt in most areas of academic life, especially in the disciplines of the social sciences, which are concerned with social relationships and institutions. A large body of empirical research and critical literature was also available by them on the general social position of women, so the symposium was directed toward the wide-ranging character and intellectual significance of the new scholarship, and toward some of its implications for social policy.

The papers that make up this book are designed to cover a range of disciplines in social science and a variety of policy issues. The first four are concerned with revisionist analyses of social science, and two of these cut across disciplines. In her Introduction, Carole Pateman points to the need to reopen such central questions as the relationship between nature and society and the concept of the 'individual'. Jacqueline Goodnow provides a review—in areas ranging from psychology and economics to music and history—of challenges to the way in which social scientists choose certain topics as 'significant', certain methods as 'proper' and certain interpretations as 'logical'. The next two papers raise questions of interpretation, method and underlying assumptions in specific fields. Patricia Grimshaw's central concern is with history, Fay Gale's with anthropology and human geography. Both document the invisibility of women in the historical and natural landscape, and explore the impact on their disciplines of assumptions about women's lesser status.

The next set of papers concentrates on the analysis of public policy, although all the discussions are informed by the new scholarship in social science. Bettina Cass and Meredith Edwards are both concerned with the broad field of economics. The former emphasises the effects of particular assumptions about the nature of work, the latter the effects of assumptions about families and the distribution of income. In the final two papers, Hester Eisenstein and Jocelynne Scutt examine recent legislative attempts to promote equality and ask how far assumptions built into the law and into the nature of the state impede the use of legislation as a vehicle for reform.

The order of editors was decided by the toss of a coin. The last stages of the work were completed while the editors were Fellows at the Stanford Center for Advanced Study in the Behavioral Sciences, and the help of the Spencer Foundation and the National Endowment of the Humanities is gratefully acknowledged.

List of Authors

Bettina Cass (Sociology)
   Department of Social Work, University of Sydney.

Meredith Edwards (Economics)
   Department of Employment and Youth Affairs, Canberra;
   Canberra College of Advanced Education.

Hester Eisenstein (Sociology)
   Office of Equal Opportunity, Premiers Department, N.S.W.

Fay Gale (Human Geography)
   Department of Geography, University of Adelaide.

Jacqueline Goodnow (Psychology)
   School of Behavioural Sciences, Macquarie University.

Patricia Grimshaw (History)
   Department of History, University of Melbourne.

Carole Pateman (Political Science)
   Department of Government, University of Sydney.

Jocelynne A. Scutt (Law)
   Law Reform Commission Victoria, Melbourne.

Introduction

CAROLE PATEMAN

Social science has always been a controversial field. Theoretical approaches and empirical methods have been the subject of heated and continuous debate, and charges and counter-charges about the propagation of ideology rather than the pursuit of objective research and science, and claims about conservative or critical theory, are all too familiar. Recently, however, the well-worn arguments and the broad terrain of social science itself have been put into a very different perspective by the rapidly growing body of new feminist scholarship. Not only does the new research open up long-neglected areas of inquiry but, much more importantly, the parties to many of the old controversies now begin to appear as allies on some crucial matters, and fundamental challenges are being posed to the assumptions and concepts in which social science is grounded.

For the past decade, evidence accumulating shows that the study of the 'social' has been a peculiar endeavour that has largely focused on the ideas and activities of only half the actors who constitute the social realm. This evidence is presented in Jacqueline Goodnow's remarkably wide-ranging examination of the way in which women have been ignored by social scientists, and of the efforts now being made to remedy the neglect and to discover what the inclusion of women will entail for the disciplines of social science. The latter question lies at the heart of the problem of women, feminism and social science. Can women's lives, experience and relationship to men be brought into the centre of the present framework of social science? Or is a radical restructuring of this area of intellectual life required for an adequate study of all our social interactions?

In earlier times, feminists tended to see the development of social science as an aid to women's emancipation. Some social scientists, in the manner of present-day sociobiologists, turned to alleged biological facts to confirm that the social subordination of women was

inevitable, but scientific, objective social inquiry was seen as part
of the general movement away from what John Stuart Mill[1] called
'the old world of thought and practice', the old world of hierarchy
and supposedly natural subjection, towards freedom and equality
for all individuals. The contemporary position is rather different.
The new feminist scholarship has shown that what is at issue goes far
beyond a sin of omission that can be remedied in a straightforward
way by now paying due attention to women and women's social
position; the objective and scientific status of the social sciences is
thrown into doubt.

The conclusion drawn by feminist social scientists is that the scope
and subject matter of social science have been constructed through
the exclusion of women and familial relations. The patriarchal construction of social science means that the study of women's lives and
the relationship between the sexes cannot be placed on an equal footing with the present objects of inquiry merely by adding women to
the existing conceptual framework; nor is it enough (to use the popular phrase cited by Goodnow) to 'add women and stir'. To do so is to
attempt to incorporate matters into social science that give meaning
to the 'social' through their very exclusion. To many people, including social scientists, this may seem an exaggerated claim. Surely, it
will be argued, with the requisite willingness to make the appropriate
revisions, women and feminist research can be accommodated and a
new dimension added to social science. The crucial point here is that
such a Whiggish view of intellectual development presupposes that
the concept of the social is unproblematic. That is, the object of
investigation in social science—the social or society—remains unquestioned. But it is precisely the concept of the 'social' itself that the
new scholarship on women is challenging.

In its modern sense, and social science is a specifically modern
discipline, society is seen as a sphere that is *sui generis*. The modern
concept of the social is of a realm divorced from Divine will; and,
most importantly for the present argument, the social is also separated from the natural ties of kinship, or, more narrowly, from natural familial or sexual bonds. Natural or ascriptive bonds stand in
contrast to the conventional relationships of society. The social, the
public world, gains its meaning from what is excluded from it, from
that with which it is contrasted and to which it is opposed.

These remarks may seem commonplace enough, but what has
gone unnoticed until recently is that understanding the social in this
way, and, hence our also understanding of the object of study in social science, excludes women, and the activities and sphere seen as
naturally theirs, from the scope of scientific inquiry. Recent feminist
work in my own field of political theory is particularly important in
the task of disentangling the complex ramifications of the patriarchal

character of social science. The question that must be asked is: Who inhabits the social world? The obvious answer is that individuals interact in and participate in society, which suggests that both women and men are present in the same fashion. The 'individual', we all learn, is everyone and anyone; it is a universal or sexually neutral category. However, one of the most far-reaching and exciting discoveries of the new scholarship in political theory is that the 'individual' is masculine.

The emergence of the 'social' is part of complex theoretical and historical developments in which the traditional view of a hierarchy of natural inequality and subordination was replaced by the assumption that individuals were born, or were naturally, free and equal to each other. Social and political theory textbooks are written as if there is no doubt that this new 'individual' can be of either sex. But a careful reading of the classic texts shows that, from the outset, women were excluded from the status of 'individual'. John Locke is a key theoretical figure, both in the development of the 'social' and in the seventeenth-century battle over the question whether men were born free or in subjection. Locke's defence of natural freedom was victorious—but most of his commentators fail to notice that the victory was for men alone. Locke's separation of 'paternal' power (the power exercised in the household) from other forms of power was crucial in formulating the concept of a society divorced from kinship, but the separation was equally important for the modern subordination of women. Despite his individualism, Locke agreed with his patriarchalist opponent Sir Robert Filmer that women remained naturally subject to men. In agreement with Filmer, he states that a wife's subjection to her husband has 'a Foundation in Nature'.[2] One cannot be both naturally subject and naturally free; women were therefore held to lack the attributes of the 'individual'. But it was 'individuals' who had the capacities that enabled them to take their place, as civil equals, in 'society', the sphere of universalism, rights, property and contract. The social or public realm was divided from the household, the private sphere where natural inequality held sway, and women were thus also divided from men and placed in subordination to them.[3]

The patriarchal character of the conception of the 'social' and its construction as a masculine realm has rarely been acknowledged. The eyes of social scientists are so firmly fixed on the public world that its division from, yet integral relation to, the private domestic sphere is 'forgotten'. This means that some fundamental problems in social science are glossed over, including the uncertain status of the family as a social or natural association. There is also, both in theory and in policymaking, as the following chapters indicate, a similar uncertainty whether the family or the individual is the 'basic unit' of society. Natural subordinates are subsumed, for social purposes, into the person of the naturally free individual who owns property, protects his interests, makes contracts, follows the career open to his talents and exercises citizenship. 'Individuals' go into society, but the individuals in question are men who, as heads of households, 'represent' women, or their wife and their children, in the social world. None of these problems can be resolved while the assumptions and concepts on which social science is grounded continue to treat the 'individual' as a universal category while simultaneously taking for granted the separation of the private and the public (that is, the sexes) and women's subordination to men. Three centuries after Locke's 'victory' over the doctrine of natural subjection, now that women have almost won the fight for formal, civil recognition as individuals, the full implications of the victory are becoming apparent. The granting of almost equal civil status with men has served to highlight the beliefs and practices implied in women's social subordination and to reveal the separation of the private and the social as a political problem.

The discussion in this volume graphically illustrates how women's subordination to men and their uncertain position as 'individuals' are reflected in the work of social scientists and the deliberations of social policymakers. For example, the 'individual' is a property owner and the being who, from the perspective of geographers, inhabits and transforms the landscape. Fay Gale shows how the association of men with property is so deeply entrenched that it has been virtually impossible for white politicians, bureaucrats and lawyers to see Aboriginal women as landowners. To be sure, the doctrine of *terra nullius* denied male Aborigines the status of property owners, but all men, even the conquered, have the potential to be admitted into the category of 'individual'. The result is that consultation over land rights and sacred sites has been conducted only with Aboriginal men.

Geographers are concerned with the urban as well as the natural landscape. They have paid a good deal of attention to urban transport and journeys to work—and the question of work is a theme that runs throughout the book. Nor is this surprising, for work is another category that lies at the heart of the problem of women and social science. Once again this familiar term, seemingly so transparent in its meaning, hides as much as it reveals. The 'individual' is not only a property owner but a worker; workers, too, are masculine. Work is another activity located in the social realm, outside the domestic, private sphere. A worker 'goes out' to work. Our cities and transport systems, as Gale discusses, are built on the tacit understanding that only men travel to work, leaving their wives and children behind them. This understanding of work also helped reinforce the division between the social realm of men and women. Men, as husbands and fathers, became breadwinners for their wives and families, and women were seen as their economic dependants.

Bettina Cass shows how this conception of marital and familial relations developed in Australia from the latter part of the nineteenth century and became enshrined in official social policy and the bargaining of the trade union movement for a family wage. The idea that the wage was paid not to the worker as an individual for work performed, but to the head of a family, meant that wages to other participants in the paid workforce—such as women who had to work to support their families—were rarely sufficient to live on. It may be supposed that all this lies in the past; women are now seen as workers in the same sense as men and, now that minimum wage rates apply to both sexes and we have equal pay legislation, the wage has finally become an individual not a family wage. However, because of the sexually segregated character of employment and the conviction that women's primary task is (unpaid) child rearing, not 'work', women are still usually found in the low-paid and part-time sectors of the labour market. Recent feminist research also reveals that the attitudes and practices of the workplace reflect and consolidate wider relationships of power and subordination between the sexes,[4] and that women's status as a 'worker' and 'individual' is still precarious.

Moreover, as Cass documents, the assumption that women are economically dependent on men has been incorporated into the tax system and payment of social benefits. We may no longer use the language of Locke, but women are still seen as the 'natural' dependants of socially independent individuals. One consequence of this perception is that women are much more likely than men to be poor, especially if they have to support themselves and their children. Yet even if a woman is also a wife, it does not necessarily follow that her standard of living is a high as her husband's. Economists and other social scientists usually take for granted that the resources of the breadwinner are equitably distributed to dependants but, as Meredith Edwards emphasises, we know very little about the actual distribution of income within households, and the comfortable assumption that breadwinners are benevolent may well be unrealistic. As long ago as 1825 William Thompson,[5] a co-operative socialist who took individualism seriously, insisted that the interests of wives and children could be protected only if they were regarded as individual interests and not subsumed under the interests of the head of the family. This argument did not, however, impress economists or policymakers. Edwards concludes that inequity between the sexes will continue until the individual, not the family, becomes the unit for the tax and transfer systems. However, this would imply that women have a secure status as individuals, which in turn, would mean the transformation of the patriarchal structure of the family.

The problems raised for social science by the patriarchal concepts of work and the worker extend much further than the field of economics or wage and social welfare policies. The most heated controversies in social science have usually involved marxist and other writers on the left, but they, too, are now targets of feminist criticism. In history, for example, the emergence of social and labour history is conventionally taken as the radical alternative to the familiar history of kings, generals and parliament. But Patricia Grimshaw shows that this history is also men's history. Whether conservative or radical, history is assumed to be made in the public, social world, and the radical historians have explored and portrayed the lives of common men as workers, unionists and political activists in complete isolation from their position as husbands, fathers or lovers, which is assumed to be irrelevant to their public activities.

It is also worth remarking that in Australia, the treatment of the developing sense of national identity, with its myths of mateship in the bush, Anzac and Gallipoli and, more recently, the triumph of a yacht sailed by men, could not be more overtly masculine. To bring women's part in making history into the concept of 'history' will transform radical history, perhaps even more than the more conservative *genres*, because the former rely heavily on the concept of class. Whether in its strict marxist sense or used more loosely, 'class' depends on a view of the worker and occupational classifications that presupposes the sexual division between the private and public spheres.

It has been claimed that Marx's categories are 'sex blind'[6] so that feminism could be used to supplement and complement Marx's insights by scholars in a variety of disciplines. However, this is far too generous a view. Marx's theory, like the liberal theories he criticised, is ostensibly universal but actually patriarchal, embodying sexual domination rather than being blind to it. Marxist and other social scientists investigating the class structure have, when they have considered women at all, almost always assumed that women occupy the class position of their husbands, that they can be subsumed within class as indicated by their marriage to a 'worker' or bourgeois 'breadwinner'. In contrast, feminist scholars have shown how difficult it is to fit women within the conventional class categories if we are granted an independent identity.

If class is less relevant to women than men, then analyses of the class character of the state by radical social scientists will also be of limited use in understanding the position of women. The problem of the state and the law is addressed by Hester Eisenstein and Jocelynne Scutt, who examine recent legislative attempts to obtain some measure of social equality for women. For over a century women have fought against discriminatory laws and attempted to change and use the law to realise the liberal democratic promise of equality of citizenship and equality of opportunity. The federal Sex Discrimination Act now stands as a symbol of these struggles—but is it more than a symbol? Contemporary feminists, too, have argued that the law, like other aspects of public life, is patriarchal. A writer quoted by Eisenstein states firmly that 'the state is male', which hardly suggests that women's position will be greatly altered through legal processes. Eisenstein, however, sees this as too simple a view and is fairly optimistic that affirmative action, at least, offers a real possibility of change. Jocelynne Scutt is less hopeful. She argues that in certain respects recent reforms have undermined the protection against violence already available under both common law and the criminal law. By making it appear that equality has been already achieved, legal reform may make action more difficult, not easier, for women.

The legislative changes of the past decade all extend the formal recognition of women as individuals, but although the problem of women's social subordination to men has now been brought into public discussion, the fundamental character of the challenge it poses, both theoretically and practically, is not always acknowledged. In social science the concepts of both the individual and the social—and the relationship that properly should exist between them—are now placed in question. One problem that must be confronted, therefore, is whether the masculine category of the 'individual' can ever include both sexes, or whether a radically revised understanding of what it means to be an individual is required. Again, the inclusion of women within history, within the landscape, at work and within the state on an equal footing alongside men, breaks down the very separation between the familial and domestic spheres and the social world on which academic social science is founded. Thus a reconceptualisation of the social is also required, and these are no small tasks. The most profound and complex problem of all that must be addressed is the significance of sexual difference in social life. Can social science and our institutions and policies give due weight to sexual difference and also provide for civil equality and full membership in social life for both men and women?

Contemporary social scientists have not recognised the relevance and importance of these questions. The great social scientists of the past struggled with them and, almost to a man, they arrived at patriarchal conclusions. If the patriarchal assumptions and arguments are not to continue to direct our theories and our research and the pretence that the categories of social science are universal is to be abandoned, the fundamental problems must be taken up once again. The relationship between nature and society, between individuality, equality and difference, between the particular and the universal, and how these engage with the distinctiveness of and commonality among women and men, must return to the centre of social scientific inquiry. Some very hard work must be done to restructure the theoretical basis of social science if it is to become the study, by women and men, of the whole of human social life.

1 Topics, Methods and Models: Feminist Challenges in Social Science[1]

JACQUELINE GOODNOW

Few people can now be unaware of changes in the amount of attention given to the position of women and the effects of gender—of being male or female. The popular press carries reports of inequality and sexual harassment, plus arguments for and against an Anti-Discrimination Bill. Universities have seen the emergence of women's studies courses, new journals and a spate of books and articles.

It is temptingly easy to set much of this ferment aside, to regard it as saying little about the way social science proceeds. The material may be segregated into its own small corner, labelled as relevant only to women ('women's issues'), as 'pure polemics', or as 'more complaints about the oppression of women'. It is also often difficult to find a shape or structure in much of what is written about women and gender: to discover, in the words of a colleague, 'what the fuss is all about'.

Those easy dismissals and the lack of obvious shape are sources of regret. They disguise the fact that much of the new scholarship (labelled 'feminist' or otherwise) contains a number of interesting challenges to social science: challenges to the topics chosen for research, the methods used, the concepts and frameworks brought to interpretation. These challenges are not simply objections; they are often fresh looks at old problems. They bring an awareness of questions not previously asked, of limitations to our knowledge, and of the consequences of thinking about men and women in particular ways. Finally, these challenges often contain specific proposals for proceeding in a different fashion, allowing us to gather a different understanding of the lives of both men and women.

Challenges form the focus for these papers, providing a thread that runs through a range of disciplines. My goal is to provide a general shape: a broad picture of challenges across several disciplines, allowing the subsequent papers to add more detail and to focus on particular discipline areas. For some of you the picture will not be new, and I can hope only that some of the examples will be fresh, as will be some comments on recent trends. For those to whom the picture is new or has been incomplete, I hope my comments will provide a helpful overview and will persuade you to look with an alert and questioning eye at data, methods and concepts in your own and other disciplines.

I shall inevitably concentrate on some challenges more than on others, if only because of my own values. The study of women and their position in society has brought challenges at a variety of levels, ranging, in Evelyn Fox Keller's words, from 'those that even the most conservative scientists ought to be able to accept' to those that end by arguing that the presence of bias in theory and method is so extreme that orthodox science must be completely rejected.[2] My own position is that such rejection is unwarranted. I do not regard all we consider as knowledge as expressing only ideology, nor do I see the critique emerging from feminist scholarship as a completely new tradition. We have all increasingly come to recognise that the development of knowledge is shaped by political and social contexts: that science is 'a social process'.[3] What most feminist scholarship does is to point to some particular forms and degrees of shaping and propose some alternatives. In the best sense of the word, it is 'rethinking'.[4]

In the task of creating a broad sweep, I have encountered one particular problem. A number of ideas have acquired for me such a taken-for-granted quality that it is sometimes difficult to look backwards and locate a specific source, especially since the study of gender is a field where I read but do not keep references. At the same time, I did not wish to write a review directed towards noting every possible source. I have partly solved that problem—partly in the sense that it still does not sit easily with me—by taking several steps. I have reread issues of a particular journal and followed a number of leads contained within it. This journal, *Signs*, is a multi-disciplinary 'journal of women in culture and society'. I have noted sources with which I associate particular ideas (others may have different associations). I have drawn from some earlier critiques of the social sciences; in particular, critiques by Ruth Bleier[5], Kathleen Grady[6], Evelyn Fox Keller[7], Mary Parlee[8], Naomi Weisstein[9] and Marcia Westkott.[10] I have also drawn from a new set of multi-disciplinary papers on 'a feminist perspective in the academy', papers asking how much impact that perspective has had, and where it departs from established perspectives.[11]

These sources serve the purpose of bringing out the issues I see as general. To them may now be added the symposium papers. These are anchored more firmly in specific disciplines and often in the Australian context. They also offer an expanded discussion on several issues that I can mention only briefly. I have accordingly noted in this paper places in which a particular issue may be followed up profitably in the subsequent papers.

The overview in this paper contains three main sections: the first is devoted to challenges dealing with the choice of research topics, the second to methods and the third to the models or frameworks brought to the interpretation of data. The three aspects are inevitably interwoven and, at heart, are all aspects of interpretations or models. I shall, however, treat them initially as separate, largely for the sake of providing a ready shape to a diverse literature. In each of those three main sections, I shall review some changes that have occurred and some continuing debates. I have also attempted to choose examples from a range of disciplines or from areas of general interest.

The final section asks how we may break away from past limitations and move towards further rethinking.

The Selection of Research Topics

I start with research topics for two reasons. First, the selection of research topics has always been a marker for what is regarded at a given time as significant and feasible. To work on a problem outside a given range is often to run the risk of being regarded as displaying poor judgment by opting for a problem that is either 'unimportant' or 'impossible'. Second, a change in the amount of attention given a particular topic often signals a change in the acceptability of an earlier way of defining a problem, or a rise in the number and weight of objections to an old view.

Research on women and gender is no exception. To illustrate that point, I shall single out three topics that have recently been given increased attention. For each, the underlying change is the recognition that earlier neglect was less a question of feasibility than of values and prevailing concepts.

The three topics are analyses of work not paid for in money, comparisons of males with females and the presence/invisibility of women. I shall follow an overview of these with the question: Is all now well? The question provides a way of introducing some current comments about shortfalls that still remain.

Work not paid for in money

We now see far more research than before on the sociology of housework, on divisions of labour within households, and on 'volunteer' or 'community' work (cf. Ferber,[12] Hartmann,[13] Oakley.[14]) We also see an increasing number of arguments to the effect that surprisingly little is known about relationships between paid and unpaid work, between what have been called public and private forms of labour or public and private sections of the economy, or between the sphere that is tagged as 'the family' and the sphere that is tagged 'the economy'. Eli Zaretsky's work is one source on this topic;[15] another is a recent chapter by Gillian Bottomley.[16]

Underlying these changes is the recognition that defining work in terms only of money is narrow, and that there is an arbitrary quality in the dichotomy between work and non-work (especially if the latter is then associated with leisure) and in the dichotomy between public and private (especially if the latter is then associated with 'less important'). Bettina Cass's chapter in this book provides a more detailed account and a particular extension to Australian decisions about wages and their regulation.

Also underlying these changes is the recognition of consequences to particular dichotomies and particular definitions of work. One general consequence is the temptation to define 'women's work' or 'women's activities' as 'insignificant', since they are 'not work'. Another is the creation of gaps and distortions in our accounts of societies and economies, inevitable whenever the work of half the population is not taken into account.

Comparisons of males with females

The rise of research reports on this topic is apparent in a wide variety of disciplines. The reports range from analyses of income levels and property rights to analyses of occupational and voting patterns, equality within the law, ways of speaking, ways of working and the occurrence of depression. Fay Gale's chapter adds an intriguing comparison of male and female approaches to the use of a landscape and to the way one travels to work, a comparison affecting not only our understanding of the way in which space is used, but also policy decisions about roads and transport in general.

Within this research wave, psychology has added a particular concern with testing assumptions found in many disciplines and often offered as explanations for differences in the social positions of men and women. These are assumptions about the 'nature' of people: their styles, preferences, personalities, abilities. Is it true, for instance, that women are more emotional, more nurturant, more sensitive, more 'verbal' and less 'spatial' in their thinking, less interested in the usual forms of achievement and more interested in interpersonal relationships? A further addition, from several disciplines consists of questions about whether any observed differences are signs of strength or weakness. Some of the current debate within feminist writing, for instance, concerns the implications of defining as strengths qualities presented earlier as weaknesses. For some, this is a productive escape from a derogatory view of women, helping to avoid the imitation of men in the course of acquiring autonomy.[17] For others, this 'lyric romanticisation' is not much different from earlier views that have supported giving women subordinate positions.[18]

Overall, research on this topic may be described as directed towards four questions: What exactly is the state of affairs? How do differences begin? How are they maintained? What consequences follow from viewing similarities and differences in particular ways?

Underlying the first of these questions is the argument that social scientists have in the past not looked for relevant data or have too readily accepted data that confirms some established stereotypes. In many cases, it has been pointed out, social science has constructed an image of women that was then either not tested or had at best only a marginal fit with the data. Ruth Hubbard has made this point with particular clarity in her analyses of 'women looking at biology looking at women'.[19] Naomi Weisstein[20] and Stephanie Shields[21] have made it for psychology. In his comments on the papers given by Bettina Cass and Meredith Edwards, Don Aitken made it again for analyses of voting patterns, noting assumptions that the direction of influence is from husband to wife and children and the failure of early research designs to allow for the specific testing of such assumptions.

Underlying the second and the third questions is the recognition that in the past social scientists have too easily accepted explanations based on 'nature' or 'choice'. They have also, it is argued, accepted too easily the argument that the way things are at the moment is the way things have always been, an assumption that turns out to be no more true for property rights than it is for the position of women in the 'official' hierarchies of Christianity and Judaism (cf. Marcia Guttentag and Paul Secord,[22] and Rosemary Radford Reuther[23]).

Underlying the fourth question is the recognition that consequences follow from particular ways of defining the 'personalities', 'skills', and 'styles' of men and women. Entry into particular occupations provides an example. We may find amusing arguments that women are not fit for political decisionmaking because of their tendency towards emotional storms around times of menstruation. It is less amusing, however, to find the argument advanced by a social scientist that the entry of women into fields such as architecture or engineering should reflect the 'fact' that women are 'more verbal' and 'less spatial' than are men in the way they process information.[24] As Helen Lambert's[25] review notes, the data do not yet provide a totally consistent picture of such 'facts'. Even if they did, the extension from group data to the education of individuals is hardly warranted.

The presence and visibility of women

The last topic I shall select as displaying change relates to the presence of women. A great deal has now been written on women in history, religion, literature, politics, and in the accounts of any science. The research covers three main questions: Why have there been 'so few'? Why have those who were prominent become so 'invisible'? Who are the other 'invisible' groups?

Underlying those questions is the recognition that 'official' accounts of history and of the nature of many societies pay extraordinarily little attention to the presence of women, or to the presence of any groups other than those seen as 'important' or as 'dominant'. Studies of paid work, for instance, have generally been studies of whites as well as of males, and seldom extend to work 'below a certain level'. Studies of Australian history usually provide little space or analysis for Aborigines, any more than U.S. history usually provides for blacks or American Indians.

Underlying these questions is the recognition that a contributing factor to invisibility is the way social scientists proceed. To the extent that we think in terms of work as paid work only, or in terms of importance lying only in the public world and in the exercise of public power, accounts will always pay little attention to the activities of women or of other minorities. For women, one alternative proposed is the systematic exploration of areas such as the home and the family, liable to bring out women's specific roles. This is, for example, the argument offered especially by Gerda Lerner.[26] For all neglected groups, one alternative lies in 'the new social history', to borrow a phrase from Patricia Grimshaw's chapter documenting the nature of everyday life and its significant events, rather than limiting oneself to officially significant dates, to 'the succession of popes, presidents, and pitched battles' as against 'the lost history of humanity'.[27]

Finally, underneath questions about the visibility of women is a recognition that questions generated by asking about women spark questions about phenomena that apply to both men and women. That general sparking is less obvious than the emergence of material specifically about women. Let me give some examples. One has already been mentioned; the concern with other 'invisible' groups, a concern that includes not only attention to the point of view from which accounts are written but also a focused interest on the extent to which several 'invisible' groups are like each other, and on the meaning of 'subordinate' or 'minority' status.

A second example is the study of passages or transitions over the life cycle. The study of women's lives has provided a major part of the data in this area. It has also prompted a general reanalysis of what is meant by 'life crisis', contributing such concepts as 'normative crisis' (a concept describing change as an expectable, healthy part of life rather than only as a disaster).[28]

The third example is less psychological. It comes from Elizabeth Wood's analysis of women in the world of music. Wood notes the recent increase in research on women's contributions, and the documentation of limits placed on women's opportunities. For women who did become visible, she also proposes a particular set of factors:

> Given creative traits of independence, initiative, discipline, concentration and self-esteem, the exceptional women musicians have invariably had the advantages also of birth in an educated *musical* family and a degree of financial security, both of which have helped them acquire technical training and prepared them to enter professional networks.[29]

Wood's analysis may be applied to the study of entry and progression in any profession. So also may some general questions she asks: What are the conditions under which an individual is allowed or encouraged to become a patron—even a knowledgeable patron—but not a performer? Or allowed to become a teacher (though still not a performer)? Or, if a teacher, confined to the teaching of students who are the same gender as oneself? Wood proposes the last question in the context of noting women such as Louise Farrenc, who was allowed in the nineteenth century to teach at the Paris Conservatoire, but only to teach women. The general question, however (i.e., who is thought to be an appropriate teacher for a given group, and why?) could be extended to any form of teaching and to any set of restrictions (from men not being seen as fit for the position of 'infants' mistress' to women not being seen as able to teach boys).

The shifts in research topics signal that change is occurring. They do not mean that all is now well, or that the reanalysis of underlying assumptions is now complete. To give some sense of continuing challenges and rethinking, let me return to each of the three topics and then raise a general question about 'significance'.

We are still some distance, it is argued, from an effective recognition of unpaid work and of an integrated account of several forms of labour. Cora Baldock and Bettina Cass have made this point most strongly.[30] I shall add some comments from Eleanor Leacock, an anthropologist commenting on a 1980 bulletin of the World Conference of the United Nations Decade for women.[31] That bulletin notes adverse effects on women from industrialisation, a reminder that the effects of development are not gender-neutral. It also notes that women's contributions as unpaid family workers have generally not been counted in a country's gross national product, regardless of whether that work consists of domestic, child-rearing, or agricultural work and even in countries where unpaid agricultural labour is a large part of a country's labour. Work that occurs in informal economic sectors and in family settings still appears to be invisible, even though its economic importance has become a source of frequent comment, comment summarised in Leacock's article and represented by the whole issue of the journal (*Signs*) in which that article apeared.

A peculiar feature of work on comparisons of males and females is the preoccupation with origins. Among academics and in the popular press, work on sociobiology and on behaviour patterns among non-human primates attracts an attention that seems to me far in excess of what it warrants as an explanation of the contemporary scene. At the least, such accounts 'ignore 5 million years of exuberant evolutionary development of the human brain'.[32] Even more seriously, the concern with origins obscures attention to the questions: How is any difference, regardless of origin, sustained? How does it come to be regarded as 'natural' or 'inevitable'?

For a number of scholars, part of the answer lies in the way the world is represented: in the symbolic universe presented to us in art, literature, religion, advertising and education. These images become an accepted part of the way we think. They also create for us a sense of normal and expectable behaviours for men and women: a range that is always restricting and often demeaning.

The analysis of images and their effects cuts a wide swathe through disciplines. It occurs, for instance, in Simone de Beauvoir's analysis of how myths and images in daily life perpetuate the notion that women have in the eyes of men the status of 'the other': cut-off, separate, and always 'second',[33] a status and image that women also often come to hold of themselves. The analysis of images recurs in studies of religion, noting that all the gods in Christianity and Judaism are male, that women have currently little or no representation among official figures, and that Biblical accounts of 'good' women place them consistently in a serving and subservient role (cf. Rosemary Radford Ruether).[34] It is to be found in analyses of fairytales, witnessed by the amusing title of a 1979 book by Madonna Kolbenschlag: *Kiss Sleeping Beauty Goodbye*. It also surfaces in many analyses of language, images in advertising and, to choose a less well-known field, in analyses of drama. Nancy Reinhardt[35] for instance, points to the way in which tragedies with women as central figures (e.g., Medea, Antigone) have often been labelled as 'problematic tragedies' (classical tragedies are traditionally about public figures who fall from high official places). She asks also about the impact of the expectation that an audience or a patron, for literature or visual art, will be male or female, a question prominent in John Berger's analysis of 'ways of seeing'.[36] On a less academic plane, Reinhardt points to the way that 'light' plays are often set within houses rather than in the public arena, often within the women's areas of the house, perpetuating an association of women with private life and with lesser significance.

All such comments raise a number of interesting research questions; questions, for instance, about relationships between reader and text, performer and audience, artists and purchasers of art. They also raise questions about policy, with one of these being the impact of rewriting texts in non-sexist language. All such questions, however, take second place when we give our primary attention to the *origins* of male/female differences, or are persuaded by the implication that current patterns are 'natural', inevitable and unchangeable.

The topic of presence and visibility of women brings out the aspects of unease to which I wish to give most attention. It is true, as many acknowledge, that a few figures of women now adorn landscapes where previously they did not appear at all. These additions, however, are only a first step.

What else may be needed? One is the continuing necessity to break the association of women with 'women's issues only'. Activities that involve only women are significant; it is easy, however, to see women as restricted to those activities. Some specific comments on this problem are related to the invisibility of women in history. A contributing factor, Gerda Lerner proposes, is the way scholars look for the role of women only in movements regarded as being 'women's issues'.[37] That bias, she argues, has led to a concentration on women as working for votes for women or for access to techniques for birth control, with little attention to women's activities in reform movements that affected both men and women. The recognition of that bias underlies the strong current interest of some scholars in women's role in the general trade union movement. It also underlies William Leach's correction to the history of the movement for suffrage.[38] 'Votes for women', he documents, provided one issue in a general reform movement that advocated wider education, a reduced romanticisation of marriage and a reduction of secrecy in society: secrecy about marriage, hygiene, prisons and other 'sensitive' subjects.

A second needed step is illustrated by comments from Myra Jehlen:

> Inside the world of orthodox and therefore male-oriented scholarship, a new category has appeared in the last decade, the category of women. Economics textbooks now draw us our own bell curves, histories of medieval Europe record the esoterica of convents and the stoning of adulterous wives, zoologists calibrate the orgasmic capacities of female chimpanzees. Indeed, whole books of "women in" and "women of" are fast filling in the erstwhile blanks of a questionnaire—one whose questions, however, remain unquestioned. They never asked before what the mother's occupa-

tion was, now they do. The meaning of "occupation", or for that matter of "mother", is generally not at issue.[39]

Jehlen's comments are part of her concern that, in the process of filling in blanks, what may develop is an isolated scholarship with little capacity to bring about any rethinking of the accepted categories, terms and assumptions. A certain degree of distance helps one rethink; too much, however, may reduce opportunities to change the views of others, and may produce what some have called a 'ghettoisation' of research.

This concern, I consider, could only have emerged after the first gap-filling steps were taken, but is likely to be more and more prominent as those steps are completed.

A similar concern is expressed by U.S. historian Carl Degler.

A number of college textbooks, it is true, now mention or discuss women to an extent not known ten years ago; a few more famous women are pictured or described, and perhaps more paragraphs are devoted to women in the workplace than before. But the shape of the American past, that is to say, the structure through which we pass on our history to students, has remained almost unchanged. .... Because history ... has been the story of what men have done ... the content and the divisions—periodization historians call it—are largely determined now by the interests of men.[40]

This larger concern with the structure of history is also prominent in Patricia Grimshaw's chapter of this book. I shall add only that Degler is concerned with the development of an integrated history, one that is 'useful to both men and women ... any new, integrated history must be truly composite ... It must not be simply history written from the standpoint of women. That will not serve the purpose of men, who also need history, however much .. women's history may right the imbalance from which traditional history has suffered for so long'. The 'achievement of such a history' Degler expects to be 'difficult and lengthy in accomplishment' but 'worth attempting, because only through a common past can all people relate to one another, and understand who they are as well as where they have come from. With an integrated history, women as well as men will attain historical depth'.

The concern of many feminist scholars in the face of such proposals is the same as that of many people facing proposed mergers: that is, they wish to have an impact but consider that the merger may well be delayed until the two parties—in this case the two histories—are closer to equal in strength. Until such time, to adapt some comments by Nannerl Keohane[41], simply adding a few women to standard accounts of history or social patterns may amount to the prescription: 'add but don't stir'.

I would not wish my comments on a change in research topics to be interpreted as meaning that choice is now value-free. Graduate students still often feel that they should avoid topics that are 'women's topics' (pregnancy, childbirth, single mothers, widowhood) for fear that they will be regarded as 'not serious scholars'. This avoidance is not unique to Australia. Pauline Bart[42] reports, for instance, a comment addressed to Alice Rossi, asking in effect how a sociologist of her standing came 'to be stuck in an area like marriage and the family'. The holding back is particularly strange when the phenomenon of interest applies to both men and women but the best examples are to be found in the lives of women. If one wished to study response to changes in life patterns, for instance, it would certainly be found advantageous to use concepts derived from the analysis of change in the lives of women, and the best examples may well come from current changes within the lives of women.

Nor do I wish to propose that topics become of interest only when they can be related to the lives of both men and women. There are phenomena that appear predominantly or solely in the lives of women or in the lives of men. No one would suggest, however, avoiding research on such topics as the election of popes, male initiation ceremonies, the way battles are fought, men in history, or cancer of the prostate simply because these are 'men's topics'. Topics that are 'men only' have never been thought to be insignificant because of that restriction.

I shall leave this question of 'trivial' and 'significant' research with one last comment. The concern with 'non-seriousness' is so strong that even some established scholars will feel a little hesitation about programmes in which all the speakers are women. They may even be tempted to search for 'the token male' to increase respectability or acceptance. The hesitation, and the readiness with which references are made to men who write on 'women's topics' or in 'feminist' fashion—are further signs of the remaining presence of values in the definition of 'significant' research.

The Use of Particular Methods

Challenges to the standard methods of social scientists take a variety of forms and often follow from a change in viewpoint. Within history, for instance, the recognition of invisibility for the 'common' man or woman has brought with it a recognition of the need to consider sources and documents that are usually ignored: from diaries and memoirs to bills of lading, records of birth and deaths, 'the pious tract intended for servants, the medical case history, and the mute monument'.[43] Combined with such sources is often a new attention to statistical analysis. The limitations of such methods are often noted but, as Patricia Grimshaw also points out in this book, a shift in method has had to follow the awareness of a need to shift topic and point of view.

A similar point is sharply made by Mary Brown Parlee[44] commenting on the choice of control groups. She cites a case where a group of biomedical and social scientists wished to add a comparison group of women to a longitudinal study of ageing that had been following a group consisting only of males for about twenty years. What group of women should one choose? The biomedical scientists argued for the female siblings of the male sample on the basis of physiological similarity. The social scientists argued for a group of women comparable to the men in education, intelligence and professional activity, on the grounds that these social dimensions are known to affect ageing. Parlee points out that 'far from being simply a methodological issue, the choice of a "control" group serves ... to define the perspective that will dominate the research'. It is also likely, she suggests, to affect the conclusions reached: the sibling match being more likely to bring out sex differences, the 'social' match more likely to diminish them.

To allow a review across disciplines, I shall concentrate on four points. One is a set of challenges to the *units* often used in social science. The second is a set of challenges to the nature of sampling. The third covers two pervasive assumptions that often accompany particular forms of sampling but may also be separate from it: the assumption of gender-neutrality for phenomena that appear unequally in male and female populations, and the assumption that one sub-group can be taken as speaking for the whole population. The fourth section asks: what kind of variable is 'gender'?

The choice of unit

I have already mentioned one form of this concern among historians. This is a concern with the way in which the structure of historical accounts is shaped by a division into periods that are usually based on changes in the activities of a privileged sub-group (e.g., Degler).[45] Among sociologists, family historians, psychologists, and economists, an equivalent concern is with the use of the family as a unit. Breaking down the family unit has taken a variety of forms. Juliet Mitchell,[46] for instance, has argued the need to think of the family as serving several separate functions: sexuality, reproduction, socialisation. Jessie Barnard[47] has argued for separating the several roles that may be played by the one person. The roles of wife and mother, she comments, are often in conflict with one another. Wives are often expected to be passive and dependent while mothers, to be effective, are more often expected to be strong and resilient.

To provide slightly more detail, I shall turn to the discipline of economics. Meredith Edwards's chapter provides an example. She notes especially clearly the limitations of analyses that treat families as a single unit and that regard income transfers within the family as occurring harmoniously and automatically. I shall add to her paper some comments I found noteworthy in an article by another economist, Heidi Hartmann.

Hartmann[48] summarises a series of historical studies of the family and proposes that one of the reasons for conflicting interpretations lies in the definition of the family as a group with unified interests. She argues that the definition of the family as an active agent with unified interests is erroneous, and proposes instead that the family is 'a location where production and redistribution take place', often in the presence of conflict and struggle. In this view, the family is a collection of individuals who negotiate issues concerning the production of goods, money, and children, and the redistribution of such goods as pay cheques. This redefinition of the family unit Hartmann then brings to bear on data gathered from time-budget studies of housework; studies covering the time spent on it and who does it. Her redefinition does not deny that households do act at times with unified interests. It does urge, however, a more thorough analysis of households and the presence of both mutual dependence *and* conflicts of interest. A number of similar proposals for the description of bargaining and decisionmaking within families—together with a description of studies—are provided by Marianne Ferber[49].

The nature of sampling

Challenges to the way in which social scientists build a data base or sample a population take a variety of forms. They cover comments on failures to analyse for gender differences, to sample both males and females when the phenomenon occurs in both, to be fully alert for accuracy in reporting, and to recognise bias in the way individuals are defined, even when counted.

In any sample that includes both males and females, it is now almost routine to ask if there are male-female differences, in much the same way that one would check for the effects of differences in socio-economic status. At least within psychology, such analysis became routine only within the last ten years. Before then, analyses for gender differences—certainly reports of such analyses—tended to be procedures followed more often by female than by male scholars.[50] The arguments for such analysis are in many ways similar to arguments for analysing for the effects of socio-economic status; that is, the status of men and women is not the same, they are socialised towards different goals and it is unlikely that their physical or social experiences are the same.

Analysing for any male-female differences assumes the inclusion of both males and females in a sample. In much of social science, we start with the assumption that certain variables will be taken into account in any sampling, unless there is a specific reason why not. Age, socio-economic status, nationality come to mind. Why not gender? After all, a question about 'male' and 'female' is one of the first questions asked about a new child or a new colleague. We live, it has been said, in a gendered world, extending a gender description (a naming as 'he' or 'she') to all kinds of objects: cars, boats, the moon, nature. Why, then, do we not find gender built into research with as little question or thought as we give to age or socio-economic status? If it were, we might have fewer accounts of society in which women are invisible or in which their perspectives are assumed, without checking, to be the same as those of men.

In many ways, sampling by gender has almost reached that status. It would be difficult to publish an article in many psychological journals without a reference to the gender of the sample or without an explanation if the sample were restricted to one gender. That has again become the case in the last ten years or so, facilitated greatly by an editor's decision—for a journal in which people wished to publish—that he would not accept articles that did not follow such guidelines. Prior to that decision, restriction to a one-gender sample was frequent and often thoughtless. I have, in fact, myself been guilty of using and reporting without comment an all-male sample for a study of decisionmaking, eliminating women after a pilot study on the grounds that a substantial proportion did not find the problem 'interesting' and did not 'work at it'. I would now continue with both men and women in the sample and regard as an important research problem the issue of why a sizable number of highly intelligent students labelled the problem as 'not interesting', or 'not my sort of thing'. I can only plead that this was in 1950. With most social scientists, I have learned the error of my ways.

Are there any occasions when double sampling would not be in order? I had, I must admit, come to think of it as routine, to apply it like a standard recipe unless questions of serious inconvenience forced me to ask whether I really needed both males and females. (In the course of studying some aspects of child-rearing, for instance, I have so far interviewed only mothers.) Several colleagues, however, have pointed out that such a procedure can become almost as unthinking as the earlier unthinking acceptance of samples restricted to one gender. A similar point is strongly made within Fay Gale's chapter of this book. Routine sampling for both genders, the new argument runs, has been a useful corrective to past procedures. It is surely legitimate, however, to sample for only one gender when such sampling is appropriate and thoughtful. One such case would be where a phenomenon occurs predominantly in the male or the female population. Another—the case especially mentioned by Fay Gale—occurs when the preceding studies in the field have been based on all-male samples, supplying a data base that already allows a comparison and that needs the contrast of an all-female sample. The critical issue is the match of the population to the topic and a careful avoidance of the assumption that a single-gender sample enables one to draw conclusions about both males and females.

My hesitations about one-gender sampling may simply reflect some of the academic history of my time. It is a salutary shock, for instance, to discover that the classic theories of achievement motivation were based on all-male samples and to realise that such a basis, until it came to be challenged by women, had not registered as odd in the way that it now would. Routine sampling for both males and females, together with analyses for gender differences, would have made such an outcome impossible. Perhaps we have now reached a point where more flexible procedures can achieve the same goals of attention to the experiences of women and the development of theory that applies to both genders.

Data on frequency are often critical to our understanding of events and to our development of policies. How widespread, for instance, is divorce, child abuse, depression, or participation by males in routine housework? For such questions, the nature of the counting is critical, together with sources of bias to the count.

Among feminist scholars, perhaps the most popular examples of problems in determining frequencies are incest and rape. Incest is of particular interest given the contrast between the emerging data on its frequency, and the definition of it at one time as 'the universal taboo'.

Beneath such specific examples is a question that applies to all areas of social science: When is inaccuracy particularly likely to occur? The closer looks now being given to what has been called 'family violence' (covering wife-beating, incest and child abuse) argue for paying careful attention to who is doing the counting and the reporting, to the forms of report and—a point less often considered—to the way the event being counted is first defined. More specifically, scholars of 'family violence' point out that errors are especially likely in areas

- where a phenomenon is thought not to occur or to occur only in certain sub-groups (child abuse and wife-beating fall into this category: they were once regarded as the province of 'the lower classes');
- where the phenomenon is thought to occur but is defined as

'not really a problem' or 'a crime' (rape is an example in this category);
- where the report is likely to lead to a negative result;
- where the phenomenon is defined in a way that meets the interests of a powerful group or that builds on some supporting definitions (examples are the tendencies to define family matters as 'private' matters or to view wives and children as forms of property);
- where the phenomenon is defined in such a way that a large number of events is excluded. The view that rape does not occur in marriage, or can be counted only if accompanied by physical violence regardless of consent, is an example. (The definition of sexual harassment is another, as Jocelynne Scutt makes clear in her chapter.)

Such points emerge with special clarity in discussions of causes and policies in the area of 'family violence and rape'.[51, 52] They contain, however, some generally useful ways of expanding past discussions of frequency problems that usually appear under the heading of 'social desirability'. Feminist scholars—particularly in areas of family violence, discrimination, or sexual harassment—are reminding us that in addition to reports being biased by the 'social desirability' of particular statements, frequencies can be distorted by the definition of an event and by a too-ready acceptance of numbers that fit one's expectations.

Challenges to the way in which men and women are defined are particularly relevant to disciplines within the social sciences that may legitimately lay claim to a consistent sampling of both men and women, and to routine analyses for gender differences. Demography and perhaps part of political science fall into this categroy.

Even when counted, however, women are often defined in their relationship to men or to children. The objections to a compulsory description of oneself as 'Miss' or 'Mrs', while men retain a single form ('Mr') is part of the objection to this way of proceeding. So also are comments to the effect that we have neglected as a research topic the relationships of women to other women. It is that recognition which has given rise to a new interest in the nature of sisterhood, in mother-daughter relationships beyond childhood and in pressures towards 'compulsive heterosexuality': stresses particularly clear in the works of Adrienne Rich.[53] It has also given rise to an increasing research interest in 'women's houses', women's groups, and the formation of convents, religious sisterhoods, and communal groups such as the *béguines* in medieval times.[54, 55, 56]

I wish to bring out especially a number of challenges clustered around the definition of status. The challenges are threefold. One is to the frequent definition of the entire family by reference only to features of the husband. His income, occupation or education is often taken to define the status of the whole family unit.

The second challenge is to the use of measures for males or females that have built into them a lower status for women. Income is one such measure. Ruth Blau suggests some alternatives in a discussion of the relative status of men and women in the U.S.A.: 'in this country very different conclusions would be reached if we stressed comparisons of educational attainment and de-emphasized occupational distributions, or if we studied the occupational prestige or status of women rather than their wages'.[57]

The third and last challenge is to the use of single markers for status. Out of the objections to income as a measure have come arguments for the need to use several measures and to give more research time to asking how these measures are interrelated for men and for women (cf. Abigail Stewart and David Winter[58]). It is interesting to note that similar proposals are emerging from the area of primatology, where analyses of the nature of dominance have led to proposals that status may vary a great deal from one context to another, and in the past might have been too readily assumed to be adequately measured by behaviours in a small number of situations.[59]

Beneath many of the specific comments about sampling are challenges to two pervasive assumptions. Both are forms of generalisation that are not logically warranted.

The first generalisation has to do with the way we relate a particular phenomenon to gender. We may assume that a phenomenon is found in one gender only when it is in fact found in both. The allocation of 'midlife crisis' to women only (under the label of 'menopause') is one example. So also is the allocation of nurturance only to women and assertiveness only to men.

We may also proceed as if a phenomenon were general, applying to both men and women, when in fact the data do not indicate that at all. This unwarranted assumption of gender neutrality is widespread. It occurs, for instance, in discussions of infant mortality, referrals for learning disability, retention rates in high school, maths anxiety, illiteracy in the Third World, applications for welfare benefits, or the number of families living below the poverty line. None of these phenomena is gender neutral. In all of them also, the presence of an uneven male-female ratio must say something about the nature, the etiology and the context of a phenomenon and, if it is a 'problem', about the kind of corrective or preventive policies we might develop. Take, for instance, the fact that in several 'modern' countries boys are far more often referred than are girls for learning disabilities or 'emotional maladjustment'. The ratio of referrals for boys compared with girls ranges from 5:1 to 10:1.[60] Such ratios must say something about the original problem or about the nature of referral. To ignore them, as gender neutral labels tempt us into doing, is to forget part of the data we should be working from. As one corrective step, we may need to become more cautious and more inventive in our labelling. 'The feminisation of poverty', for instance, is a label that contains a ready reminder that households with a solo female parent are heavily over-represented in families below the poverty line.

The second generalisation is that one sub-group speaks for all is often the real target behind objections to sampling only one gender. The sample is restricted. The conclusions drawn, and the label given to the study, are often not. To make that issue concrete—at the risk of making it seem a 'trivial' matter of 'only language'—let me cite a comment by anthropologist Judith Shapiro on the titles of two books. One book is an 'account of a northern Australian Aboriginal society by two male anthropologists who relied on male informants and presented analyses of such institutions as marriage . . . from a male point of view. Subsequently the same society was studied by a woman anthropologist who analyzed the marriage system from the women's point of view. Her book was titled *Tiwi Wives*. The other was called simply *The Tiwi of North Australia*.'[61]

The use of data based on only one gender is a form of sampling that may be forced on anthropologists or be particularly appropriate to the research topic. The more important part of Shapiro's example lies in her argument that the titles illustrate the assumption that the views of one sub-group are a sufficient account, or are the significant account, of a phenomenon. Titles such as 'the Tiwi' imply that the views of male informants (even in an area such as marriage) represent the official or correct accounts, if not the only or the real account of Tiwi society.

It is precisely this type of implication that is criticised by many scholars. In broad terms, it takes the form that what is often represented and accepted as the 'real' view of a society, of history, of human nature, or of 'good' literature and 'good' art, is the point of view held by people in power or regarded as in power. Power is more often held by, or attributed to, men than to women. Men, in effect, are taken as speaking for women as well as for themselves.

Are general conclusions ever drawn from samples restricted to women? There are some occasions where the actions or viewpoints of women are taken as representing the whole of a phenomenon, even when men and women are both involved. The clearest example is the use of the term 'parents' when the sample contains mothers only. Such usage implies either that parenting is carried out only by mothers, or that the contribution of fathers is insignificant. Both implications are meeting increasing objections from social scientists, most the them male (cf. Frank Pederson,[62] Michael Lamb,[63] Ross Parke,[64] Graeme Russell,[65]). Neither assumption—that men speak for all or that women speak for all—is good thinking.

The use of gender as a variable

Up to this point I have been stressing some specific proposals about changing methods. They bring us inevitably, however, to some more general questions about gender as a variable. What is its relationship to established variables such as class or status? Is it a variable to which we may ultimately pay less attention than we currently do? If so, what alternative dimensions might we use to differentiate among individuals? These questions bring out some ongoing debates.

The terms 'sex' and 'gender' are used by some scholars as interchangeable ways of referring to male-female differences. Others prefer 'gender' to refer to most male-female differences, on the grounds that gender carries with it the notion that male-female differences are less matters of biology than they are 'socially constructed': that is, matters of custom, law and convention that may vary across cultures and across historical periods, carrying associations that go well beyond any physical difference. This use of gender, referring to the way male and female are defined, underlies the argument that the topic of concern in women's studies should be not the study of women but the study of gender, covering men and women but with each studied in their own right rather than as speaking for each other.[66] It is this use of gender that underlies also Sandra Bem's proposal that a major topic for research should be the acquisition of 'gender schemas': a set of ideas that define as appropriate for men and women particular skills, preferences, personalities and self-concepts, and that act as filters shaping our perceptions and interpretations of events.[67]

I shall boil down a complex debate—well documented in Lydia Sargent's[68] collection of papers—by noting that there are scholars who see these two as separate variables, intersecting with one another. There are other scholars who see gender or sex as the primary variable. Let me illustrate the debate by referring to Caryl Churchill's play *Top Girls*. She assembles in that play a wide variety of women, including Pope Joan, Patient Griselda, a highly placed Japanese courtesan and a woman executive moving up the contemporary corporate ladder. What unites these four in Churchill's presentation is not economic class but the way in which being women and in particular giving birth to children places them at risk. In all the societies they represent, child-bearing is an event with consequences that they as women cannot control, since the control rests with men. In a visual form, the play expresses the argument by scholars such as Shulamith Firestone[69] to the effect that gender is a variable that has primacy over economic class. For a lively exchange on the same issue in the context of philosophies of education, the reader may wish to note letters to the editor of the *Harvard Educational Review*, written by David Slive[70] and Jane Roland Martin.[71]

The relationship of gender to class is one source of unhappiness with classical Marxist accounts of society. Despite the recognition that Marxist theory gives a useful attention to conflict, control and oppression, the combination of Marxism with feminism has been described by one scholar as an 'unhappy marriage'.[72] Part of that unhappiness is the increasing recognition that socialist states have not necessarily brought equality for women.[73] Part of it is a more general concern with a relative inattention to gender and a focus on paid work. Any theory will need amending if it starts from a narrow definition of work and if it defines power only in terms of access to paid work and its products, without reference to power in terms of the ability to control the way one's own body or sexuality is used. An insistence on class alone, for instance, is not likely to account for the way a society approaches issues of abortion, birth control, sterilisation abuse, domestic battery, rape, incest, lesbianism, sexual harassment, prostitution, female sexual slavery, and pornography, to borrow a list from Catharine Mackinnon.[74] Mackinnon also provides a nice summary statement: 'Feminist theory asks Marxism: What is class for women?'

My comments about gender and a further variable, 'status', may be relatively brief, given the earlier comments about the need to define the status of women in terms other than in relationship to men, and to consider several markers of status rather than assuming that one's favourite measure is sufficient.

The issue I wish to single out is the equating of women with subordinate status. When people assume that women are a protected, favoured group ('well cared for' and virtually members of a 'leisure class'), it makes sense to issue the challenge that women are in fact a minority group (defined in terms of access to power rather than in numbers) and to argue that the position of women is similar to that of slaves, servants or employees. It also makes sense to present the status of being married and 'working at home' as the equivalent of being caged, however gilded the cage might be. Such challenges have been frequent in the past and to a large extent, they still make sense. To them, however, are being added some qualifications. I shall draw these from a chapter written by Carl Degler[75] although he is by no means the only one to make them.

One qualification is to the notion of minority group-servant status. Women are a very special minority group in the sense that they are numerically half the population, are found at several income or class levels rather than clustered into one, and are frequently told their work is critical even if it does not appear in most accounts of significant work. In addition, one of the usual markers for minority status—ability to intermarry with the ruling group—does not hold. 'Insofar as women are concerned, that test not only fails to apply, its reversal is close to the truth. Intermarriage by women with the master class (men) is actually the principal source of women's oppression, not the sign of their acceptance.'[76]

Women are also not identical with slaves, servants, or other employees. They may 'seem to have something in common since they are all subordinates'.[77] There are, however, differences, leading Degler to conclude that 'if one is going to talk about women as subordinates, and certainly one ought to if one's analysis is going to be realistic, then we need to recognize that in such a situation they are *sui generis* too. We need a fresh and more imaginative way of defining their subordination than simply drawing on what we know about the subordination of slaves or workers.'[78]

A second qualification has to do with the use of domesticity—of working at home—as an indicator of status. Its value as an indicator, Degler points out, may vary from one time to another. A rise in the number of women who are at home may signal in one century an exclusion from the activities of the public world. In another, it may represent an improvement in status: 'not so much a prison as a way-station on the road to greater autonomy'.[79] That comment may well elicit from many the response that the way-station often turns out to be a permanent dead end. The essence of Degler's argument, however, is the need for care in arguing from any particular single marker of status: 'There is a danger of being anachronistic by interpreting the meaning of women's lives in the nineteenth century by the standards of the twentieth'.[80] The reality is that the 'concept of female status is a complicated and slippery one'.[81]

One of the problems in attention to gender is that it may itself perpetuate the notion that the only critical feature of individuals is their being males *v* female. The emphasis may have unhappy consequences. It may add an air of reasonableness to a world segmented by gender, perpetuate the exclusion of women from many 'male' activities and suggest that men and women are in no sense alike.

Are there alternatives? Let me briefly mention a few proposals. One is that the major dimension, at least for activities and power, be that of public-private rather than from the start male-female. All societies may be regarded as adopting a public-private distinction. The problems of exclusion then begin when men are assigned only to the 'public' sphere while women are assigned only to a private world of family, children, and 'finer feelings'. Michelle Rosaldo[82] provides both arguments for the distinction and some reservations about its complete adequacy, a line of argument to which Linda Nicholson adds.[83]

A second alternative pays more attention to the thoughts of individuals than to their settings. I have in mind the degree of attention given to the importance of 'consciousness raising' and to a proposal such as Mackinnon's[84] that a major social factor, and by extension a major way of describing individuals, is the extent to which people are aware that what is presented to them as the one 'real' world, the one natural order, is in fact only one of several possible worlds.

A third comes from a psychologist, Sandra Bem. Bem has made several contributions towards the goal of breaking down the dichotomy of male-female, with its implication that certain qualities belong only to men while others belong only to women. One contribution has been the term 'androgyny', designed to apply to individuals who combine within themselves qualities usually attributed to only one gender. The androgynous individual may be, for instance, both nurturant and assertive. (A summary of this position, together with some expansions, qualifications, and an analysis of underlying assumptions, is provided by Janet Spence.[85]) A later contribution from Sandra Bem is the proposal that individuals and societies may be differentiated in terms of the extent to which they adopt 'gender schemas':[86] that is, the extent to which they view the world (from activities to probable skills and personalities) in gender-segmented fashion. The goal of formal education and of child-rearing, Bem argues, should be people who are 'gender-aschematic' and a world in which activities and styles are so open to males and females that the designation male-female will lose much of its current force. Can that state be reached without a return to women being invisible, judged inferior, or losing self-esteem and a pride in their own qualities? That question I am still mulling over.

Concepts and Interpretations

At base, all challenges to the selection of research topics or of methods are challenges to the overall frameworks we use to view the world. To keep the material within bounds and to give it a focus, I shall concentrate upon the frameworks brought to bear on a particular phenomenon: *contemporary differences between men and women in social position and in style.* That focus also has the advantage of bringing out some lines of debate that cut across disciplines.

I shall start with some ongoing arguments related to whether, in considering the source of difference, one stresses a model of choice or of control, a model of patriarchy or capitalism and a model of nature or of demand. I then wish to take up some general challenges to the usefulness and accuracy of a number of dichotomies and associations that often mark the way in which males and females are considered in the social sciences.

Sources: choice or control and discrimination?

Economist Nancy Barrett describes economics as the discipline where this issue has been most prominent. In her analysis, the difference between men and women (or blacks and whites) in the labour market—especially the difference in wages—has been a very useful test for theories based on differences in preference or in productivity, whether those theories are written in terms of neoclassical economics or in terms of human capital. All theories accounting for differences in terms of choice or ability, she argues, have difficulty in accounting for the persistence of differences when men and women are equally qualified and equally interested. That difficulty in its turn is part of the argument that one should reverse the usual argument that 'economic status determines social status. Rather, economic status may well be a reflection of social worth or status judgements .... Women ... are economically discriminated against because society does not value women's work as highly as that of men.'[87] In effect, the basic problem is one of perceived significance or value. The argument helps make sense especially of shifts in the prestige (and financial rewards) of various occupations, from teaching to typewriting; prestige drops as the number of women in the field increases.

The rejection of choice as the only factor or as the major factor in one's activities, however, is not limited to economics or to standard occupations. An interesting case in point is an analysis of variations in the extent to which women novelists in Victorian England were able to get work published, an analysis based on a sampling of archives for all manuscripts submitted over given periods. Tuchman and Fortin use that data as a way of supporting a cited statement from Virginia Woolf: 'To account for the complete lack not only of good women writers but also of poor women writers, I can conceive of no other reason unless it be that there was some external constraint upon their powers.'[88]

Sources: patriarchy or capitalism?

This debate is related to arguments about the extent to which a variable such as 'class' can account for the position of women. It is also related to debates about the interaction of family and social forces. How far does the nature of the family shape society, and how far does the reverse apply? (That type of question underlies a great deal of argument about whether the primary goal of social change should be a change in the way parenting is carried out or a change in, say, the access of women to paid work or their more equal treatment in the areas of welfare and law.) To condense a wide-ranging debate, I shall use one quotation arguing for an interaction:

much of the debate .... over whether patriarchy or capitalism is the primary cause for women's subordination focuses on which domain is more important. To a considerable extent, those who stress domestic inequalities centre on patriarchy, while those concerned with the public domain emphasize capitalism ... It is clear that capitalism builds upon and reinforces the sexual inequalities engendered in those preindustrial societies where private property and commodity production have already led to stratification and the formation of nuclear, male-headed households.[89]

Sources: nature or social demand?

To this line of debate I wish to give slightly more space than given to the previous two. This is partly because it has generated a new line of research and partly because it brings out with particular clarity an aspect to be found also in debates about choice and about 'family' *v* 'social' forces: namely, the link between arguments about sources and decisions about policy.

The best-known parts of this debate would certainly be those related to sociobiology, especially to the study of non-human primates. Many a paper and book has been written in favour of 'the inevitability of patriarchy' and of 'male dominance'[90] (Goldberg uses the former term to refer to forms of organisation beyond the family, the latter to refer to 'couple' relationships and to relationships within the family). Inevitability is argued for on the grounds of behaviour patterns in other species. It may also be argued for by pointing to the way that a 'subordinate' status for women (not simply a division of labour) is to be found even in the earliest of human societies or at a very young age.

I shall not attempt to give a quick Cook's tour of arguments and counter-arguments in this area. Some useful summaries are already available: by Helen Lambert[91], for example, on arguments from hormonal research, from Donna Haraway[92] and Ruth Bleier[93] on arguments from primatology, and from Ruth Hubbard and Marian Lowe[94] on arguments from evolution. Ruth Bleier comments that if one is looking for justifications for current society, 'a primate model can be found to demonstrate any set of human characteristics or social interactions'. In effect, whatever one seeks, one can find.

Instead, I wish to draw attention to two questions: Where does one look for research on alternatives to a model of 'first origins'? (It is not enough to simply find fault with one framework.) And why the fascination with 'first origins' or 'biological' bases?

An alternative appears in research about response to changes in situational demand. It is easy to see that women move in and out of the paid labour force as a function of demand. Both Australia and the

United States, for instance, saw a major move of women into the paid labour force during World War II (a label that itself reflects a framework). Both countries also saw the emergence of justifications for child care centres, with reassurances about any possible harm to children. Does a demand factor apply also to qualities of style or personality so often assumed to involve qualities that are intractably male and female by nature?

There is now a fair-sized body of research on changes in style and personality as a function of situational demand, especially in adult life. I have in mind, for example, research on men who become deeply involved in parenting,[95] on women who re-enter the paid work force[96] and on men and women who retire from paid work or who shift from one part of the life cycle to another.[97] All such cases document changes in style and personality. They reflect, within the context of gender, a wider shift within psychology and sociology towards a greater attention than was given earlier to 'adult socialisation' and to changes in response to demand. The 'new look' at ageing, for instance, argues against inevitable decline in one's ability and for effects from changes in the demand to be quick and alert, combined with the stereotype that one will 'naturally' become slower and less intelligent as one ages.[98]

In effect, there is a model, emphasising demands and expectations, that provides an alternative view to differences based on 'nature' or even 'early socialisation', and that can generate active research. A model of demand underlies as well an often-cited proposal from the area of primatology. This is Jane Lancaster's[99] proposal as to how some 'harems' come about.

> For a female, males are a resource in her environment which she may use to further the survival of herself and her offspring. If environmental conditions are such that the male role can be minimal, a one-male group is likely. Only one male is necessary for a group of females if his sole role is to impregnate them.

The fascination with 'first origins' is a point that has given me more pause for thought. There is a certain absurdity in our preoccupation with great apes, early human societies and hormones as explanations for social inequality or for current arrangements between adult men and women. No one suggests, for instance, that we should construct housing or dress ourselves in the way that chimpanzees or orang-outangs do. No one suggests that we account for current economic arrangements in terms of bargaining among lemurs, or current production techniques in terms of tool using among hunter-gatherers. Moreover, we all know that most social phenomena have multiple causes. Why, then, the fascination with 'first origins' as explanations for the current social positions of men and women?

I would like to present a proposal I find especially intriguing. This is Helen Lambert's[100] proposal that the location of an 'innate' base is linked to social policy. Her argument basically says we do not feel compelled to take compensatory action for disadvantages we can call 'natural'.

> An unexamined but crucial assumption is the general notion that differences among persons justify social inequality. Biological (usually meaning intrinsically determined) differences are often regarded as more reasonable bases for unequal social rewards than are differences that result from variations in the environment, which are held to have more of a claim to compensatory special treatment. There is more consensus on the moral obligation of a society as a whole to make retribution, as it were, for differences shown to be caused by imperfections in the social system (e.g., discrimination) than to compensate for differences in natural endowments. In this view it becomes important to determine whether an observed difference is due to biology or to society.

In effect, a perfectly reasonable interest in the behaviours of other species or other societies acquires a surplus meaning and a status as evidence for the justification of current social practices that is not warranted. An interest in 'origins' has a legitimate place in social science. Its interpretation as the cause of current arrangements is hardly logical. I cannot resist another comment of Lambert's in this respect:

> The peculiar arrangement whereby many women receive economic rewards for their social contributions (in child care, homemaking, and community work) only indirectly via their husband's income, is neither morally nor practically required by the fact (if indeed it is a fact) that women are biologically better parents than men.

Dichotomies and associations

I have been dealing so far with three specific lines of debate about possible sources to contemporary aspects of men's and women's lives. Each presents a specific challenge to some established frameworks. I wish now to consider some challenges to pervasive ways of thinking.

One such general challenge is to the way in which we interpret observations and think about men and women in terms of dichotomies. The objection is particularly to the association of the pair of terms male-female with several other contrasted pairs of terms: public-private; instrumental-expressive values; production-consumption; effective-ineffective; objective-subjective; rational-emotional; significant-trivial.

Such dichotomies have several consequences. They divide the world into segmented parts. They make it difficult, as noted earlier, to think about the way in which spheres so neatly segregated interact with one another or about the way lines are crossed (e.g., males being expressive, women being assertive, depending on context). They readily become a base for concentrating only on one segment (on production, on rationality, on the activities of males). They may also become the basis of social control. 'Rational' behaviour, for instance—the 'natural' province of men—may become a valued goal that undercuts the status of 'emotional' women and denies the legitimacy of anger. It may also give a higher status to research on logical thinking and problem-solving than to research on emotion. Such stress on the political nature of the concept of 'rationality' is perhaps best known in the form of arguments from Jurgen Habermas.[101]

Along with these dichotomies go several associations that again make it difficult to think clearly about the positions of men and women and that, absorbed into our thinking, also become part of our actions. I wish to draw out three of these, in part because upsetting these associations is the goal of many challenges to established ways of thought and in part because one association (of women with victims) is displaying some recent change.

The first association has to do with women and silence. A paper by Nannerl Keohane[102] will serve as my source. Keohane notes that 'speech, discourse, and voice have been effective metaphors for political activity since the Greeks'. She also notes the prevalence of advice to women that they are at their best when they neither speak nor are spoken of: advice starting from Aristotle quoting Sophicles to the effect that 'a modest silence is a woman's crown'. The association, Keohane points out, gives rise to a sense of strangeness when women speak in public places and to the ready judgment that when their voices become assertive, women also become 'shrill' and 'unattractive'.

The second association—of home with haven—has been the target of a two-pronged attack. Both prongs are aimed at upsetting the assumption that women at home are always in a happy position, protected and sheltered by men who make sacrifices to provide that protection and who need a quiet, stress-free retreat on their return from a stressful workplace. One prong of the argument points out that the home is often not a haven for women.[103] It is, in contrast, the most common site for physical abuse. The other prong looks more closely at 'the heartless world'. Doris Lessing, for instance, in her novel *Summer Before the Dark*, has her main character return to paid work and begin to wonder if she had been providing solace and balm for that pleasant world over many years.

The third association is that of women with victims. The most visible trend in research on women has been towards documenting a record of oppression and vicitimisation, of being pawns in a game in which others have been the movers. That documentation has been needed if only to counter the assumptions that women live sheltered, happy lives, protected by men and provided with all that they could want. Nonetheless, it is wearying to find oneself described endlessly as a victim and as an object acted upon rather than as acting. It is also difficult to think in terms of an effective link to reformist action from the position of victim or object.

I find it encouraging, then, to see a shift towards more documentation about the way women have coped with difficulty or have exercised power. Let me pull out three indications.

One is research on changes in fertility. As Carl Degler[104] notes, 'Changes in fertility have long been a concern of demographers'. He argues, however, that 'generally, in explaining those changes, ... demographers have paid little or no attention to women as decision-makers. They have treated fertility as a masculine concern, that is, something which responds to the economic or social needs of men.' Degler is one of the historians who now argue that the explanation of change must take into account 'the special interest (and autonomy) women have had in exerting some control over their fertility'. The image of some decisions being made by women would be in closer correspondence with the way in which birth control is usually treated as their responsibility.

A second indicator is research on women as acting, as being agents. An example is the emphasis on women as acting sexually, choosing rather than being only sexual objects. Another example is the study of women fighting discrimination or harassment. That line of thought does not deny the frequency with which women have been victims or the frequency with which explanations have taken the form of 'blaming the victim' (a term that has become common usage for the way in which the poor are held responsible for their own poverty, or women are described as inviting rape). It does point, however, to the need to consider how one can present an integrated picture of people as both agents and objects, or at least progress to a less uni-dimensional picture than is provided by an exclusive stress on victimisation.

The third and last indicator is an editorial from *Signs* in the summer of 1983, expressing a concern with the 'empowerment' of women. As that editorial noted, 'critiques of male power must continue for as long as that power exists (and it shows at this point no real sign of diminution). At the same time we have reached the stage at which we must turn equal attention to our own empowerment; think ourselves powerful, think ourselves agents, not objects.'

Looking Forward

Given these several challenges to the way in which social science often proceeds, how do we move forward? Where do we go from here?

I have noted throughout the paper a number of occasions where rethinking has given rise to a change in specific research directions: prompting attention to new topics or proposing a change in methods. At this stage, I wish to make a number of more general points. My view of ways forward is necessarily personal. There are, of course, several viewpoints within the current debates.

First, let me deal with some proposed ways forward that I do not find congenial. One is a state limited to despair and outrage. Though there are frequent grounds for anger, despair seems to me no way forward (my own attachment to rationality is undoubtedly strong). A second is disengagement from the mainstream of social science. I noted in the opening section that for some scholars the only solution lies in disengagement, withdrawing from the usual structures of academia or from involvement in policy. A certain degree of disengagement is often helpful in promoting rethinking. Too much, however, does not promote either of the two strategies that Donna Haraway, using an image from analyses of women writers, sees as needed: rewriting old stories in new form or creating completely new stories. Haraway's comments, made after reviewing several critiques representing most social science as fictive and impossibly distorted, reflect my own feelings. She repeats Ruth Hubbard's caution that women, after noting androcentric or male-oriented accounts of the world, 'should not produce mirror-image "estrocentric" stories, except perhaps as joke and parody'.[105] Nor should they retreat into a relativism that places them outside any participation in action, any possibility of shared politics.

> Feminists do not wish to adopt the mask of having no position, mere spectators on the sidelines of the history of science. Corrosive skepticism cannot be midwife to new stories.

What general steps are open for all scholars, once they decide against disengagement? One is a state of greater alertness to the way that values affect social science. In concrete terms, it has been suggested that, in any analysis of current policy, we ask consistently: Who benefits? Who controls? Who decides? Those questions are very much part of the analyses offered by Hester Eisenstein and Jocelynne Scutt. They are also part of a continuing reanalysis of past policies. It affects Rousseau's reputation as a liberal, for instance, to realise that he did not see education as extending to women.

Equivalent questions may be proposed for data or for any set of observations. I have suggested the need to ask, with an eye to gender, a question that is part of standard criticism in any science: Does the nature of the sample match the nature of the conclusions? Nannerl Keohane cites Ellen Boneparth as the source of two related questions: 'Who is missing from this picture? And why?'[106]

This concern with missing or invisible people is linked not only to the nature of any critique but also to proposals that social scientists take positive steps to see that their students do not come to perceive research as a male activity. The moves towards removing barriers in employment, and towards citing women, are such steps. In Keohane's argument, 'seeing women's names cited more frequently accustoms all readers to expecting that women scholars will be taken seriously as scholars'.[107]

Citing women in a way that signals the presence of women scholars, is a move that may seem strange. In the old days, the reference lists in many journals followed the practice of initials for males and full first names for females. Many of us at the time did not like the distinction, feeling it to be based on a misplaced extension of other distinctions (almost a condescending courtesy), and were pleased to move to a system where all authors were anonymously initials only. From that history, it is interesting to note the emergence of reference systems that give full first names for both males and females.[108] The underlying argument in such a change is either that the gender of an author may be useful information in evaluating background or that the number of women scholars is now reaching a point where it is effective education for students to become aware of their sizable presence. Changes in the use of the term 'black' provide an analogy. A form of address or reference that might once have been assigned and used as a sign of lesser status has shifted to being part of positive self-esteem and pride. With some sense of unfamiliarity, I have deliberately given in the text of this chapter first names and surnames. I feel some uncertainty in doing so, but the shift in practice does force questions about assumptions built into forms of reference.

I also find positive the proposal that we take a direct look at the feelings that often accompany research on women and gender. One persistent feeling I have mentioned is the sense that topics seen as related primarily to women's lives are less 'significant' than those related primarily to the lives of men. Becoming alert to the presence of such a feeling, and coming to look carefully at its validity and its source, are steps forward.

It is helpful to bear in mind that significance may not lie in the activity itself. In Margaret Mead's often-quoted words, 'Men may cook or weave or dress dolls or hunt hummingbirds, but if such activities are appropriate occupations of men, then the whole society, men and women alike, votes them as important.'[109]

That judgement may be less true than it was. As Judith Shapiro notes in commenting upon the effects within anthropology of regarding women as valued informants, one may begin to discover 'women who have their own ideas about what is important in life', and to ask about the conditions under which a woman's sub-culture supports or challenges a society's dominant values.[110]

In similar fashion, we may well look directly at the feelings of anxiety and irritation often provoked by studies of women and gender. As Eleanor Leacock[111] and Fay Gale have noted, it can be disturbing to have to change one's viewpoint, to give up some long-held assumptions, to part with some familiar dichotomies and to recognise that one has been myopic. It is also disturbing to be presented with an image of oneself as oppressor, as enemy, as a collaborator or bystander (however innocent) in discrimination and disadvantage. Part of that difficulty was recognised some time ago by Florence Nightingale, who achieved a reputation as 'a great complainer' and noted that: 'men are angry with misery. They are irritated with women for not being happy.... To God alone may women complain, without insulting Him!'[112]

Is it possible to avoid a defensive, confused or hostile stance in response to criticism or proposals for change? I started this paper with one such proposal and shall end with it. *All* social science is based on a readiness to wonder how a state of affairs comes about, rather than regarding it as so natural or inevitable that it does not come up for question. *All* social science proceeds also from a readiness to examine assumptions, to find better methods, and to recognise errors in logic. As Patricia Grimshaw notes in her chapter, one never takes any particular account of history as the 'really real', established forever. The study of women and gender is in this sense a major spur to what effective social science is consistently about: the retelling of old stories and the writing of new ones, and the recognition that both are always needed.

2 Women in History: Reconstructing the Past*

PATRICIA GRIMSHAW

A Yankee feminist of evangelical Christian mould, Miss Jessie Ackermann of the American Women's Christian Temperance Union, first (in 1913) pointed bluntly to the absence of women from published accounts of Australian society, and she undertook to redress this imbalance. She was utterly frank and matter-of-fact in attributing the cause of this omission of women's lives in her study, *Australia From a Woman's Point of View*.

> So far as I am aware, a woman has not yet written a book on Australia. Those which have appeared present the man's point of view; consequently, the position of women in the country which pioneered them into citizenship has hardly been touched upon, much less properly set forth in its vital bearing on national life.[1]

Jessie Ackermann was imbued with the sense of women's moral and spiritual superiority to men that she shared with so many first-wave feminists. She was confident that women's special gifts and roles had played a significant part in the establishment of this new society and in the texture of social life in the early twentieth century. In her own spirited and idiosyncratic style, she set out her views on pioneering life for women, even going to Hansard to read 'for weary hours' to reach an intelligent understanding of the passage of the women's vote in the country's legislatures. She emphasised not only the public but also the private world of the country's inhabitants. 'Glimpses of Home Life in Australia', 'Mothers, Children, and the Birth-rate', 'Men in Australia As Husbands and Fathers', were some of the categories she chose for organising her observations, as well as 'Women of Australia As Citizens', 'Some Laws Relating to Women and Children' and 'Women and Wages'. Her sense of women as significant

*I should like to acknowledge the help of my colleagues Susan Janson, Greg Dening, John Lack and Charles Sowerwine in the preparation of this paper.

agents and actors in Australia's past and in the present that she described was in stark contrast to other accounts of the country's situation. There is little evidence that her gallant effort to describe women's experiences, and the efforts of those women who came after her, to retrieve women's experiences affected in the least the major paradigms that were already accepted as predominant in Australia's intellectual discourse.

In writing on women in history, I wish to make observations on a range of interpretations that this title can allow; on the way in which women have figured in mainstream historiography; on the way they have written and continue to write about women in history; on the way history is affected when women become a central focus. My argument is that the current preoccupation with women's history is transforming traditional academic history because it challenges that hierarchy of significance and those central categorisations of the past that have previously defined the discipline's boundaries and substantial interests. In Australia, as in other Western countries, women have recorded their own and other women's lives to celebrate their own woman-centred version of the past, yet such writing had no impact on mainstream, male-defined historiography in which the accepted myths of the past rigidly excluded women's experience. Over the past decade, however, a new women's history has emerged, which is taking the writing of women's past out of a separate and subordinate sphere. Its practitioners are mainly confident, highly educated women, energised by current feminism, who do not seek merely to add material about women to history as it has been traditionally conceived. By placing women at the centre of their focus, they are challenging conventional historical constructs in such a way as to throw a fresh and illuminating light on the total fabric of past societies.

The events and circumstances of the past are dead and vanished; the study of history cannot discover the 'truth' about the past. Historians reconstruct from the relics of the past, from writings and oral traditions and from the remnants of material culture, interpretations of past life, interpretations that are necessarily moulded by the historian's own social context. The relics of the past are often extensive; but partial, fragmentary and confusingly haphazard and random. Historians must inevitably select material to use from these relics, and that selection must be based on a sense of relevance derived from their own preoccupations and those of the audience for which they write. This is not to deny that the practical daily experience of the historian—the search in the archives—can seem an agonisingly slow, laborious search for valid and soundly based generalisations and hypotheses. It is, however, to cast doubt on any historian's claim to be definitive.

In John Stuart Mill's essay on the social relations between the sexes, 'The Subjection of Women', written over a hundred years ago, he commented on people's ignorance of the influences which shape human character and referred to the writing of history in the following way.

> History, which is now so much better understood than formerly, teaches another lesson: if only by showing the extraordinary susceptibility of human nature to external influences, and the extreme variableness of those of its manifestations which are supposed to be most universal and uniform. But in history, as in travelling, men usually see only what they already had in their own minds; and few learn much from history, who do not bring much with them to its study.[2]

His insight has been reiterated on many occasions since. History, in E.H. Carr's definition, is 'a continuous process of interaction between the historian and his [or her] facts, an unending dialogue between the present and the past.'[3]

As the intellectual discourse and ideological constraints of a society change, therefore, in response to changes in the material and political structures of society, so, too, do approaches to historical reconstruction alter. What appears a clarifying and persuasive version of the past to one generation is not necessarily acceptable to another or to certain social groups within that generation. This relativism, however, in no way suggests that the style and substance of historical reconstruction do not matter, because it is problematic rather than definitive. A sense of history is vital to an individual's sense of personal and social identity, to a society's establishment of a cultural tradition, and to the models of the world which that society wishes to transmit to its young and to posterity. History is not an esoteric exercise; it forms part of an essentially political discourse that is rooted in the present.[4]

Over the last century, academic historians have produced a great many interpretations of the past in liberal, left-wing and conservative histories, theoretically or empirically based. They have at least one factor in common: academic history has almost totally ignored the past experience of women. History has concentrated on power and the powerful in the public sphere, on the growth of states and governments, on wars, revolutions and diplomacy, on the broad contours of economic change and the political movements it has generated. Conventional history has been the tale of great events and those connected with them: kings, generals, prime ministers, diplomats, popes and lawyers, with a sprinkling of scholars and artists. Few women, except those who by virtue of high birth and ascriptive right were thrust into positions of public prominence, figured within such accounts of a country's past.

The issue is not, of course, whether women *had* a history. They have shared the world equally with men; they have lived, breathed and had their being in the same lands, they have been equally affected by social change, they participated equally in the processes of constructing and transmitting culture, and in the nineteenth and twentieth centuries they have increasingly entered the public arena of human life that has been the historian's province. Yet that massive area of human concern has been most partially recorded by those intellectuals who presumed to write our society's history. In Gerda Lerner's words, 'The history of women has a special character, a built-in distortion: it comes to us refracted through the lens of men's observations; refracted again through values which consider man the measure. What we know of the past experience of women has been transmitted to us largely through the reflections of men: how we see and interpret what we know about women has been shaped for us through a value system defined by men.'[5] What academic historians have told us about women has been negligible.

When the subject of the sexual bias of history is discussed, the objection is frequently raised that most men as well as women have been left out of history and that this is the perfectly reasonable result of history's essential emphasis. Most men, like women, were marginal to major historical change; where they were not, they entered historical accounts. The objection continues that conventional history includes women as well as men in the sense that it isolates those events that most narrowly influenced women's lives as well as men's: wars, depressions, the rise and fall of government. Women's interests and needs were integral with men's in a society in which their lives were closely bound together: conventional history is the history of what was important for them both. As Berenice Carroll has pointed out, women were presumed to be living out their lives in essentially changeless roles, irrelevant to intellectually vital questions.[6]

Women undeniably do not constitute a minority group in history in exactly the same way as do ethnic, religious or geographically contained segments of a population who have been subjected to social discrimination and ignored in history. Like other minority groups, women have had certain personal characteristics attributed to them on the basis of biological differences, have been prescribed certain roles on the basis of these supposed characteristics, and have been heavily censured for moving outside those roles.[7] But women's history cannot be seen as the same in character as black history, working-class history or migrant history: half the blacks, half the working class, half the migrants are women. Hence the issues touched upon in women's past are essentially more wide-ranging and complex than the history of other 'minority' groups. Women have been integrally involved in all aspects of a country's past. They have been white and black; they have been native-born and newcomers; they have been plantation owners' wives and slaves, ladies of the manor and serfs, mistresses of a bourgeois household and scullery maids, owners of the means of production and factory operatives.

We are nevertheless justified in speaking of 'women's history', despite the extent to which women shared the cultural expectations and conditions of life of men of their class, race and time. In Western society, gender divisions have been so deep that despite the bonds between women and men, women's experiences have often been profoundly different from men's; they have been differently affected by the same events, they have participated differently in social processes.[8] The gender dichotomy of our society has meant that women's lives have been more closely related than men's to the family and to private life, their participation in public life has been more hesitant, and in some senses women have had a separate culture, a different world view, even from that of the men with whom their lives were closely bound. Marriage and parenthood had different meanings; work had different constraints; women responded differently to famine and revolution, to wars and depression.[9] Their relationships with each other, with kin and with community have been different from those of men.

That separate sphere of women has not, of course, been an equal one, but has been defined in ways advantageous to male dominance in a patriarchal society. Women were divided by class, certainly, but within each class they have constituted a subordinate group in ways that for certain women, have entailed severe oppression. A second justification for speaking of 'women's history', therefore, is that women's social participation, disadvantaged in comparison with men, raises common questions about women's social status, their strategies for coping with inequality and the reasons for changes at times in their social position, which require careful study at the particular level of women's experience. As Hilda Smith maintains, it is necessary 'to view the development of women's history from the feminist perspective of women as a distinct sociological group which has experienced both overt and covert controls through legal, political, and social restrictions'.[10]

Women were subordinate in a patriarchal society, and suffered again by being subordinate in the patriarchal process of history writing. Once it is accepted that women had a separate past, it becomes clear that the problem of women's history is not the question of whether women 'made' history or not, but a question of the discovery of tools with which to interpret women's past. To a certain extent conventional history, of course, simply ignored women's presence even when women were participants in a process under examination. It is nothing short of amazing to see how 'citizen', 'worker', 'the voter', 'the city dweller', 'the settler', could all be designated male, even where this was palpably incorrect. But by and large, women have been ignored in academic history because the questions asked of the past have been irrelevant to women and the canon of significance has deemed their own experience trivial or unimportant.

The historians of women's history are countering this situation in a spirited attack on conventional historiography. If traditionally trained historians viewed the demands of second-wave feminists for a sense of identity, rooted in a sense of women's past, as an article of faith and hope rather than as a goal capable of achievement, those historians must now reassess their view. In 1976 the American historian, Carroll Smith-Rosenberg, wrote, 'Placing women at the center of our analytical scheme, we have sought to construct models encompassing the complex interplay between the macrocosm of social structure and belief systems, the microcosm of family structure and the existential experience of being female.'[11] Together with Natalie Zemon Davis and Joan Kelly-Gadol,[12] she persuasively asserted that women's history was thereby forcing scholars to turn to new sources and new interpretative models, to rethink causation in the past, to rethink periodisation and, overall, to re-evaluate the accepted canons of conventional history, observations that are increasingly being realised. Sceptics will doubtless cling to firmly entrenched notions of relevance. J.H. Hexter wrote that historians look where the power to make change resides:

in the councils of the princes, in the magistracies of the towns, in the membership of the great leagues of traders, in the faculties of the universities—and they found men. On the occasions on which they happened to find women they usually noted the exception; but through no conspiracy of the historians the College of Cardinals, the Consistory of Geneva, the Parliament of England, the Faculty of the Sorbonne, the Directorate of the Bank of England and the expeditions of Columbus, Vasco da Gama and Drake have been pretty much stag affairs.[13]

By this standard, women's history will not add anything to the store of human knowledge, but its aim is different from Hexter's formulation.

One might invite such sceptics to consider the effect of Federation on the lives of Australian women in 1901. The Federation movement and its eventual success loom large in our history books, yet one could argue that the event had little relevance for women's lives. On the other hand, another issue at the turn of the century was critically important for women: the spreading knowledge about birth control and public acceptance of fertility control. Does not that mark a rival and highly significant change in women's history? We could further suggest that to have been born, married, given birth, followed a husband to another state, suffered a severe illness or been the subject of domestic violence or marital breakdown, to have entered or left the workforce or to have had a death in the family, were events of far greater significance in girls' and women's lives in the year 1901 than they are now. The process of discovering ways to put such events into a context and to persuade some people that they were relevant to the major issues of the country's economic and social change must inevitably prove creative and constructive for the discipline as a whole.

While women's history has developed its own particular focus over the past decade, it has not done so in isolation from other initiatives in the discipline. Women's history has emerged from a complex interaction of two areas: the concerns of the contemporary feminist movement and the growing field of social history, refurbished as it has been in fresh new garb since the 1940s and 1950s. In terms of influential theoretical insights, socialist feminism has particularly enlarged the areas of concern of women's history. In *Woman's Estate*, Juliet Mitchell redefined women's past in the light of New Left revisions of socialist orthodoxy, and queried the use of one major issue: the relationship of individuals to the means of production or to the economy as the pertinent indicator in life experience. Past socialist theory, she said, had 'failed to differentiate woman's condition into its separate structures, which together form a complex—not a simple—unity'.[14] Women's lives were a specific unity of different elements and the variations of women's condition in history resulted from different combinations of those elements: production, reproduction, sexuality and the socialisation of children. She initiated a debate within Marxist social theory which has been very influential, particularly as many feminist historians are left-wing.

Social history and women's history have also overlapped in their concerns, and to some degree women's history can be defined as part of the new social history. Social history has concerned itself with the 'underside' of history and has explored the use of sources in creative new ways to study family life, community experiences and the sorts of public institutions disregarded by conventional history—prisons, schools, brothels, factories and religious expression below the level of church hierarchies. This search has established a context for many women's lives that was previously unremarked, nowhere more usefully than in the patterns of family life among the poor, for whom few literary sources remain. The methods of the French historical demographers in outlining the life cycles and interaction of the poor through family reconstitution have been particularly fruitful: to begin and end with essentially political questions to be answered from ready literary sources has not probed the life experiences of poor women, nor indeed of most unexceptional women of the middle classes. The debt of women's history to the methodologies pioneered by social historians is very considerable.

Some women's historians, such as Wini Breines[15] and Rayna Rapp[16], however, have parted company with social historians over their treatment of women in particular areas. In some senses, women's history treats questions outside the range of new social history; women were not only part of the 'underside' of history. Women's historians are examining women in politics, the professions and the arts, as well as in the upper classes and as the wives of powerful men.

In addition, many social historians neglect the political issues concerning women that women's history has inherited from feminism. In the family history of the American colonial period, for example, historians have tended to concentrate on the father-son relationship rather than the mother-daughter one; other family historians have ignored issues of 'sexual politics' and few have cared to pursue the lot of single and widowed women. As Olwen Hufton said at a 1983 seminar on single women in early modern Europe, the demographer notes the decline in the marriage rate at times of economic depression. She wished to discover how women survived economically in hard times when they could not marry.

Elizabeth Fox-Genovese has mounted a fierce attack on so-called 'bourgeois radicals' who find 'consciousness' a dirty word and who, she alleges, dislike intellectual history.

> On the tendentious claim that only a phenomenological description of existence and its conditions affords 'good' history, these establishment radicals indiscriminately chronicle poverty, demography, sex, love, work, mobility, marriage, childbirth, and bird-watching. Social behaviour—that which exists in the eye of the professional observer—becomes a catchall capable of absorbing anything from sainthood to deviance, sadism to masochism, with no capacity for differentiation.[17]

She also stated with some sarcasm that women's history was alive and well in its ghetto. This seems to me a pessimistic view, both of the potential of social history in general and of women's history in particular, although her trenchant criticism hurts because it contains some truth. In the hands of historians who are not basically interested in women's issues, social history can remain uninformative on the key questions that feminist historians wish to raise. Dealt with in this way, women's history may simply add descriptive information to a version of the past still dominated by male-oriented paradigms, even if the subject matter is fresh. Overall, the fact that social historians have adapted models drawn from the social sciences has enormously enriched our attempts to reach past societies. The ethnographic approach to reconstructing past cultures can be particularly exciting in its complexity and in the hands of an historian such as Natalie Zemon Davis it enables issues of gender to be subtly and fully treated. With feminist theory, new social history and an upsurge of interest in women's issues generally to enliven its approaches and preoccupations, women's history is a lively and significant direction in the discipline.

To criticise past history writing and to assert the potential of women's history to alter historical consciousness, it is perhaps best to dwell on one country's historical experience. I now intend to review these issues in relation to Australian historiography, which, though less extensive and newer than the history writing of other kindred Western countries, reflects the same preoccupations and influences.

Ann Curthoys and Anne Summers, two women who have made highly significant contributions to women's history in Australia, first drew to our attention the neglect of women in Australian historiography. In an article she wrote for *Arena* in 1970, in which she discussed a short overview of women's history written by Ian Turner for Julie Rigg's collection of essays, *In Her Own Right* (1969),[18] Ann Curthoys pointed out, 'Women do not appear in most Australian histories in any important way. The nature and effect of the family in Australian society is not discussed. Sexual habits and beliefs have not been studied, nor have the rate and reasons for the entry of women into the work force'.[19] Ann Summers's assessment of Australian historiography's neglect of women was even more trenchant: 'Most Australian history works are so closed, so suffocating, so self-assured in their preoccupation with the activities of men that such questions could not even occur to the reader. To read them is to be lulled into the false assumption that women did not even exist.'[20]

It would be difficult to point to a national historical tradition that more clearly represented a celebration of white male achievement. Astonishingly little about women in Australian historical works was written before the past decade. The earliest histories of Australia, written by such men as Parkes, Pember Reeves and Coghlan around the turn of the century, presented the history of Australia as a tale of exciting progress, the taking of a continent, the establishment of an outpost of British civilisation of an improved nature, the federation of colonies into a promising new state.[21] Such men began a process of myth-making, of aligning a reading of the past with the search of men of their generation for a sense of identity as Australians, that has had a powerful influence on Australian history for much of this century. Certainly if short histories of Australia may be regarded as a distilled version of the 'really real' stories about the past, women get short shrift. Ernest Scott saw history as 'a record of the doings of men living in communities ...' when he wrote *A Short History of Australia* in 1916, and there is no sense in his book that 'men' meant 'human beings'. As he moved through 'The Land and the Squatters', 'The Dawn of Constitutional Government', 'Australia and the Great War', 'Imperial Relations and the Australian Spirit', the actors were unambiguously men; cause and effect were assessed in male terms. Scott was a feminist and he did note the entry of women to the University of Melbourne together with their political enfranchisement; events in which he was personally interested. However, only a handful of women—Mrs Aeneas Gunn, Elizabeth Fry and Mrs John Macarthur—were mentioned, and when the Henty brothers took up 'their unauthorized abode at Portland, with flocks, herds, poultry, and a serviceable whaling ship', their wives' presence went totally unremarked.[22]

In his *Australia*, published in 1930,[23] W.K. Hancock had an index entry for cattle, sheep and rabbits, but not for women. Caroline Chisholm's work for immigrant women and a few women prominent in the arts were noted briefly. Henry Parkes, Hancock wrote, landed at Sydney with a 'wife and child and three shillings'.[24] This was one of his few mentions of a female actor, akin to the allusion by R.M. Crawford in *Australia*, published in 1952, that a more substantial house implied that 'the squatter had overtaken his first outlay of capital; it generally implied that he was bringing a wife to the bush, and so transforming its social life'. (This view of women as appendages to man's projects was suggested yet again in Crawford's history in an acknowledgment at the beginning that speaks volumes for the contribution of women to academic history: 'To Miss Kiddle for her digging on my behalf'.) Interestingly, Scott's sense that first-wave feminism had been a landmark in Australia disappeared as it receded in later historians' memories. Once again, Manning Clark's *A Short History of Australia* made only passing mention of a few notable women (Caroline Chisholm, Nellie Melba, Queen Victoria, Elizabeth Macarthur, Barbara Baynton, an anonymous convict girl and her mistress), and added to the pool of interest in women's past by one sole question that he raised but did not pursue: whether the imbalance of the sexes in the convict period might have instigated male domination of women in Australian society.[25]

For writers of the so-called 'radical nationalist tradition' in Australian historiography, boundary riders, shearers, convicts and labourers might have replaced governors, business entrepreneurs, squatters and prime ministers as a central focus of their tale, but writers such as Brian Fitzpatrick, Robin Gollan, Ian Turner and Russel Ward, despite a left-wing egalitarianism, continued to emphasise the role of men in Australia's past. Men, emphatically, were the movers and actors in those social processes from which a distinctively Australian character evolved. Russel Ward in 1958 depicted the Australian as male in *The Australian Legend*.[26] He said he did not intend to write 'yet another cosily impressionistic sketch of what *wild boys* we Australians are', but he described the stereotypical Australian as 'a practical man, rough and ready in his manners and quick to decry any appearance of affectation in others. He is a great improviser ... He swears hard and consistently, gambles heavily and often, and drinks deeply on occasion.' Not only did Ward fail to ask about the stereotypes of Australian women, but he explained the development of the 'typical Australian' from the *absence* of women on the frontier. It would be difficult to imagine more successfully obliterating women from current Australian identity and from history. This was symbolically registered in the index of *The New Britannia*, Humphrey McQueen's New Left rebuttal in 1975 of the radical nationalist historians: 'women, ignored, page 13'.[27]

That mainstream history (or 'male-stream history' as Canadian feminist Mary O'Brien has called it) ignored women's lives might not have precluded serious treatment of women's experience at the level of the monograph or specialised study. In choice of subject and categorisation, the preoccupations of Australian historiography generally ignored or pre-empted attention to women's lives all the way through to the level of local histories of Australian communities. A patriarchal society generally disregarded women's importance except in a separate sphere that was not considered the realm of academic history. Women, as well as men, usually acceded to such definitions about the past and few current women's historians over the age of forty can have escaped this earlier socialisation. I myself questioned such values very belatedly: my early venture into women's history, a study of the women's suffrage movement in New Zealand, was possible because the subject fitted into the traditional historical canon.[28]

While the few academic histories dealing with women that appeared in Western historiography were usually the work of women, Ann Curthoys was right to point this out as atypical: 'Female historians have been affected by a desire to succeed as *people*, to submerge their feminine identity and by an abhorrence of the feminist stereotype.'[29] As Anne Summers pointed out, our earliest female historians, Marion Phillips and Myra Willard, wrote in precisely the style of the men. She might have also pointed out, too, that very few women in Australia were ever in a position to be academic historians. Until 1960, no woman had ever been appointed to the history staffs of the universities of Tasmania, Queensland and Western Australia; Sydney and Adelaide had one long-term appointment each (Marjorie Jacobs and Kathleen Woodroofe) and only Melbourne had more than one (Jessie Webb, Kathleen Fitzpatrick and four women in part-time or senior tutoring jobs). If we consider a slightly broader group, women who formed part of male intellectual circles, it may be more accurate to say that their response to women in history was divided. When such intellectual women attempted to write general Australian history, they adopted the male model of significant issues. On the other hand, the same women could write about women if they treated women separately.

General historical accounts of Australian history produced by women, then, differ little from the textbooks of men. *My Australia* by Marjorie Barnard and Flora Eldershaw, published in 1939, told how 'rum, wool, gold succeeded one another as key commodities and, in a widening world, the claims of labour became the crux of Australian political life. Like the pillars of Hercules, the two great issues of markets and the standard of living flank this modern sky.' They reported further that 'it was a man's world ... The life of the road was the norm. Within its limits it demanded a high standard of courage and endurance, of resourcefulness and, above all, of mateship, the solidarity of men against the bush.' The writers saw themselves as presenting 'a shape of history, a review of the raw material from which we shall mould our future'[30]. It is difficult to see its relevance to women's future.

The story of Australian mateship and an economic periodisation of Australian history typified other women's general histories. Mollie Bayne and Mary E. Lazarus included an historical chapter, 'The People Before Us' in their 1940 book, *The Australian Community: A Critical Approach to Citizenship*, and those people were the usual band of explorers and governors.[31] To the modern eye the title of Kylie Tennant's 1953 history *Australia: Her Story*, looks decidedly promising.[32] But the female possessive referred incongruously to that masculine entity, Australia, land of male convicts and male gold diggers (though Tennant tried, unlike most writers, to recreate something of the atmosphere of early Australia through character sketches and use of dialogue). *The First Hundred Years*, produced in 1954 by Helen G. Palmer and Jessie MacLeod in 1954, was in the same mould.[33] Perhaps the only general history which deviated at all from this pattern was Margaret Kiddle's inauspiciously titled *Men of Yesterday: A Social History of the Western District of Victoria* published in 1961, in which she treated such aspects as homestead life in the 1840s, sketches of squatters' wives, the education of squatters' daughters, prostitution and attacks on black women.[34] Such references, however, constitute a tiny percentage of the whole book: one suspects that Margaret Kiddle felt justified in addressing these subjects at all because she included 'social history' in the title, evoking an old British historiographical tradition that allowed treatment of women along with aspects of manners and mores. Yet some of these same women who were part of the Australian intellectual world could and did treat women's past experiences in separate studies. It was as if the 'separate spheres', of the two sexes were mirrored in the society's history. Kathleen Fitzpatrick, whose biographical attention had been turned to Sir John Franklin, wrote in 1975 a history of the Melbourne private school, the Presbyterian Ladies' College,[35] Margaret Kiddle (1950) wrote a biography of Caroline Chisholm;[36] Mollie Bayne (1942) recorded the experiences of women in World War II,[37] Marjorie Barnard and Flora Eldershaw (1938) wrote on women for Australia's sesquicentenary,[38] and both they and Kylie Tennant in novels showed sympathetic understanding of their fellow Australian women. No male academic historians dealt with women's past in such a way. The factor of these historians' gender was the significant stimulus to their interest.

In *Damned Whores and God's Police*,[39] Anne Summers pointed to the way in which female art forms have been adjudged 'to occupy a distinct universe, one which is apart from and inferior to the male, which is unself-consciously upheld as the universal model'. Further, she continued, 'The second form of exclusion has been that of critical neglect'. Yet to women artists themselves, and to those women who appreciated their creativity, this work was meaningful. It could also be said that this separate women's history writing merged into a separate stream of Australian women's history, largely ignored by academia, but perhaps giving at least middle-class women some sense of community with women in the past. This earlier tradition of writing on women was a muted voice in the process of historical reconstruction, but it demands the respectful attention of those now sympathetic to women's efforts to sustain a sense of identity as Australians in this century.

While the writers of this earlier women's history were educated women, they emerged from a range of middle-class backgrounds: genuinely well-read, highly educated women were the minority. E.M. Clowes (Evelyn Mary Mordaunt), author of the 1911 study, *On the Wallaby Through Victoria*,[40] viewed the state of Victoria through a woman's eyes and apologised in advance for the gaps in her knowledge. In her previous eight years in Victoria, she said, her nose had been close to the grindstone, 'while life has resolved itself for the most part into a mere struggle for existence ... I have edited a woman's fashion paper, of sorts ... I have written short stories and articles, I have decorated houses, painted friezes, made blouses for tea-room girls, designed embroideries for the elect of Toorak ... I have housekept, washed, ironed, cooked. Once I made a garden, drew out estimates, engaged the men, brought soil and manure, shrubs and plants'.

This was not the style of background to which the Oxbridge-educated historians of Australian universities would lay claim. Yet, like Jessie Ackermann's account of Australia published two years later, E.M. Clowes's study showed an insight into women's past and present experiences that portrayed them in a constructive fashion. She relied on oral sources a good deal, and recounted an old pioneer woman's account of the bush, 'the one-roomed house, with rough log walls, mud plastered, and roofed with bark; the log fire on the open hearth, with the kettle slung above it, ready to warm milk for the young lambs, who lay on sacking before the fire, or shared the bed...'. She described the lives of squatters' wives left alone in huts in the early days in isolation and fear and added, 'For the good of Australia and the Australians, the history of such people ought to be written.' She told of the poor return that dairy farmers' wives received for their butter before the establishment of central butter factories, of the shearing carried out by the families of small 'cockies', with 'all the family being called upon to help, the girls in carrying away the fleeces, and even clipping the belly-wool for their brothers'. She described the petty privations and self-denial of young working girls and students living away from home, and the army of charladies, with 'work-bowed figures, the roughened hands, the tired faces, with their bright, eager eyes, all victims of the golden lure of the west, where the Victorian husbands seem to cast their conscience as easily as a snake casts its skin'. She gave the celebrated governors a short shrift: they simply signed bills and otherwise concentrated on 'looking nice and behaving prettily, while by far the most arduous part of the position rests upon the shoulders of their wives'.

The style and substance of this earlier women's history were various, yet they served one purpose; to take the reader directly into the world of women as seen by women. The considerable number of autobiographies written by women served this function. Why did women write them if not in an attempt to record something of their own lives and the activities of women connected with them that would otherwise be lost to posterity? They could seldom justify their enterprise on the basis of public prominence, despite the fact that these might have been exceptional women: that did not mean exceptional Australians and it was therefore unlikely that mainstream historians would find their lives worth attention. Hence Bessie Harrison Lee wrote of the temperance movement, Catherine Spence of her life and political activities in Adelaide, Ada Cambridge and Rosa Praed of their impressions of colonial Australia, Alice Henry and Dora Montefiore of feminist concerns; Daisy Bates, Dame Enid Lyons, Jessie Street, Ada Holman and so many others recorded some facets of their lives as part of a personal historical project.[41]

Some of the women who wrote autobiographies have also been the subjects of biographies undertaken by other women, another significant avenue by which women have undertaken the task of writing their history. Women undertook biographies of men; men did not write biographies of Australian women until very recently. Seldom was the material relating to a figure of respect extensive, and very often women's papers were preserved with little care. Women put together, however, a number of collections of biographical essays, ranging from series in women's journals through to published books. E. Marie Irvine wrote *Certain Worthy Women* (dedicated to the memory of her mother, 'Jessie L. Compigne—a Pioneer') in 1939, recording the lives of such women as Elizabeth Macarthur, Mary Reiby, Elizabeth Macquarie, Georgiana McCrae, Lucy Osborn, and two Aboriginal women ('Dark Stars').[42] She wrote frankly.

> It is not claimed that they were, in any dramatic sense, heroines. But that the manner in which they overcame the trials of a new country was heroic, few persons will deny.
>
> They are, I think, representative figures and worthy in the true sense of the word. If my work succeeds in rescuing the story of some of them from partial oblivion, and placing [them] before those readers who are interested in history, then any labour that the telling of the tale has cost will be more than repaid.

The writers of full-length biographies frequently made the same point. Marnie Bassett, for example, wrote of Mrs Philip Gidley King, 'It was not then the custom to recognise the part played by wives of public servants in making or marring their husband's work—in all the printed records there are no fanfares for Mrs King ... She was truly, as she was later to describe herself, her husband's partner in his labour and anxieties in the colony'.[43] The point had to be made just as vehemently, however, about women who acted in their own right in women's organisations, whose activities were similarly faithfully recorded by their fellow labourers in the Woman's Christian Temperance Union, the National Council of Women, the Country Women's Association.[44]

The attempts by women to write accounts of other women's lives tended to fall into two groups: the first, the tales of largely unknown women who mostly lived during the colonial period; the second, the stories of identifiable women who achieved some modest prominence in their lifetime. This history had an overall purpose that was more than purely descriptive; it had a moral motivation. Gerda Lerner has categorised this style of women's history as 'compensatory history' including the history of so-called 'women worthies', a phrase coined by Natalie Zemon Davis to describe biographies of able women: she suggested that the European versions had a polemical purpose, 'to provide exemplars, to argue from what some women had done to what women could do, if given the chance and education.'[45] In terms of Lerner's criticism of such compensatory history, that concentrating on the lives of exceptional women told us little about most women's experience, one might say that in Australia few indeed of these women were known at all beyond a very small group of people, nor were they as vastly distanced by wealth or education from a reasonable proportion of the population as were the European women of Davis's study. However, it was compensatory in the sense that this material attempted to add some knowledge of women to the country's historical consciousness. This early women's history was similarly 'contribution history' in Lerner's definition in its effort to describe women's contribution to society, while not challenging the central concepts at the core of the discipline. The writers had a clear message: women *did* contribute to the creation of Australia and all Australian women should feel justly proud of pioneer women's efforts, of which later Australian women were beneficiaries.

While this early women's history displayed little overt feminist sentiment, there was nevertheless an underlying resentment of the neglect women's history had suffered. It may be nearer the truth to say that the ideological position of many writers was close to first-wave feminism, which had accepted the strength of woman's case for citizenship on the basis of women's significant but different roles, imbued as these roles were with high moral and spiritual purpose. Women's history consequently needed resurrection from neglect, but could remain apart from the male version of the past.

In this spirit, groups of women prepared special women's volumes to commemorate the centenaries of Victoria and South Australia and for the sesquicentenary of Australia in 1938. It was clear that women's history would otherwise be neglected, that this was insulting to the memory of women in the past, and separate volumes would at least register their significant contribution to Australia in a style that they promoted confidently, though they clearly knew it would be separate but not equal. In their foreword to the Victorian centennial volume of 1934, Nettie Palmer and Frances Fraser spelled out the writers' object in a typical fashion,[46] saying that in this book, women of Victoria honoured the part women had played in making Victoria and Melbourne what they were in that year.

> We honour especially those who made the great venture, and came with their men-folk to this unknown land, enduring the great privations with a spirit that inspired husbands and sons to persevere in spite of all. Women did more that cook and sweep. They milked cows, dug for gold, sowed the corn, and even literally put their hand to the plough. They tended the sick and dying, they comforted the home-sick, and in every way passed down to the women of to-day their splendid heritage of courage and initiative.

They continued to say that pioneering was not confined to the early days of Victoria, but that it still goes on. Woman has gradually made a place for herself in almost all walks of life.

> She has shown the pioneering spirit in ways undreamed of by her grandmothers. Not usurping the man's place, she has been his mate in higher things as she was in the more humble. Some of the ways in which women have shown the pioneering spirit are recorded here. Their courage and perseverance have been shown in making better conditions for women and children.

A Book of South Australia: Women in the First Hundred Years had similar aims: to tell of the 'noble' part played by early women settlers, filled with 'fortitude in the face of privation and danger'.[47] In the foreword Lady Duggan reminded readers, 'Today we are reaping the benefit of their great endeavour, of their determination to win through and of their faith.' *The Peaceful Army: A Memorial to the Pioneer Women of Australia 1788 to 1938* again celebrated 'the heroism and devotion of the women who have shared, and are still sharing, the hardships of this struggle [and they] deserve all the recognition we can give them'.[48] Graeme Davison has suggested that the 'Australian legend' was promoted by urban dwellers far from the rigours of the frontier;[49] one might perhaps sense here an admiration of the urban middle-class woman for the unimaginable hardships of bush housekeeping. (They disregarded, as many have noted, the ways in which white women oppressed Aboriginal women in this process.)

The Fraser and Palmer Victorian collection told of women who 'blazed the trail' as 'firsts'—the first woman telegraphist, the first woman elected to a municipal council, as well as the early women artists and writers of Victoria. It also discussed improvements in girls' and women's education, 'citizenship', women in trade unions, clubs, welfare work, nursing. The South Australian collection was similar, with the records of women in medicine, law, arts, sciences, drama and social welfare, with a piece on pioneer women by Daisy Bates (who strangely praised the role of white women in their relations with Aboriginal women), and chapters on Mary McKillop and Catherine Spence. In *The Peaceful Army* M. Barnard Eldershaw wrote on Elizabeth Macarthur, Dymphna Cusack on Mary Reiby, Miles Franklin on Rose Scott, Eleanor Dark on Caroline Chisholm: 'Not half-a-dozen books by Mary Wollstonecraft', she wrote, 'could have been more effective "vindication" than the life of this indomitable woman'. The substance of these volumes is a useful indicator of what women thought worth preserving and asserting about Australian women's past lives.

Mary Durack wrote of Eliza Shaw, the subject of her 1976 biography *To Be Heirs Forever*, that

> Eliza Shaw was among the longest lived of the early settlers. She survived her husband, five of her nine children and most of her contemporaries, and saw out the regimes of no less than eight successive governors. Her story therefore encompasses almost the first half-century of Swan River settlement. It is to a great extent the story of her times and of the policies of local govenment, especially on issues relating to labour and land tenure that were of such vital importance to the early colonists.[50]

It was not often that these women writers were able to relate their subjects firmly to a social context in the manner Mary Durack attempted. If they did have the skills to develop a broader historical perspective, for the most part the material on women was added on to pre-existing historical framework. Of the limitations of such traditional women's history, Natalie Zemon Davis has observed,

> 'Establishing the record of female activity in the past, it nevertheless wrenched it from its historical context. Treating women in isolation from men, it ordinarily said little about the significance of sex roles in social life and historical change. And written with special goals for a special audience, it had little effect on the main body of historical writing or periodization'.[51]

In their biographies and family chronicles, however, a few of these early women's historians (such as those of Mary Durack herself, Alexandra Hasluck and Marnie Bassett) may be discerned as presaging a new approach to women's history, though the realisation was fleeting. In family histories, to begin with, women could scarcely be ignored, but were being treated alongside the history of men. Men certainly are the main protagonists of *Kings in Grass Castles*,[52] but the women are nevertheless integral in a passage such as the following, for example, when the family are leaving for new lands. The men, Durack wrote, gathered in the cattle and horses, while 'the women packed up their wagons and the drays, stacked in the rough-hewn furniture, the kitchen utensils, babies' cradles piled with clothing, tin trucks full of valued possessions from their old homes in New South Wales.' In work such as Hasluck[53] on Georgiana Molloy, and Bassett[54] on the Hentys, there is some recognition of female networks, of the importance of personal relationships within the family and of kin networks that were, in the hands of some later women's historians, turned into a tool of analysis. For the most part, however, the women's accounts remained separate from the men's. A comment by Vance Palmer in the foreword to his *National Portraits* of

1940[55] suggests implications for this independent/dependent development. He wrote that 'one obvious lack in this book is any reference to the work of women. Surely, it will be said, there have been some women in Australia of marked creative ability or personal distinction. Quite so. *The Peaceful Army*, a very fine volume edited by Flora Eldershaw and devoted to such women, is my sole but sufficient reason for not including some of them here.' The women acted separately because of male exclusiveness; their separate endeavour was then used as an excuse for their exclusion.

This separate endeavour by women to write their own history in personal terms has continued throughout the 1970s into the 1980s, because the neglect of women's past that gave rise to the genre has most certainly not disappeared. Now, however, there is an interested audience for women's personal chronicles, evident when women spoke of their own life efforts at the Women and Labour Conferences. Marilyn Lake and Farley Kelly have edited a collection of biographical essays on women for the sesquicentenary of Victoria in 1984. Women who were part of the 'underside' of history in Australia still need recovery; 'women worthies' remain little known to the public at large.[56] The situation, however, unlike the environment of the centennial writers of the 1930s, is undergoing rapid change.

In 1958, the Social Science Research Council of Australia, (since transformed into the eminently more prestigious-sounding Academy of Social Sciences) engaged the Englishman Norman Mackenzie to undertake a research project on the position of women in Australian Society. An academic gap had been noted; MacKenzie did his best to fill it.[57] Part of the reason for women's disadvantaged position, he reasoned, was clearly historical, but Australian historiography offered him little help. 'It is scarcely surprising', he wrote in *Women in Australia*,

> that we know so little about women in those early years, for few among this anonymous regiment reached officer rank. One or two with unusual gifts or fortunate circumstances could break through the barriers that, in the Victorian era, ensured that women should receive little education and even fewer opportunities to enter public life. The majority had to face more immediate problems in the domestic world to which both custom and necessity confined them.

Norman MacKenzie understood the stuff of history. Women's historians who bent their attention to the history of women in the 1970s, mostly young and stimulated by current feminism, had no such respectful notions about the inviolability of such an historical model of relevance. Drawn from a generation of women who had

had better educational opportunities than women in the past, with a wider potential readership, and strengthened by a sense of a new direction in scholarship in other Western countries, these scholars have worked separately on women's history, but with such an historiographical and theoretical range that at last women's history is clambering out of its separate sphere. The tone of the writing, the style, the issues raised, are now very different from anything intellectual women had written previously.

Anne Summers and Miriam Dixson presented the first challenges to mainstream Australian history in their germinal studies *Damned Whores and God's Police*[58] and *The Real Matilda*,[59] published in the mid-1970s within months of each other. Confronting the historical generalisations of the radical nationalist tradition, they each—with their separate radical feminist analysis—discounted the idea that Australian history involved the development of an egalitarian society based on the particular experience of the Australian frontier. Those circumstances that might have been conducive to male mateship and male opportunity had precisely the opposite effect on colonial women. Miriam Dixson pictured male immigrants imbued with the denigratory attitudes towards women common among Irish and English poor, and reaching a country where the sexual exploitation of female convicts and the harsh conditions for pioneering women served only to perpetuate sexist oppression. Anne Summers saw the sexually exploitative nature of Australia's early years giving way to a more settled society in which women were controlled by the manipulation of two dominant female stereotypes, of deviant whore and upholder of conventional morality. This was a far cry from notions of Australian history as Whiggish or communitarian progress; a new version, too, of that earlier myth about pioneer women.

Summers's and Dixson's books coincided with the publication of an unprecedented number of works on women's history, research for which had been undertaken since Ann Curthoys' original *Arena* article of 1970. There was a sound monograph from Beverley Kingston, *My Wife, My Daughter and Poor Mary Ann*[60] along with Edna Ryan's and Ann Conlon's *Gentle Invaders: Australian Women At Work 1788–1974*[61] and a collection edited by Ann Curthoys, Susan Eade and Peter Spearritt entitled *Women at Work*,[62] all appearing in 1975. Two other collections contained valuable historical chapters, Fay Gale's *Women's Roles in Aboriginal Society*[63] and Jan Mercer's *The Other Half: Women in Australian Society*.[64] Two feminist journals, *Refractory Girl* and *Hecate* were regularly publishing innovative historical articles.

Since that first spate of publication, further collections of essays have appeared, three drawn from the Women and Labour Conferences at Sydney, Melbourne and Adelaide, others concentrating on women's roles in the church, in prostitution, in the law, a women's studies reader, and a recent collection of articles from the University of Western Australia. Chapters on women's issues are now regularly included in specialised historical collections. There are now useful collections of primary source documents and published bibliographical tools to assist the women's history researcher. Further full-length studies are appearing more slowly: Drusilla Modjeska on Australian women writers,[65] Janine Burke on women artists,[66] Katrina Alford's economic history of women in early colonial Australia.[67] Many more can be expected over the next few years, as books currently being prepared for press appear, and as major research projects now under way are completed.[68]

Women's history is less developed here than in the United States or Britain, where a much larger population has supported many more scholars. This new Australian women's history is addressing itself to a full range of Australian historical issues, but in many cases fresh insights are being most effectively suggested rather than being exhaustively demonstrated while we await full-length studies. Taking the field of women's history as a whole, however, the canon of traditional history is being as significantly challenged here as elsewhere, and is even more influential than in other countries, since social history had developed only slightly in Australia when women's historians began to publish their work. In many cases then, they are undertaking research on areas in which a wider group of historians are concentrating elsewhere.

Before outlining where I think women's history is taking important initiatives, it might be worth acknowledging that scholars are not pursuing its goals in an unproblematical fashion. To discover conceptual frameworks to elicit meaning from fragments about women's past has been and continues to be a difficult task. There are sharp debates over contrasting and sometimes conflicting approaches. Any growing area of history has been subject to controversy, and since women's history is aligned to an activist movement that is itself subject to theoretical disagreements, it would be surprising if this were not the case. As Joan Kelly-Gadol said, 'Women's history has a dual goal: to restore women to history and to restore our history to women.'[69] Some women's historians may interpret the past in ways that seem unhelpful to feminist strategies for change in the present, and what energises the activists constructively is subject to disagreement. With their emphasis on class-based material oppression, socialist feminists are criticised for disregarding male dominance. Radical feminists, with their stress on patriarchy and sexual politics, are criticised for ignoring class ('If you don't think class matters, that merely means you are bourgeois'). Social historians who portray women's lives in a descriptive ethnographic fashion, particularly attempting to reconstruct women's consciousness in their own time, are suspected of insensitivity to women's sharp social disadvantages.

This argument over a stance towards women in the past may be categorised somewhat starkly by a portrayal of women as 'victims' or as 'agents' in their social environment. Sheila Ryan Johansson[70] comments that contemporary feminist writing rejects older works on women as a saga of 'Woman-the Good' or 'Woman-the-Bad', and has substituted 'Woman-the-Passive-Victim'. 'The present emphasis on the utter, total and complete victimization of women in the past leads only to the conclusion that for one half of humanity, time has meant nothing more than survival, or a cowlike submission to inscrutable natural processes and outrageous social customs.' Others have complained that to insist on the centrality of male oppression of women maintains men as the central actors, yet again, in women's past, so that women's history remains a sub-area of male history. According to Carroll Smith-Rosenberg, 'to insist on the centrality of the male-female oppressive dyad, ironically maintains men as the central actors in women's past and thus transforms women's history into a subcategory of the history of male values and behaviour'.[71] She continued her critique in this way,

> One of the principal goals of women's history has been to so re-define the canons of traditional history that the events and processes central to women's experience assume historical centrality, and women are recognized as active agents of social change. A second goal of women's history has been to explore the complexity of the female experience. The purpose of women's history, thus, is not to create a pantheon of ideologically correct heroines, but to analyze the evolution of women's roles, in the context of the effect of economic change upon a society's allocation of economic resources and power, institutional developments, and ideological conceptualizations.

Women's historians who approach women in the past from a more strongly feminist perspective, however, have cause to object to the implications in the work of those who adopt this stance. To write women's history from inside the social construction of reality of the participants themselves can weaken the restrictive force of the argument that women make their own history but *not* in circumstances of their own choosing. (It is perhaps a similar debate to the one that centred on new approaches to the history of slavery in the American South.) Historians of women will continue to develop analytical skills in response to this controversy about the historical process.

The original insight that women's history is bringing to bear on history centres not simply on the treatment of the private sphere but on the complex relationship of private to public, which is changing constantly under the impact of economic and cultural change. As social historians, women's historians are treating the personal, the private and the mundane; but women's historians are also examining the extent to which wider political and social forces have set boundaries to the private experience, and, conversely, how the public behaviour of women and men is rooted in cultural notions of gender that were learned in and were sustained by the private sphere. By demonstrating in the process how women's history is relational and can only be understood in a broader context, so, too, is it demonstrating that men's history must similarly be viewed within the context of ideas of gender. Natalie Zemon Davis has said that we should be interested in the history of both women and men, that we should not be working only on the subjected sex any more than an historian of class can focus exclusively on peasants.[71]

Within the private sphere, women's historians have tackled the history of housework, the concept of women's culture and family relationships. The mechanics of cooking, cleaning, washing, the entire material culture of the home, have been resurrected from the folk museum, and the changing meaning of 'housework' and 'housewife' has been explored. Women's historians examine the life cycle of women, from infancy through to menarche, marriage, childbirth, lactation, fertility control, maturity, ill-health and old age, together with the social roles of daughter, sister, wife, mother and grandmother. They raise questions about women's sexuality, about sexual politics, patriarchal control, domestic violence, family breakdown and divorce. Some are exploring the concept of a 'woman's culture', a different social construction of reality in which women found ways to mitigate their social inferiority in a compensatory way by finding a source of strength in common concerns. They are, moreover, suggesting ways in which cultural constraints of this world influence transformations caused by industrialisation, technological change and urbanisation; in turn they show how the demands of the powerful, of the state and of capitalist interests have monitored ideologies such as motherhood, notions of femininity and the practices of sexuality and birth control, and how political forces shaped the laws which have strongly influenced personal worlds.[72]

Conversely, women's historians have looked at women's roles in public life, and in particular their paid work experience, their role in social reform and in politics, and 'deviant' women, relating both the changes obvious over time and also certain continuities in patterns of behaviour to familial concepts. The timing of women's entry to paid work, the duration of work, the gender dichotomy of the labour force, the entry of women to professions and questions of unionisation have all been subjected to clarifying analysis, while these studies throw into new relief the history of labour. Women's social reform associations and their past feminist activism are being related on one hand to major social changes in society, rather than being treated as preoccupations of exceptional or unusual women, and at the same time are being connected ideologically, once again, to personal and familial concerns. Women's historians are examining treatment of those women whom society has designated deviant, particularly prostitutes, in a similarly complex way. Overall, they are uncovering a rich vein of material and creating new categories of relevance.

I was asked in this chapter to consider whether taking gender into account makes a substantive difference to the discipline of history: whether women's history is merely a sub-area of history or whether history is transformed once women and women's activities are included. My answer has been a positive one; I believe women's history makes a radical difference to the discipline and that a process of transformation is taking place. It would be an exaggeration to suggest that at the level of much advanced history teaching or individual research, women's history has achieved more than encouraging teachers and scholars to add missing material on women to the style of history they previously taught or studied. (This seems a substantial improvement on previous denigratory and dismissive attitudes.) This admission does not negate my view that at the boundaries of the discipline women's history is proving a radical and far-reaching innovation. The inclusion of material on women in the bicentennial history of Australia suggests that women's history is influencing historical consciousness in this country.

Women were never unimportant or marginal from the perspective of their own lives; they became unimportant only through male historical constructs that ignored or trivialised their world and dismissed efforts by women outside academia to record a past for themselves. Now that women's history is taking its place within the academy, a different view of the past begins to emerge, promising a clearer vision of the history of humankind. Writing women into history 'implies not only a new history of women but also a new history'.[73]

3 Seeing Women in the Landscape: Alternative Views of the World Around Us*

FAY GALE

Women, like children, should be seen but not heard. Often in the social sciences, however, they have been neither seen nor heard. Some geographers are now trying to alter that view; trying to include women in descriptions of the world around us. Social scientists have become used to viewing the world as men view it, through men's eyes. For natural scientists a largely male view of our environment may not matter, but for social scientists, who purport to study society, ignoring half of that population has led to a limited and skewed world view.

In my own discipline of geography, this has been very evident. Geography has traditionally defined itself as 'a study of man and his environment'. Famous landmarks in the discipline have been given titles such as 'Man's role in changing the face of the earth'. In 1982 a major text appeared entitled *Man and the Australian Environment*. Geographers have usually assumed that the word 'man' was used in the generic sense and, indeed, when queried about the sexist implications this has often been the defence given. However, a study of work contained in such volumes demonstrates that the material deals predominantly with environments and/or activities of males and that female issues are largely ignored. A pioneer in modern human geography, Carl Sauer[1], did suggest that women's role in changing the face of the Earth may, in fact, have been as important as that of men, because the food-gathering activities of women must have substantially changed the animal and plant life of a region by selecting some varieties, domesticating others and transporting species to new areas. But geographers largely ignored his plea to consider the critical

*I am grateful for the guidance and inspiration given to me by many female scholars, especially Janice Monk of the Southwest Institute for Research on Women, Arizona.

role of women, as distinct from that of men, in developing our present landscapes.

The world, Australia—these are landscapes peopled with and altered by men. Yet if social science is about people, we have been studying only half of our science. A study of the other half may show different views of the world around us. It is resisted by all but a brave few because any step towards that other side of the view has enormous repercussions for our whole theoretical framework and for the organisation and planning of society. And geographers have been especially slow to include the other half of society in the field they call 'human geography'. Recently two women geographers have described this process in an article entitled 'On not excluding half of the human in human geography'.[2] In our desire as social scientists to be accepted by the academic community and our willingness to suppress our feeling of subordination in scientific stature to the natural scientists, we have adopted their methods and narrow world view, but for us it has been much more serious. It has limited both our methods of data collection and our analytical framework.

In geography, for example, gender is of no consequence in studying rocks or geomorphological processes or distributions but, when we transferred the same methods and the same standards of analysis to the human processes, we sadly missed a major part of the data. In our desire to be scientifically acceptable, as we thought, we in fact introduced considerable bias into our studies. Sampling procedures applicable in studies of elements of the physical landscape were used, for so-called scientific reasons, as the discipline developed in areas of economic application. The transfer was not questioned because it appeared that a study of wheatfields or the distribution of wool production could achieve reliable results from working solely with male respondents. But as geographers moved further into the social sphere they continued to retain the methods and theories developed in studying the distribution of physical features in the landscape. While such methodology could be transferred with only limited discrepancies to distributions of say, crop production, the sexist bias in our methods becomes frighteningly evident when applied across the whole discipline. Human geographers are not natural scientists and the same scientific structures cannot be simply transferred. Geography is a good example of the limitations that have beset social science as a whole in its often blind and subservient following of the natural sciences, since geography's origins lie firmly in the so-called natural landscape.

The concept of a household head used so extensively in social surveys is one such bias. He is a largely mythical character who has been heavily dressed in real clothes and imbued with ideas and attitudes that control the activities of this theoretically uniform unit called a family or household. The individuals who make up any household vary considerably in a number of respects, of which age and gender are two noticeable differences. Female geographers have illustrated some of the problems of assuming the unified nature of households and not allowing for individual differences. Tivers[3], for example, says that 'by accepting the household as the predominant unit of study in human geography and by neglecting the explicit study of the geography of women, geographers have implicitly accepted the existing structure of society and prevented the examination of one of the most persistent and pervasive forms of inequality in our society'.

Indeed it is rather questionable today whether there is, in fact, such a person as a household head and, if there is, whether studying 'him' alone is of scientific value. One geographer has just completed a study of social activities in country towns by using the household head as the basis. He acquired his data by surveying a beautifully valid statistical sample of rural dwellers—except that all were male. When he used the concept of a household head and as a result surveyed only males, he said he saw no problem, since husbands would know about the social activities of their wives and be able to answer the questionnaire on behalf of all members of the family. Those of us familiar with the very different social interests of males and females in country towns in Australia are not convinced.

But even the belief, which many male social scientists now promulgate, that all social surveys should include women as well as men, is not enough. It is often little more than a realisation that the woman's point of view may add colour to the data. It rarely assumes that the woman's view, or for that matter the opinions of other members of the household, may be different or contradictory and require a totally different theoretical or methodological framework for study. Certainly social science made an important step forward when it accepted the principle that, for many studies, samples should represent both males and females but in doing so it ignored the reality that some topics are best suited to a study of one gender only. Our colleagues in physiology do not have the intellectual problem that we have. To them it is clear and academically acceptable to study only females when considering features that are solely female.

Woe betide the female scholar who goes further than merely including women in the study population and suggests that a particular study will be better or more accurate if only, or primarily, females are studied. I have recently had that experience. I have worked in Adelaide for many years and have published three separate studies of Aboriginal people living in that city. In the first two, in 1966 and 1973, I tried to work with both men and women. However in a study undertaken in 1980[4] the bulk of the material came only from women. I was looking at the household economic situation of Aborigines in

Adelaide. My earlier work had shown me quite clearly that Aboriginal women were the primary economic providers for their families; that if we keep such an outmoded concept as that of household heads, the majority of household heads are women. I therefore surveyed mainly women. Had I counted just those few male household 'heads' or taken an equal sample of male and female heads, my study would have been biased because of the relatively low number of males who could be categorised as 'heads' of Aboriginal households. I therefore decided to work mainly with women. Indeed, in Aboriginal society and probably in our society also, women can work successfully only with women, for the same reason that men, even if they attempt to study both genders, acquire reliable data on many issues only from their own sex.

However, a male colleague has heavily criticised my decision to work primarily with women. Didn't I know that it was 'accepted practice' these days to 'sample both males and females'?[5] It appears that, while some of my male colleagues now consider that they should add women to their samples, all hell will break loose on the female who decides that better results, for a particular purpose, will be achieved by focusing on women. That is apparently going too far.

The fact is that Aboriginal women in our cities are the most reliable source of household economic data. A study of poverty, household incomes, housing distribution or similar issues can best be achieved by working with a female sample. In the general Australian economy, where males are the main providers of monetary income, it is difficult for male scholars, welfare bureaucrats or policymakers to accept the hard fact of life that amongst at least one sub-group, namely Aborigines, it is primarily the women who hold the economic power, such as it is. To study this means studying females.

What I am trying to say is that, as necessary as it is to add females to our samples of males in our studies of society, we should not be content that this is the end goal. Just as there are topics best studied among males only, there are also issues best understood by working solely with females. And these are not necessarily trivial issues, as we have been led to believe.

Again it seems to me that, as social scientists cringing in our colonial mentality against natural scientists, we have been willing to accept all too easily the label of 'trivial' or 'superficial' or 'subjective' for areas that we do not think physical scientists will judge to be of high intellectual rigour. Virtually everything that concerns females is still in this shady area. The production of unpaid housework or child rearing are obvious economic areas that are ignored, as Meredith Edwards's paper in this book has shown. It therefore becomes difficult when we try to show that Aboriginal women, who usually do not work for paid labour, are household 'heads' and the primary economic decisionmakers.

We are slowly coming to realise that the world consists of males and females sometimes acting together, sometimes independently, and that the study methods should be determined by the nature of the topic and the degree to which the problem relates jointly or separately to each gender. To ignore females or to assume that they are only an extra factor, at best a further variable, is to lose a part of the world view. Plans are built, decisions made, the world constructed on the basis of these views. We have made inaccurate and often costly mistakes because of the limited scope of our science.

To illustrate this need to see females as more than an added variable, I will use another geographic example. The journey to work is one of the rather well-worn areas of study in geography. Cities have been planned, freeways built and public transport routes determined on the model that families live in the suburbs and that males travel each day between home and work. The transport system has been geared to enable men to commute daily by the shortest, fastest route at peak hours. City planning has assumed the accuracy and general applicability of this male model.

Recently studies have begun on women's journeys to work and as these have emerged they have shown that the assumed model is inapplicable in many cases. These studies have cast doubt on the basic assumption that as more women entered the workforce their journeys to work would be the same as those of males.[6] Studying female travel patterns has not just added a further variable; it has questioned the whole model on which urban planning and transport systems have depended. Taking women as a separate study has meant not just a slight adaptation of methods; it has thrown up the need for a reassessment of theory and application.

Although public transport has been designed and continues to be built (e.g., the new *O-bahn* route under construction in Adelaide) on the male commuter model, studies have shown that the transport requirements of women, especially working mothers, are different from those of men. Studies of women's journeys to work do not parallel men's journeys. Women with families try to obtain work as close as possible to their homes to minimise the extra time they spend in travelling. Manning[7] has illustrated major differences in the ways men and women in Sydney travel to work. He found, for example, that women travel much shorter distances to work than do men. In Sydney he reported that the median straight line journey to work for women was two-thirds of that for men. Because married women prefer employment close to where they live they will take lower-paid, part-time work and may refuse or be ineligible for promotion as a result. Their need to contain their travelling thus limits their range of choice in employment.

To a large degree, women's journeys to work are also different in kind as well as in distance. Women with family responsibilities tend not to take the straight commuter-type trips. Their journeys include stops and detours for shopping, taking children to and from day care or school, and visiting aged parents. Public transport in its pattern, location and fare structure is designed quite contrary to these needs and yet a large proportion of women use such facilities. Indeed, many require an extra trip a day in the opposite direction from work. The time and the cost of such requirements are seldom taken into account in planning either roads or public transport.

Furthermore, studies of women's journeys to work show that frequently when the household owns a car the male, who has the least travel problem, takes the car. Where there are two cars, the male frequently takes the larger 'family car' alone on his non-stop trip while the wife uses a smaller, often crowded car as she takes her turn at the roster of delivering her own and the neighbour's children to day care centres and schools.

Studies in both the United States of America and in Australia have shown that there are considerable differences between men and women in the means of transport as well as in the distance travelled. Women use public transport relatively more frequently than do men in their journey to work. Wekerle,[8] in reviewing several studies in the United States of America, suggests that women use public transport two to three times more regularly than do men in that country. The situation in Australia must be comparable, since, according to Manning,[9] the proportion of women in Sydney who travel by bus or who walk to work is more than double that of men.

Conversely, more men drive to work. Manning found that both single and married women used cars much less frequently than did men. He discovered that, while more than two-thirds of men in Sydney travel to work by car, less than one-third of single women and only one-half of married women had such access. Thus married women, who have previously taken work close to home to save time as well as single women who do not have such restrictions, take much longer than men per kilometre travelled. Married women tend to have the shortest trips to work but at comparatively slower speeds than men. Because of their greater use of public transport or walking, it is even more important for women to limit the distance they travel. Manning,[10] suggests that women in general travel shorter distances to work 'because they can afford to travel only by slower means of transport, and, in the case of married women, because their time is more valuable'. Thus women are disadvantaged by being forced to use a transport system built on a male model which does not necessarily suit them and as a result adds considerable cost to them, their families and ultimately to the community at large.

It is often assumed that women are most involved in the suburbs and that the metropolitan centres are largely men's places. The increasing participation of women in the city workforce has made important changes to the landscape of the city. A simple example is the growth of restaurants and boutiques. Working women have had to save time over household activities. Their diminishing time but increasing income have led to some restructuring of city centres. But the working women's role in 'revitalising cities'[11] is often ignored.

While the preference of the working father is usually for a sub-urban home and garden, this is not so often true for working mothers. They often prefer city apartments where travelling time is less, there are more services to assist with household chores and there is a variety of entertainment available to their children close at hand.

So imbued are we with the suburban ideal that large housing estates have sprawled at the edges of our cities giving horrendously long journeys for working mothers and impossible transport prob-lems for sole parents. Yet the government-subsidised housing estates built on the suburban pattern are not occupied by only model nuclear families. Here are to be found the greatest proportion of supporting mothers. In fact, some housing estates are occupied predominantly by single parents. For them the isolation and the prohibitive costs of travel are in total disagreement with the urban model. Forster[12] dis-cusses some of these problems in relation to employment for people at Elizabeth, an outer suburb of Adelaide.

Suburbs may well satisfy commuter males with non-working wives, but they do not necessarily suit either working wives or non-working supporting mothers. In ignoring such large and growing sections of our cities we are increasing the financial and social costs to the society at large. Studies of women in cities have thus challenged male con-structs of urban planning.

Prevailing theories on spatial inequality rely upon poverty, residential segregation, ethnic groupings, etc., to explain variations between different groups, but research on women must cross the variables of class, race or spatial location and it thus demands a revi-sion of existing theories.[13] The modern city with its zoning patterns, neighbourhood structures and transport system is built according to the plans constructed by males based on the male view of urban life. The urban world of many women is different. Broader theoretical models are necessary to incorporate women in the urban landscape.

My own discipline, geography, growing as it did out of studies of the physical landscape, has been slow to adjust to the fact that women, as well as men, inhabit the landscape and that their be-haviour and their effects on the environment may not necessarily be the same as those of men.

My sister discipline of Australian anthropology was a little, but only a little, quicker to realise that women offered a quite different view of the world. Until very recently the prevailing view of anthropologists, who were previously male, was, in simplistic terms, that Aboriginal men were the tribal elders who held the status, power and authority in Aboriginal society. Anthropologists had, as Diane Bell[14] so aptly notes, relegated Aboriginal women to the position of 'feeders, breeders and follow-the-leaders'.

Such a view was but a reflection of the assumed status of women in our own society. And if the superior society of Western civilisation did not accord equal status to its women, clearly no culture, especially one assumed to be hardly human, could be more developed in this respect. The view was pervasive and has dominated the whole conceptual framework of our relationships with Aborigines. Aboriginal women were merely convenient objects who helped make life more comfortable for European male settlers on the frontiers.

As female anthropologists developed their ideas and tried to relate their field experiences among Aboriginal groups to the theoretical models they had been taught, the enormous gap between theory and the real Aboriginal world became too obvious to ignore. Thus Catherine Berndt[15] wrote an article, the title of which succinctly defines the problem: 'Digging sticks and spears or, the two-sex model'.

Indeed, ever since the publication of Phyllis Kaberry's work in 1939 there has been ample evidence[16, 17, 18] to show that Aboriginal women had a significant part to play in the overall ceremonial life as well as the economic and family activities of their societies. More recently Diane Bell[19, 20] has summarised the material and added her own field work to prove beyond doubt that Aboriginal women's activities in rituals and in land relationships were real and alive, even though male observers failed to see them. Yet the anthropological profession in particular and Australian society in general, along with the academic community at large, continued to believe in the unimportant, indeed, trivial role of Aboriginal women, outside their immediate family responsibilities.

These notions have been seriously challenged as more and more female scholars have worked in the field and as Aboriginal women have been given the opportunity to speak for themselves.[21, 22] It was gradually accepted that Aboriginal women produced substantial amounts of food and that, in economic terms, they and their children were independent of men. This was in stark contrast to the predominant position of women in Western society.

It has been in the area of land ownership, however, that wide acceptance of male superiority and domination has been hardest to combat. So prevalent was the assumption that land was owned by males that the whole structure relating to land claims has been established on this conceptual model. Male politicians, lawyers and bureaucrats, firmly convinced of the reliability of the model of male ownership of land and of its sacred sites, set up a legal machinery for land rights which largely ignored women. That construct is now being challenged in many areas of Australia.

As one piece of land after another has come up for contest, either through land claims or development proposals, it has become increasingly clear that men are not the sole owners of land and sites. Women also have claim to land and there are areas sacred to women and women's rituals. Inevitably, European males working in various capacities in Aboriginal Australia saw only the world of the Aboriginal male and assumed that was a total view. Land rights and the whole consultancy process over sites became modelled on a view of Aboriginal society constructed by non-Aboriginal males. Gradually, non-Aboriginal women began to see the world of Aboriginal women and seriously challenged the whole idea of a male-dominated landscape in both actual and totemic terms. But the male assumption has cost Australia dearly.

Example after example can now be cited where the dominant Australian view of a male-structured Aboriginal society has been exploded. The site of a proposed recreation lake at Alice Springs is but one such example. It so happens that the lake was planned for a site sacred to Aboriginal women. In Australian society the engineering, construction and planning world, along with that of government, is largely dominated by male decisionmakers. Although some Aboriginal men were consulted it was not thought necessary to consult Aboriginal women. It never occurred to this whole assortment of non-Aboriginal males that Aboriginal women owned land or sites or carried out religious rituals. So strong has been the establishment of the theoretical model of male superiority in Aboriginal society that non-Aboriginal males failed even to consider Aboriginal women.

Werlatyre-Therre, a very important women's site, would have been flooded by the proposed lake at Alice Springs. When announcements were made about the construction of a dam to enable the development of a recreation lake, the women, who had not been considered, let alone consulted, began to protest. Very early in the discussions an old woman custodian spoke strongly against the suggestion. She said it was a crucial site in the whole women's Dreaming pattern of central Australia. But the male workers consulting with the Aboriginal men seemed not to hear. So tightly fixed were the theoretical blinkers that it was felt that if the site was not crucial for men it could not be an important area. It seemed impossible to imagine that women had essential rituals or that they owned and treasured sacred areas that were the preserve of women and not of men. The old woman could not be heard because every self-respecting, educated Australian knows that Aboriginal women do not own sites or have sacred rituals to which men are not permitted. As proposals went ahead a number of Aboriginal women who had strong ties with the area moved in to protest loudly and visibly. They set up camp at the site and effectively called a halt to the construction, demanding that they be recognised, just as Aboriginal men would have been considered if it had been a men's site. Once again the Australian government, that is, we, are going to pay in hard cash for the time lost, an inquiry and the exploration of alternatives, largely because our male view of Aboriginal Australia excluded women.

The economic as well as social costs of our limited theoretical constructs can be seen affecting almost every sphere of life. The assumption of male leadership and decisionmaking in Aboriginal society was no doubt gladly accepted by non-Aboriginal scientists and government officers. It suited the Western view of man's proper place. The evidence of the gulf between fact and theory is becoming greater daily.

On the basis of the model, which Australian social science constructed in relation to Aboriginal power structures, the police force made decisions that have disadvantaged both Aboriginal and non-Aboriginal women. One of the rationalisations for stationing only male officers in outback and rural areas where Aborigines were living has been the assumption that Aboriginal men hold the power, make the decisions, know the sacred sites and will communicate only with men.

Policewomen protested because these limitations on where they could be appointed disadvantaged them for promotion. Aboriginal women complained that with only male police it was not possible for women to call for assistance, obtain driving licences or be involved in a number of other issues where they felt handicapped in relation to their menfolk. But the complaints from both groups of women were, at first, ignored because they did not fit the theoretical constructs built up, albeit falsely, about Aboriginal social structure.

Perhaps even more insidious than the dangers and costs we have experienced as a result of our male-dominated view of Aboriginal society has been the enforcing of that view upon Aborigines. Aboriginal men have been selected and groomed for special positions in the public service. Aboriginal men, in outback Australia, have been taught by non-Aboriginal men to consider themselves superior. They have become so self-conscious of their position that when consulted about land or sites they are virtually too embarrassed to say, 'Don't ask us, women control that area, ask the women'.

Aboriginal women have also been similarly affected. They have been told so often that it is their men who own the land, know the only sacred sites and rituals and make the decisions. When their own life experiences disagree with the constructs being put upon them by non-Aborigines, they are confused.

Let me take a recent South Australian example to illustrate this situation. Jane Jacobs[23] has shown the extent to which Aboriginal women have been affected by the masculine-centred view of the world. In spite of the constant attempts by Pitjatjantjara women to be involved in the Pitjatjantjara land rights negotiations, the whole process was decided between Aboriginal males and non-Aboriginal males in the form of lawyers, anthropologists, public servants and politicians. Pitjatjantjara women protested at their exclusion. They hired buses to bring them to Adelaide when their male relatives came south for negotiations so as to ensure that they were not entirely neglected. But the premier and his various advisors talked only with the men. The press, along with everyone else, largely ignored the presence of the women so that few outsiders even realised that the women were there, let alone knew how they felt.

Other Aboriginal women saw this public image being put forward. It was, after all, well advertised with frequent photographs in the daily press of the 'all-male' team. The Adnjamathanha women of the Flinders Ranges assumed therefore that in Pitjatjantjara country the men were in control and that women had little influence. But in the Flinders area the women knew this was not true. Theirs was a society where women have strong positions of power and where women, as well as men, worked for land rights. When the Southern Lands Council was established, the women of the Adnjamathanha group were reluctant for their people to join. The women felt that the inclusion of Pitjatjantjara people, whose male domination had been clearly publicised, would lead to a demise of their own status.

Thus, not only have Australian males established a biased and limited view of Aboriginal society; they have even, inadvertently, imposed that view on to Aborigines who know it to be at variance with reality.

It is becoming obvious, therefore, that once we begin to see women in the landscape, to include them in our studies, much of the male-constructed theoretical base of social science is challenged. The process may be threatening but it is clear that to ignore women is costly, even in straightforward monetary terms.

Feminist scholarship is reconstructing our models of the world to include women in the landscape. It may be uncomfortable while it is happening, but in the long run our theories will be more accurate and their application less wasteful.

4 Rewards for Women's Work

BETTINA CASS

The experiences of work, rewards for work and official definitions of work and non-work constitute the most critical set of events and socially constructed meanings around which the life histories and life chances of women and men have been differentiated.

In the social sciences there has been a long tradition of scholarship in which unpaid activities carried out within the family household have been identified with non-work because they take place outside the transactions of the labour market. Gainful employment has been defined as work; domestic labour, being outside the market and regulated wage transactions, has been defined in the traditional economics literature as 'leisure',[1] and in the sociological literature as the sphere of family obligations.[2,3] As a result, in Australian social science scholarship until the mid-1970s, the labours of women who work within the household as wives, mothers and daughters, and the goods and services that their labours provide have been excluded from the annals of labour history[4], from the purview of labour market economists and economic historians[5,6], from the considerations of welfare and tax economists;[7,8] and from the sociological accounts of work.[9,10]

It is not my intention in this paper to review the significant feminist scholarship of the last decade which has explored the nature of women's work, paid and unpaid, in the household and in the workforce, and the connections between them. Rather, this paper identifies the contributions to social thought and social policies made by earlier feminist activists who from the 1920s challenged the dominant dichotomies of work and non-work, the relegation of men and women to these supposedly separate spheres of human activity and the economic, social and political injustices that women suffered as a result. These feminist challenges were made in response to the administrative, legislative and judicial processes that, from the last decade of the nineteenth century had institutionalised the work/non-work, market/domestic dichotomies, suffusing them with sex and gender connotations which legitimated these splits as 'natural', allocating rewards of income and social power accordingly.[11]

The Organisaton of Work and Non-work, Breadwinners and Dependants and Rates of Pay

I begin with the terms in which the population was officially enumerated and classified, which provides a vivid indication of governments' attitudes to paid and unpaid work, and no doubt reflected and reinforced emergent views about the rightful domestic division of labour.

Colonial and later Commonwealth statisticians, commencing with the censuses of 1891, defined employed men's daily labours as the gainful work of 'breadwinners', while women's daily domestic labours were defined as the non-work of 'dependants'.[12, 13, 14] This new classification, devised by the New South Wales statist Timothy Coghlan and the Tasmanian statist R.M. Johnston, placed wives and daughters at home (including a goodly proportion of rural women and women who assisted in family businesses) firmly in the dependent category for the first time. In the absence of a clear statement otherwise on the census form, such assistants in family enterprises, both rural and urban, and women doing domestic work without pay were classified as dependent. The result of these changes was 'to remove the functions of the reproduction and maintenance of the population from the definition of economic activity unless they were paid for in wages and salary'.[15]

Unpaid domestic workers were placed with other non-earners amongst the 'dependent': a category that included all persons dependent upon relatives or 'natural guardians', wives, children, and others not engaged in pursuits for which remuneration was paid; all persons dependent upon private charity and those whose support was a 'burthen on the public revenue'.

Deacon[16] emphasises that this work of government statisticians contributed to the official construction of gender placement, the relegation of women's unpaid work, whether as part of the household or part of the business enterprise, to the category of persons who did not work and were therefore held to be dependent on a male breadwinner, whatever the contribution they might have made either directly or indirectly to family income. Tait[17] pushes the interpretation in another direction by pointing to the significance of income definitions in the categorisation. What was distinctive, he argues, about the 1891 classification was not that workers were distinguished from non-workers, but that income recipients were distinguished from non-recipients.

What neither Deacon nor Tait notes is that the census classification contained a basic assumption of one-way income transfers taking place within the family from breadwinner to dependants. In addition it was assumed that these transfers could be equated with those received from private charity or public revenue. Wives and daughters in the household were held to be neither producers nor generators of income; were akin, in fact, to recipients of welfare. Official statistical collections retained the breadwinner/dependant classification until the post-World War II censuses, but its replacement by concepts of labour force status did not indicate that the underlying ideology of women's dependency had been superseded in other areas of public policy or private practices.

What was even more significant than the mode of statistical classification of men's work and women's work, of the remunerated and the unremunerated, was the very different ways in which the payment for breadwinners and dependants was regulated. In the labour market, the competing/conflicting interests of capital and labour over wages were represented collectively and state-regulated. The obligations of adult male breadwinners became the nub of the union movement's wage bargaining strategy from the turn of the century until the mid-1970s,[18] despite clear evidence that the capacity of the economy to pay had been the ruling doctrine in wage fixation probably from the outset.[19] Nevertheless, at the level of rhetoric and institutionalised advocacy at least, from 1905 legislative and judicial interventions established that the adult male 'living wage' (but not that of adult women) would contain a family component in recognition of men's legal obligations to their dependants.

The regulation of wage fixation to protect the earnings of adult men and their breadwinning responsibilities were *public acts* where opposing collective interests were represented and arbitrated. This must be contrasted with the treatment of women's interests as dependants. Their 'remuneration' was expected to be negotiated individually and in private within the confines of individual conjugal and family relationships. Such protections which were afforded were contained in various enactments from the colonial period which imposed upon husbands/fathers the legal obligation to maintain their wives and children. However, these obligations were rarely enforced successfully after separation.[20] In intact families, the maintenance of wives and children was left to the goodwill and discretion of the breadwinner as to fair transfers of income. This is not to suggest that such transfers from breadwinner to dependants were typified by unfairness, but to highlight the *public* character of the regulation of paid market work and the *private* character of the obligations and relationships surrounding unpaid non-market work.

One of the outcomes of the essentially private, individual nature of breadwinner/dependant negotiations is reflected in the over-representation of women and their children amongst the poor, making claims for subsistence upon colonial and post-colonial charities[21,22] and upon government agencies such as the State Children's Relief Board in New South Wales from the turn of the century and the equivalent welfare authorities in other states.[23] It was not too great a step from dependency on individual family breadwinners to dependency on government and non-government welfare agencies,[24] given the maintenance of women's 'living' wage below family subsistence level.

The principle of the 'living wage' for men had been institution-alised as a 'family wage' in Commonwealth and state arbitration tri-bunals since 1905 and 1907. Labour's demand for an ethical wages policy which would use the power of state tribunals to intervene in 'free' labour market mechanisms in which labour and capital met on unequal terms was translated into the rights of adult male workers to a basic minimum that allowed them and their families to be main-tained in reasonable comfort.[25,26] However, when it came to fixing the living wage for women, different principles were assumed to be operating. Mr Justice Higgins justified the decision he had made in the Mildura Fruit Pickers' case of 1912 to lay down a separate and lower minimum rate for jobs normally carried out by women, on the ground that women were not usually legally responsible for the maintenance of a family.[27] Similarly, Mr Justice Heydon, making the first declaration of a 'living wage' for women in the New South Wales Board of Trade in 1918, decided that the court could not consider that the female worker had any other responsibilities besides support-ing herself. The female minimum was to be determined on the pre-sumed typical case of the woman with no responsibility for depen-dants, as the male minimum was to be based on the presumed typical case of the man with legal responsibility for wife and children.[28] As a result of such decisions, the female living wage was maintained in Commonwealth and state industrial arbitration jurisdictions at 54 per cent of the male rate until the industrial conditions of World War II interrupted this pattern. Only in occupations where women's cheaper labour might lead to the displacement of men was equal pay a real consideration.

The dominant conception of wives and mothers as typically depen-dent non-earners and of women workers as having no dependants was found to be incorrect in several investigations of family and em-ployment status. Knibbs, the Commonwealth Statistician, in the first Australian expenditure survey in 1911 found that amongst the re-sponding families where both husband and wife were present, in only one-third of families was the husband the sole breadwinner.[29] Dr Marion Ireland's survey of women in Victorian manufacturing industries in 1928 found that almost 30 per cent of the women interviewed were helping to keep or were wholly supporting other family members. This proportion understated the real incidence of women's support of dependants because 46 per cent of the employees surveyed were juveniles, most of whom did not earn a wage sufficient to assist in the support of others.

In 1937 Muriel Heagney, trade union researcher and activist, appeared as witness for the Australian Council of Trade Unions in the basic wage inquiry in the Arbitration Court, supporting the claim for an increase in the basic wage rate for women to 60 per cent of the male rate. Heagney's case rested on the evidence collected in her book *Are Women Taking Men's Jobs?* (1935) which showed that women workers, both single and married, were required to support children and other family members on their inadequate wages. Women's lower wage rates had been a critical issue in the Depression when a greater proportion of women were compelled to find work because the breadwinner was unemployed, or because combined family income was too low for the family's subsistence. The burden of family support was borne by women at all times, but this burden increased during times of unemployment.[30] The court rejected the claim for an increase in women's base rate to 60 per cent of the male rate on the grounds that industry's capacity to pay would be severely extended and that it was not proven that women employees typically supported others. The court and later the Arbitration Commission held firm to notions of the 'family wage' when rejecting the unions' and women's organisations' claims for an equal basic (later a minimum) wage for women from 1937 until 1974. However, from 1931 (at least) the capacity of the economy to pay, the ideological nub of the employers' case, had gained explicit ascendancy as the guiding principle in wage determination.

Despite the accumulating evidence of women's paid work supporting others, in wage fixation the assumption that women's market work should provide only for their own frugal needs persisted until the abnormal industrial conditions of 1940–45. Even though remuneration for women's market work was subjected to arbitration, and even though the conditions of their paid work were subjected to official inquiry (the Royal Commission on Female and Juvenile Labour in Factories and Shops, 1911–12), the outcome of such interventions did not, paradoxically, provide protections for women in paid work. The *Report of the Royal Commission on Female and Juvenile Labour in Factories and Shops* presented a volume of evidence on women's low and inadequate pay, their almost complete lack of protection by unions, the fatigue generated by their poor working conditions, the lack of industrial safety and the virtual absence of opportunity to acquire skills and certification by apprenticeship, but the overriding concern of the *Report* was with the protection of women and girls from the moral and physical damage that factory work was firmly believed to inflict on their childbearing capacities.[31, 32, 33]

The purpose of all such state interventions was to 'protect' women's obligations in the domestic arena; their procreative capacities and their obligation to provide care for children and husband. The enforcement of women's dependency came from two directions: firstly, through the maintenance of a sex-segmented labour market where men's jobs and women's jobs were demarcated by job training, custom, arbitration court judgments and union compliance that consolidated unequal rates of pay; secondly, through the maintenance of household activities as a domain of private relationships, where the husband's obligation to support was left largely to the exercise of goodwill. Further, the assumption that women were or at least should be supported legitimated the belief that their wage needs were less than those of men.

It could be said that the division of labour thus entrenched lay at the very heart of state-regulated capitalist labour relations. Two sets of work incentives might be maintained by the construction of men as breadwinners and women as dependants: incentives for men to 'sell' their labour in the market, and incentives for women to provide their labour unpaid in the household, in return for their keep and the affection of those of whom they took care. However, this is merely a representation of the official ideology. The investigations of Knibbs[34], Ireland[35] and Heagney[36] showed that another set of work incentives were operating, impelling wives and mothers into paid market work (often unrecorded in the official statistics) so as to augment family income. As the Royal Commission on the Basic Wage[37] and Piddington's[38] popularisation of it documented graphically, the so-called male 'living wage' had never been sufficient to provide for the needs of more than husband, wife and at best one child. In families at the lower levels of the earnings distribution, even where there was a male 'breadwinner', women's earnings were also required for family subsistence.

Or, as Eleanor Rathbone argued robustly and repeatedly in Britain from the 1920s until 1945[39, 40, 41] and as Jessie Street argued in Australia[42], the concept of the 'family wage' could not be relied upon to ensure that breadwinners distributed to dependants what was their due. No authority was vested with the power to ensure that adequate intra-family transfers were made. For both of these reasons, 'dependants' also became 'breadwinners'—but rarely at rates of pay that would allow the woman in married-couple families to become the principal breadwinner or, as census forms designated it until 1976, the 'head of the household'.[43]

The Feminist Challenge

Feminist thinkers and activists inside and outside the labour movement, in different periods, challenged the dominant dichotomies: the construction of women as dependants, men as breadwinners and supporters; the organisation of paid market work and its reward so as to maintain these distinctions and inequalities.

What was distinctive about feminist political work and the thinking that informed it was the refusal to accept the dominant classifications of breadwinner/dependant; the recognition that domestic activities represented work of value; that women who were presumed to be supported were also themselves supporters, both through paid and unpaid work; that the 'family wage' was inadequate in providing for the needs of both breadwinner and dependants, firstly because it was set too low and secondly because there were no guarantees that the wages of the breadwinner were distributed equitably within the family. What this work did was to extend the efforts of Piddington, who in his Memorandum to the *Report of the Royal Commission on the Basic Wage*[44] and in his polemical booklet *The Next Step: A Family Basic Income*[45] had delineated the individual rights of children to income, separating them off from the father/breadwinner's right to a living wage with a family component. Women in the labour movement and in feminist groups outside the labour movement (the United Associations of Women, the National Council of Women) delineated the individual rights of mothers to an income, disaggregating further the collective interests of the family as represented by the male breadwinner.

Feminist thought reconceptualised the household as an arena of non-market work and social caring, an arena of women's labour that contributed both to the well-being of family members and to the well-being of the nation, through women's diligent attention to the care of children and breadwinners. They demanded that such labour required government-regulated income support for the mothers of dependent children: 'direct provision' to mothers on behalf of their children to recognise the *separate rights* of women and children to income, and they mobilised around the issue of motherhood or family endowment in the period 1920 to 1945.[46, 47, 48, 49, 50] Family endowment would provide a necessary supplement to the basic wage in families containing children. In being paid to mothers it would recognise the economic contribution of women's unpaid child-care and domestic labour.

There was a second and related thrust in feminist thought and advocacy, a critique of the 'family wage' principle. Inquiries such as the Basic Wage Commission[51] and the New South Wales Industrial Commission's Inquiry into the Living Wage[52] had demonstrated the inadequacy of ruling basic wage rates in meeting the needs of the domestic unit for which they were determined. Unionists were clearly aware of these inadequacies, but some feminists went further to challenge the fundamental assumptions of the family wage that legitimated wage injustice to women employees by denying their family obligations, and prescribed wives' debilitating dependency on their husbands' income. Muriel Heagney and Jessie Street reconceptualised women's market work as equal in value to men's market work and women's needs as identical to men's needs. From the mid-1930s they mobilised around the issue of equal pay, Heagney from within the union movement, Street from her base in the United Associations of Women.[53] Some feminists connected in their thinking and their strategies the deceptively separate spheres of market work and domestic work, arguing that social policies that provided the mother with financial support to recognise the costs of children were the necessary counterpart to wage justice for women in the labour force.[54, 55, 56]

Class allegiances differentiated feminist advocacy. Labour movement women saw allowances to mothers through the tax/transfer system *augmenting* the inadequate basic wage that must, nevertheless, retain its family component. Kate Dwyer in New South Wales in the 1920s and Heagney in the 1930s and 1940s were not prepared to jettison the unions' historic wage bargaining strategy and risk a reduced share to labour. Rather, they mounted arguments for cash transfers to mothers as universal redistribution recognising the increased costs that women incurred in rearing children, accompanied by extension of the 'family wage' concept to women (as Heagney argued in the 1937 Basic Wage Case). Street, however, advocate for both equal pay and child endowment, held that the introduction of equal pay required an accompanying cash transfer scheme to provide direct income for mothers and their children, but unlike trade union women, she did not support the family wage principle.[57, 58] Where feminist thought and advocacy converged was in recognising that cash transfers to mothers of dependent children outside the wage system was essential if, in Heagney's words 'men and women in industry were to meet on more equal terms than is possible under present circumstances'.[59]

In addition, there was feminist consensus on the issue of which parent required income support—the parent whose domestic work went unrecognised. In the words of Jessie Street commending the Commonwealth government child endowment legislation of 1941,

> We realised the enormous difference it would make to mothers, not only to have the extra money, but to have it paid to them. For many mothers this was the only money that they were entitled to in their own right and it gave them the first taste of economic independence.'[60]

The basic thrust of feminist thought and activity in this period was to call upon *collective* processes of regulation, i.e., various state agencies, to revalue women's market work, to reassess women's needs as supporters and to recognise the contributions and costs associated with women's non-market work. This position reflects a view that feminist interests could prevail upon the state to distribute and redistribute income to women more equitably through market earnings and through the tax/transfer system. This position also reflects the refusal to accept the work/non-work dichotomy and its assumption of untroubled, equitable private transfers from breadwinner to dependants.

The Family Wage Superseded

The family wage principle was not abandoned in wage fixation until 1974, at precisely the time when women market workers finally won both equal pay for work of equal value and an equal minimum wage. There was no transferral of the concepts of family needs, or breadwinning obligations to remuneration which applied equally to men and women—rather, the wage was described finally as an individual wage. But there was a long history of feminist activism before this outcome was achieved.

In the Commonwealth Court of Conciliation and Arbitration (later the Commission) in 1926, 1937, 1950, 1969 and 1972, claims were made by the combined unions, supported strongly by various women's groups, for the implementation of a uniform basic wage to apply regardless of gender (in 1937 the claim was more modest). These claims were met by the response from employers and from the Court that such a demand was impossible to implement. Not only was the extension of the family wage concept to women beyond the capacity of industry to pay, but such a move would contravene the traditional basis of Australian wage fixation: that the male was still the family breadwinner and that the introduction of an equal minimum wage would sacrifice the fundamental advantages that the wage system gave to the normal family unit.[61, 62]

Even in the 1972 equal pay case, after the introduction of 'equal pay for equal work' (i.e., for women working in predominantly male occupations) in 1969, and after the introduction of 'equal pay for work of equal value' in 1972, the Commission rejected the claim for an equal minimum wage on the grounds that:

Ever since the minimum wage has been the subject of debate it has been presented by unions and considered by the Commission as including a family component ... However the unions now argue as a simple matter of equity that females should receive the same minimum wage as males. We reject that argument because the male minimum wage ... takes account of the family considerations we have mentioned.[63]

The contradictions of the family wage issue are clear: despite the fact that the 'minimum wage' and the 'total wage' concepts introduced in 1966–67 were not defined as a family-needs based wage and despite the fact that the capacity of the economy to pay had been confirmed as the ruling wage fixation doctrine in the post-war period, when it suited employers and when it suited the Commission (i.e., when both were rejecting the claim that the minimum wage be extended to women), the family wage principle was brought forward as a significant consideration.

In the 1974 national wage case, when the minimum wage concept was extended finally to women following the claims of the ACTU, the National Council of Women, the Union of Australian Women and the Women's Electoral Lobby, and the legislative intervention of the Commonwealth Labor government, the Commission rejected totally the notion that the minimum wage could continue to have a family needs component. The Commission was defined as an industrial arbitration tribunal, not a social welfare agency, and the care of family needs was deemed to be principally a task for governments.[64]

Commentators at the time suggested that the long process of dismantling the family wage concept (which had gained momentum in the period 1966 to 1974), had resulted in a lowering of the real value of the minimum wage, requiring the addition of a cash transfer to dependent housewives.[65] The implication of Downing's argument was that equal pay for female employees had resulted in the relative impoverishment of the families of male employees—that an upsetting of the balance of the breadwinner/dependant relationship had resulted when men and women in industry met on more equal terms. According to Downing at least, a cash transfer to dependent wives was required to redress the imbalance. Unrecognised in this explanation of events was the fact that the family needs principle had long been a part of the rhetoric, but not the substance of wage fixation.

---

*The sex-based segmentation and segregation of the Australian occupational structure has been exacerbated by industrial changes in the recession (Cass, 1981 *Unemployment and the Family*, SWRC Reports and Proceedings No. 7, Sydney, Social Welfare Research Centre, University of New South Wales.). In 1981, 81.2 per cent of the female workforce was employed in occupations where women were over-represented; only 8.2 per cent were employed in occupations where women were under-represented and 10.6 per cent were employed in 'gender-free' occupations. Of the eighteen occupations in which women were concentrated, 6 contained over 60 per cent of women (clerical workers, shop assistants, stenographers and typists, teachers, housekeepers,

Poverty research had demonstrated that the minimum wage (even with the addition of child endowment) was barely adequate to meet the needs of a family with two children, and quite inadequate for larger families.[66] Nevertheless, the legal recognition of equal pay was achieved as the rhetoric of the family needs doctrine was finally abandoned.

It must be noted that the full realisation of equal pay for work of equal value remains unrealisable while men and women continue to be employed in a sex-segmented labour market.[67]*

The Family Wage Reconstructed

Changes in wage fixation implemented in the period 1950 to 1975, beginning with the setting of the women's basic wage at 75 per cent of the male rate after women had 'proved' their efficiency and reliability in their war work[68] and ending with the extension of the male minimum wage to women in 1974, resulted in women market workers' needs being defined as equivalent to men market workers' needs. But neither men nor women were then presumed to have family needs that could be used as a relevant argument in the determination of wages. The care of family needs was relegated to the tax/transfer system.

Paradoxically as the concept of the family wage for adult male labour (originally introduced to protect adult male low wage earners) was progressively abandoned in wage fixation—a transposed version was extended in the tax system where it provided greatest monetary benefit for adult male high-income earners. Effective public expenditure support was used to protect the breadwinning responsibilities of (generally) male taxpayers with dependants. The categorisations of work/non-work, support and dependence were effectively transferred to the concessions for dependants in the tax system, concessions that provided direct benefits not to the dependants, but to the breadwinner. Such concessions assumed that men with family responsibilities

---

cooks, maids and nurses) (Office of the Status of Women, 1983, 'Women's Contribution to Economic Recovery' *in Information Paper on the Economy* for National Economic Summit Conference, April 1983, Canberra, Australian Government Publishing Service, page 19). In addition, vertical segregation of the labour market continues to place women in jobs characterised by little status, authority and job autonomy. In August 1966, 3.3 per cent of the female workforce was employed in administrative, executive and managerial jobs; in August 1983 this proportion had fallen to 2.6 per cent (see Table 1). In the same period, the proportion of the male workforce in administrative, executive and managerial jobs increased from 8.4 per cent to 9.3 per cent.

Table 1 Employed persons: Occupation by sex 1966–83

	1966	1970	1974	(August) 1978	% 1980	1981	1982	1983
Males								
Professional, technical	8.3	9.3	10.8	11.7	12.1	12.4	13.5	13.6
Administrative, executive and managerial	8.4	8.1	8.5	8.4	8.6	8.5	9.3	9.3
Clerical	8.6	9.1	8.4	8.2	7.8	7.9	8.3	8.1
Sales	6.0	6.0	6.0	6.8	6.7	6.7	6.5	6.6
Farmers, fishermen, timber-getters	11.9	10.4	9.5	8.8	8.8	8.8	8.7	9.2
Transport and communication	7.9	7.8	7.6	7.5	6.9	7.2	7.1	7.4
Trades, production-process, labourers	44.5	45.0	44.4	43.3	43.5	42.9	41.1	39.9
Service, sport and recreation	4.4	4.4	4.8	5.3	5.5	5.5	5.6	5.9
Total	100	100	100	100	100	100	100	100
Females								
Professional, technical	13.3	13.0	15.1	17.6	18.8	17.8	18.9	19.2
Administrative, executive and managerial	3.3	2.2	2.1	2.1	2.4	2.5	2.6	2.6
Clerical	30.1	32.4	33.7	33.5	32.4	33.8	33.8	34.6
Sales	13.4	13.5	13.0	12.7	13.1	12.9	12.5	12.6
Farmers, fishermen, timber-getters	4.4	4.0	3.2	3.6	4.1	4.4	4.3	4.0
Transport and communication	2.5	2.5	2.4	2.1	2.1	2.0	2.1	2.0
Trades, production-process, labourers	16.0	15.2	14.0	11.3	10.2	10.7	9.5	8.9
Service, sport and recreation	17.1	17.2	16.5	17.1	16.9	16.0	16.2	16.1
Total	100	100	100	100	100	100	100	100

Sources: A.B.S. *The Labour Force Australia*, 1978, Cat. No. 6204.0., March 1980, pages 61–62
A.B.S. *The Labour Force Australia*, August 1980, Cat. No. 6203.0., December 1980, page 17
A.B.S. *The Labour Force Australia*, 1981. Cat. No. 6204.0., February 1983, page 61
A.B.S. *The Labour Force Australia*, August 1982, Cat. No. 6203.0., November 1982 page 25
A.B.S. *The Labour Force Australia*, August 1983, Cat. No. 6203.0., September 1983, page 25

had reduced capacity to pay tax, and also assumed equitable transfers of tax savings within the family from breadwinner to dependants—the same assumption underlying the family wage.

Tax/transfer treatments of family dependencies have a long history: a tax deduction for dependent children was included in the Commonwealth income tax system from its introduction in 1915 and a deduction for a dependent spouse was introduced in 1936.[69] Such tax treatments represented a variation of the family wage principle: namely, that the taxable income of breadwinners should be adjusted according to their family responsibilities. The tax savings made by taxpayers in respect of dependent children and a dependent spouse had a regressive impact: as deductions from taxable income until 1942, when the Labor government replaced them by a system of rebates, and again from 1950 to 1975, dependants' deductions were of more value to higher income earners in higher marginal tax brackets than they were to lower income earners.[70, 71] These deductions were effectively indexed against inflation in two ways: through government increasing the basic rate, and through the working of the deduction system itself which rose as incomes rose with inflation (National Population Inquiry).[72]

Tax treatments were generally applied to the principal income earner's taxable income, usually the man's income, since here they represented the highest value. Husbands/fathers who were taxpayers gained tax relief if they had dependants, and higher-income family men gained the greatest savings. The notion of the family wage transposed to the tax system acquired new class connotations: no longer used to protect low-income male employees, but to provide greatest monetary advantage to high-income husbands.

Meanwhile, what had become of the system of cash transfers to mothers introduced in 1941—the transfers that feminists had seen as an essential counterpart to equal pay, and an essential redistribution to mothers incurring extra costs in the rearing of children? The critical issue is that, unlike wage fixation, these were not subjected to routine review of their value, and, unlike tax deductions, they were not automatically indexed against inflation. The only form of guaranteed income redistribution to women recognising their child-care responsibilities eroded in real value through the long boom while the regressive system of tax concessions for husbands/fathers increased in real value. These contradictory processes disadvantaged all mothers, both market and non-market workers, and particularly disadvantaged pensioner and beneficiary families and low-paid workers' families with little or no taxable income who were unable to benefit from tax concessions. In ways that appear to be much more subtle and hidden than the categorisations of work/non-work, breadwinner/dependant made explicit in census enumerations, in wage fixation and in the daily experiences of family and paid work relationships, tax/transfer treatments reinforced the breadwinner/dependant relationship. Tax concessions for breadwinners had the ultimate protection of effective indexation; cash transfers for mothers in respect of their dependent children were provided with no such protection.

Nor does the abolition of dependants' deductions and their replacement by rebates in 1975 and the introduction of family allowances in 1976 alter this analysis. Because of the indexation of the rebate for a dependent spouse and the non-indexation of family allowances, the period 1976–82 saw the erosion of the real value of cash transfers to mothers with dependent children and the increase in the real value of tax rebates for husbands with a dependent spouse.[73, 74]*

The tax/transfer system could be seen as having little to do with the concepts of work and non-work, but this would be a false view. The tax/transfer system has developed in conjunction with the system of primary distribution from earnings: tax treatments to adjust tax liability according to demands made on the breadwinner's income; cash transfers in respect of dependent children to recognise the costs that women incur in child-rearing. Relative priorities in public policies reflect and reinforce dominant views of the value of male work and male breadwinning and the relative lack of value accorded to women's non-market work, particularly their child-rearing. It could be claimed that the clear priority given to tax treatments and the more erratic and unpredictable treatment of cash transfers inhere in the different characteristics of the tax system and of the transfer system. Tax expenditures are relatively hidden from public visibility— cash transfers are all too visible, particularly in a period of recession. But this explanation does not touch the nub of the *gender* issue: it is the treatment of distribution and redistribution to women which is given low priority. The minimum wage lost its family connotations when women gained the male equivalent: even if this was mere rhetoric, it was significant rhetoric. There is every indication that if child allowances had remained as rebates in the tax system they would have been indexed. Having been transferred from 'wallet to purse', the question of indexation was no longer considered relevant.[75] The priority given in the tax/transfer system to benefits for taxpayers with a dependent spouse (defined as one with little or no independent income) could be read as reinforcing the traditional pattern of work incentives: providing disincentives to the labour force participation of wives with dependent children. Such an emphasis would be consistent

---

*In 1979–80, the dependent Spouse rebate provided tax savings for 45 per cent of male taxpayers in married couple units and for 2 per cent of female taxpayers in married couple units (Keens and Cass, *op. cit.*).

with the alleged redundancy of married women's labour force participation in a period of high unemployment.

Working Part-time, Caring Full-time

Perhaps the most insightful message from the work of the early
feminists is that we must connect our analyses of the market and the
domestic: that their alleged separation is an ideological device that
reinforces the power of the market and the powerlessness of caring
work, in terms of relative remuneration, social participation and political influence. Taking my theoretical emphasis from a contemporary
feminist scholar, Margaret Power,[76,77,78,79] my concluding case
study will explore the connections between women's paid market
work and women's unpaid, domestic, caring work in the recent economic recession.

In the Depression of the 1930s, women experienced less recorded
unemployment than did men, because of the intense sex segregation
of the workforce. Highest rates of recorded unemployment were experienced in the building and construction industries and in heavy
manufacturing industries, predominantly employers of men, while
the service industries, domestic service, light manufacturing and retail trade, where women were concentrated, were less affected.[80]
This did not mean that women's jobs were unaffected by the Depression: on the contrary, many worked part-time or at reduced wages.
However, it is clear from the work of Muriel Heagney[81] and the evidence that she gave at the 1937 Basic Wage Inquiry that women's
work was essential for family support in the Depression, and more
women were compelled to find work in the female sectors of the occupational and industrial structure. However, public and political argument at the time centred on the attack that women were displacing
men in the labour market and contributing to their unemployment:
hence the title of Heagney's book *Are Women Taking Men's Jobs?*
Women who were without work were unlikely to get unemployment
benefit (and this was particularly harsh where they were not part of a
family) and little relief work was provided for women. As Power[82]
notes:

> Despite the intense social pressure on women to withdraw from
> paid work, they kept working. Economic necessity ensured that
> they stayed in employment ... Women did not ease the crisis by
> being expelled from the labour market; women contributed to so-
> cial stability, however, in that they were blamed for the severity of
> the crisis.

Table 2 Shares of the labour force, shares of unemployment, and unemployment rates by age and sex 1966–82

%	AGE (Years)					
	15–19		20–24		25 & Over	
	Males	Females	Males	Females	Males	Females
1966 (August)						
Proportion of labour force	7.1	6.6	8.2	5.0	54.0	18.8
Proportion of unemployed	11.2	16.3	6.9	8.9	31.4	25.0
Unemployment rate	2.5	4.0	1.4	2.8	0.9	2.1
1970 (August)						
Proportion of labour force	6.1	6.3	8.9	6.1	52.0	20.9
Proportion of unemployed	12.3	14.4	7.9	8.6	26.7	29.7
Unemployment rate	2.9	3.6	1.3	2.0	0.7	2.1
1974 (August)						
Proportion of labour force	5.7	5.4	8.6	6.1	51.0	23.2
Proportion of unemployed	12.2	15.3	10.4	9.3	25.6	27.2
Unemployment rate	5.0	6.7	2.9	3.6	1.2	2.7
1978 (August)						
Proportion of labour force	6.3	5.3	8.3	6.3	49.0	24.4
Proportion of unemployed	16.6	15.7	11.9	9.6	27.5	18.7
Unemployment rate	16.5	17.2	8.9	9.6	3.5	4.8
1980 (August)						
Proportion of labour force	6.2	5.6	6.4	6.6	48.3	24.8
Proportion of unemployed	15.5	17.9	12.2	10.2	25.7	18.6
Unemployment rate	14.8	18.9	8.5	9.1	3.1	4.4

1982 (August)						
Proportion of labour force	5.9	5.0	8.7	6.6	48.4	25.4
Proportion of unemployed	14.4	12.9	14.5	8.7	30.2	19.3
Unemployment rate	16.4	17.1	11.3	8.8	4.2	5.1
1982 (October)						
Proportion of labour force	5.8	5.1	8.7	6.6	48.3	25.5
Proportion of unemployed	13.0	12.4	13.4	10.0	30.8	20.4
Unemployment rate	17.5	18.8	11.9	11.7	4.9	6.2

Sources: ABS *The Labour Force Australia*, 1978, Cat. No. 6204.0
ABS *The Labour Force Australia*, August 1980, Cat. No. 6203.0
ABS *The Labour Force Australia*, August 1982, Cat. No. 6203.0
ABS *The Labour Force Australia*, October 1982, Cat. No. 6203.0

Table 3 Changes in employment by age and sex: Full-time and part-time workers, 1974–83

('000)

Age	15–19		20–24		25–34		35–44		45–54		55–59		60–64		65 and over		All Employees	
	M	F	M	F	M	F	M	F	M	F	M	F	M	F	M	F	M	F
Full-time workers																		
1974	294.5	253.2	479.7	303.0	962.2	295.2	749.6	238.0	720.5	227.7	258.1	62.2	184.5	25.5	61.7	12.1	3710.9	1416.9
1983	223.8	182.9	467.3	341.6	1024.4	375.0	902.1	291.8	644.2	199.5	261.2	56.8	113.4	21.4	33.8	6.8	3670.3	1475.9
changes	-70.7	-70.3	-12.4	38.6	62.2	79.8	152.5	53.8	-76.3	-28.2	3.1	-5.4	-71.1	-4.1	-27.9	-5.3	-40.6	59.0
Part-time workers																		
1974	31.8	46.4	18.6	50.3	16.6	161.2	9.2	152.5	11.2	112.1	7.4	33.6	12.0	20.7	29.5	14.4	136.2	591.2
1983	66.8	91.4	31.7	68.1	39.0	215.3	29.1	247.6	24.1	147.6	16.3	45.3	14.7	19.1	19.0	11.6	240.5	845.9
changes	35.0	45.0	13.1	17.8	22.4	54.1	19.9	95.1	12.9	35.5	8.9	11.7	2.7	-1.6	-10.5	-2.8	104.3	254.7

Source: A.B.S. The Labour Force Australia 1978. Cat. No. 6204.0, March 1980, pages 42–43
A.B.S. The Labour Force Australia August 1983. Cat. No. 6203.0, September 1983, page 18

But women's contribution to social stability went beyond their paid work and their role as scapegoat, they were also responsible, as ever, for household work and caring work—for stretching subsistence and below subsistence reduced earnings and unemployment sustenance. Histories of the Depression in Australia[83, 84] and in Europe[85] have given us glimpses of the survival strategies employed by the women in families, in particular their attempts to maintain order and structure in daily life; to create regular meals and makeshift clothing—and in most cases we can discern the hidden self-denial of these non-market workers. Some of Peter Travers's respondents who had been young unemployed men in the Depression in South Australia, living in their parental home, could not recall any personal deprivation, and they surmised that perhaps their mothers had been making sacrifices.

What then does this historical anecdote suggest for our understanding of the economic recession? In the period 1974 to 1982 (Table 2) adult women's share of the labour force has increased by 2.8 percentage points while adult men's share has fallen by 2.6 percentage points. Adult women's recorded unemployment rate increased by approximately eight percentage points (for those aged between twenty and twenty-four) in this period; the corresponding figure for men in the same age group was an increase of nine percentage points. Unemployment rates for women aged twenty-five years and over increased by 3.5 percentage points; the corresponding figure for men was an increase of 3.7 percentage points. Without even considering the dimensions of hidden unemployment which has its higher incidence among adult women[86] it is clear that women were not left unscathed by the job losses of 1974–82. However, Table 3 shows the extent of job loss and job gain in full-time and part-time work for men and women in the period 1974–83. What is clear is that increases in adult women's employment (aged twenty to fifty-nine) have been greater than increases in men's employment: women had a net gain of 352 800 jobs, of which 60 per cent were part-time; men had a net gain of 206 000 jobs, of which 37 per cent were part-time. Table 3 shows the concentration of full-time job loss for both men and women at both ends of the life cycle, for young people and for people over the age of forty-four. It seems clear that the deterioration of the job market has fallen inequitably on younger and older workers; has fallen on adult men since 1980 predominantly in the building and construction industries, and in the heavy industrial manufacturing sectors;[87] has fallen on adult women predominantly in manufacture, wholesale and retail trades and in the service industries.[88]

An understanding of the sex-segmented and segregated nature of the job market enables us to understand these differential impacts, and in particular to understand the increase in women's part-time

Table 4   Part-time employment, as percentage of all employment, 1974–83

		1974	1980	1981	1982	1983
15–19	M	10	18	17	20	23
	F	16	27	28	31	33
20–24	M	4	6	5	6	6
	F	14	18	17	18	17
25–34	M	2	3	3	4	4
	F	35	38	36	36	36
35–44	M	1	2	2	3	3
	F	39	46	45	47	46
45–54	M	2	3	3	3	4
	F	33	41	42	43	43
55–59	M	3	5	4	5	6
	F	35	39	41	41	44
60–64	M	6	11	10	9	11
	F	45	46	46	44	47
65+	M	32	31	35	35	36
	F	54	57	59	59	63
All	M	4	5	5	6	6
EMPLOYEES	F	29	36	35	36	36

Sources: A.B.S., *The Labour Force Australia*, 1978, Cat. No. 6204.0, March 1980, page 42–43
A.B.S., *The Labour Force Australia*, August 1980, Cat. No. 6203.0, December 1980, page 16
A.B.S., *The Labour Force Australia*, 1981, Cat. No. 6204.0, February 1983, pages 45, 47
A.B.S., *The Labour Force Australia*, August 1982, Cat. No. 6203.0, November 1982, page 18
A.B.S., *The Labour Force Australia*, August 1983, Cat. No. 6203.0, September 1983, page 18

work in the recession. From 1974 to 1983 the incidence of part-time work increased for all employees, by 2 percentage points for men and by 7 percentage points for women, but this aggregate hides the significance of age as well as gender in the distribution of part-time work (Table 4). The greatest increases in part-time work were experienced by both young men and women, but from that point the experiences of the sexes diverge. The increase in women's part-time work as a proportion of their total employment increased markedly in the age groups 35–44 and 45–54; in the age group 25 to 59 women are on average ten times more likely than men to be employed part-time. This must of course be related to their responsibilities as non-market workers, in particular to their responsibilities as child-carers. The labour force participation rate of married women with dependent children decreases according to the age of their youngest child: where there is a pre-school child only 11 per cent of women are in full-time employment and a further 18 per cent are in part-time employment; where the youngest child is of primary school age, these proportions increase to 20 per cent of women in full-time employment and 30 per cent in part-time employment; where the youngest child is of secondary school age, full-time employment increases to 28 per cent and part-time employment remains at 30 per cent (Table 5). There can be little doubt that the increase in part-time employment for women in the age group 35 to 54 in the period 1974 to 1983 can be attributed to the job needs and the income needs of mothers.

As Margaret Power identified for the 1930s, women's paid work is clearly critical in a period of job insecurity. However, part-time work for women does little to alter the domestic division of labour: housework and child-care remain the duties of women even though men may 'help out' more than they once did. The 'double burden' remains the essential characteristic of women's market/non-market work.[89] Adult women's increased labour force participation rates in the post-war period have not resulted in the convergence of women's and men's paid work histories: rather, women with children have typically added part-time, intermittent, paid work to their unpaid domestic work and their child-care responsibilities[90] while employed men have continued to be dominantly full-time workers, identifying the domestic domain with leisure or with 'helping'. The consequences of these partial changes have been to consolidate a further sex-segmentation of the labour force into full-time, relatively secure, well-rewarded work with the possibilities for advancement, non-wage fringe benefits and some control of decision-making (where men predominate); and part-time, poorly paid, insecure work with few possibilities for further training and advancement, and few non-wage fringe benefits (where women predominate). This dichotomy continues to be legitimated by the belief that women will be at least partially supported by a male breadwinner. Conversely, women's part-time, intermittent, paid work justifies their continuing responsibility for unpaid household work, child care and the care of elderly and sick relatives.

In connection with women's continuing responsibility for non-market caring work, it must be noted that a role has been forged for these labours in the current recession. This is a fourfold role: provision of unpaid household work to stretch incomes, provision of emotional support for the victims of recession, provision of unpaid household care for the elderly and the ill when funding levels for institutionalised and community services are inadequate and provision of unpaid volunteer or poorly paid semi-volunteer work in the community.[91,92,93] The demands of the New Right that women retreat from their pursuit of paid income in the formal labour market and move back full-time into unpaid work in the home and the community (similar to the attacks on working women made during the Depression of the 1930s) serve clear ideological purposes: to reactivate the traditional breadwinner/dependant bond as the cornerstone of the stable, pre-recessionary society.[94, 95]

Table 5   Labour force status of married women by age of youngest child present, Australia, July 1982

Married women with youngest dependent child aged	In the labour force				Not in the labour force	Total
	Full-time	Part-time	Unemployed	Total		
0–4	10.9	17.8	2.6	31.3	68.7	100.0
5–9	20.4	30.1	3.6	54.1	45.9	100.0
10–14	28.4	29.6	2.5	60.4	39.6	100.0
15–20	28.0	26.1	1.3	55.3	44.7	100.0
Total	18.8	24.4	2.7	45.9	54.1	100.0

Source: A.B.S., *Labour Force Status and Other Characteristics of Families, Australia, July 1982*, Cat. No. 6224.0, Table 24.

Recent feminist analyses have clarified the nature of the transfers that are actually occurring in the non-market household sector: a transfer of goods and services to children, sick and elderly relatives and to able-bodied men, provided by the women who are assumed to be supported. Rather than seeing only a one-way set of income transfers from breadwinners to dependants, congruent with the receipt of 'welfare' (as the 1891 Census categories enshrined them), these analyses uncover a system of hidden and unpaid welfare services provided by women.[96, 97, 98, 99, 100]

Women, Income Distribution and Poverty

Paradoxically, the providers of the 'hidden welfare system', because of their caring obligations, are vulnerable to poverty. The nominal achievements of equal pay for work of equal value and of cash transfers to mothers that recognise (in a residual way) the costs incurred in the rearing of children, have both contributed to an increased overall share of income to women in the period 1968–69 and 1981–82 (Table 6). The ratio of women's to men's income overall, and in respect of each principal source of income, has shown a consistent increase, especially since 1973–74. This is particularly significant in relation to income from wages and salaries, where the ratio increased from 0.48 in 1968–69 to 0.64 in 1981–82. However, the ratio of female to male income from all sources was still 0.48 in 1981–82, predominantly because of the much higher proportion of women than of men whose principal source of income is derived from government social security benefits or transfers (including family allowances): 45 per cent of women compared with 18 per cent of men. The proportions of both men and women deriving their principal source of income from government benefits have increased since 1968–69, for men by 11 percentage points, for women by 4 percentage points, reflecting the impact of the recessions from 1973–74. But women remain 2.5 times more likely than men to derive their income principally from government income support. This indicates the extreme importance of the tax/transfer system for women. It also demonstrates the outcome of the gender divisions of paid work and unpaid work, resulting in the unattainability of wage and income equality for women while the sex-based division of labour persists in the family and in the labour market.

Poverty research demarcates the extreme manifestation of income inequality: income insufficient to meet needs (usually measured stringently according to official or semi-official criteria). The income units most vulnerable to poverty in 1978–79 were single-parent fami-

Table 6 Principal source of income, gross mean annual income and ratio of female to male mean incomes: 1968–69, 1973–74, 1978–79, 1981–82

		Principal Source of Income							
		Wages and salaries	Own business trade, farm or profession	Share in partnership	Govt. soc. sec. benefit or other transfer	Superannuation or annuity	Interest, rent, dividend	Other	Total
1968–69 (1)									
% gaining principal source of income from:	M	76.2	6.3	6.7	7.3	1.2	2.1	0.2	100
	W	42.8	1.5	4.9	41.7	0.8	7.2	1.2	100
Mean annual income	M	3,450	4,780	4,480	860	2,750	2,880	3,010	3,390
($)	W	1,670	2,050	3,080	400	1,640	1,160	1,820	1,180
ratio W:M	R	0.48	0.43	0.69	0.47	0.60	0.40	0.60	0.35
1973–74 (2)									
% gaining principal source of income from:	M	75.1	6.2	6.3	9.3	1.0	1.9	0.3	100.1
	W	46.1	1.4	4.8	41.0	0.5	5.3	0.9	100
Mean annual income	M	6,060	7,870	6,500	1,440	4,310	4,000	4,130	5,710
($)	W	3,160	3,950	4,770	740	2,470	1,540	2,430	2,160
	R	0.52	0.50	0.73	0.51	0.57	0.39	0.59	0.38
1978–79 (3)									
% gaining principal source of income from:	M	67.1	5.8	8.3	15.0	1.4	1.9	0.6	100.1
	W	41.4	1.3	6.6	43.2	0.5	6.2	0.7	99.9

		Col 1	Col 2	Col 3	Col 4	Col 5	Col 6	Col 7	Col 8
Mean annual income ($)	M	11,570	13,580	10,560	3,040	9,310	6,910	6,270	10,170
	W	7,050	8,170	8,640	1,980	6,760	3,210	4,830	4,720
	R	0.61	0.60	0.82	0.65	0.73	0.46	0.77	0.46
1981–82 (4) *									
% gaining principal source of income from:	M	57.0	15.9	included	18.2	1.5	5.9	1.5	100
	W	32.9	9.1	on left	45.5	0.7	10.3	1.5	100
Mean annual income ($)	M	16,910	13,301	included	3,741	12,450	5,564	4,587	13,020
	W	10,852	9,888	on left	2,626	10,407	4,204	4,045	6,230
	R	0.64	0.74		0.70	0.84	0.76	0.88	0.48

Sources:
1. Commonwealth Bureau of Census Statistics, *Income Distribution, 1968–69*, Part 1. Ref. No. 17.6
2. A.B.S. *Income Distribution 1973–74*, Part 1. Cat. No. 6502.0
3. A.B.S. *Income Distribution, Australia, 1978–79*, Individuals. Cat. No. 6502.0
4. A.B.S. *Income of Individuals, Australia, 1981–82*, (Preliminary) Cat. No. 6501.0
* In 1981–82, the two categories, own business, trade etc., and share in partnership were aggregated.

lies with children (of which 90 per cent were headed by women); non-aged single women; couples in the early years of family formation, particularly where the major breadwinner was not in full-year, full-time work; low income couples with three or more children; the long-term unemployed.[101, 102]

The best guarantee against poverty in an income unit in 1978–79 was the employment of at least one adult in full-year, full-time work, while an even stronger guarantee was the presence of two adult income earners. Being a woman appeared to generate sufficient 'disability' (to use the concept of the Commission of Inquiry into Poverty[103])—i.e., inadequate income, to create a disproportionate risk of poverty: non-aged single women were vulnerable to poverty, a process exacerbated by motherhood and by old age. Whereas the rate of poverty among all income units in 1978–79 was estimated at 9.3 per cent, among non-aged, women-headed income units the rate was much higher: 19 per cent of non-aged single women and 41 per cent of women single parents were estimated to be living in poverty[104]. What should be noted is that the poverty of women with dependants and of families with dependants is also visited upon the children: 12.3 per cent of children were estimated to be living below the poverty line in 1978–79, compared with 8.3 per cent of adults.[105]

The following processes have contributed to the higher incidence of poverty amongst women-headed income units, and amongst children in the period 1974–83.

- The increase in the rate and the duration of unemployment.
- The increase in the numbers and proportion of single-parent families in receipt of pension or benefit—i.e., where the parent is excluded from paid work.
- For those in paid work, the increase in tax liability, borne disproportionately by low income, two-parent families where both parents are employed. (This is one of the consequences of the favoured tax treatment given to single-income families with a dependent spouse—regardless of the income of the taxpayer.)[106]
- Decreasing public expenditure in real terms on cash transfers for mothers with dependent children.
- Inadequate expenditure on child-care facilities to provide support for employed women which dependent children.
- The persistence of unequal pay for women in a segmented labour market.

Like the women and children of former decades making their claims upon charitable institutions and the state welfare authorities, it would appear that women and their children are disproportionately represented among those whose opportunities for paid market work and secure income have been adversely affected by the recession and by public policies. Women may become poor when they have no male breadwinner and/or when they are excluded from full-time, adequately paid work by age, unemployment or family responsibilities. Women may remain poor because of the persistence of unequal pay in a sex-segmented labour market. The tendency of the tax/transfer system to provide increased real support to taxpayers with a dependent spouse at the cost of decreased real support to mothers with dependent children has contributed to the poverty of women and children. These priorities in the tax/transfer system symbolically represent the rewards that accrue to employed men who have maintained the dependency of their spouse.

Conclusions

This analysis has identified apparent continuities in the public policy treatment of paid and unpaid work and their respective rewards. Even though the official construction of the breadwinner/dependant dichotomy analogous with the work/non-work dichotomy was removed from government statistical measurement, and even though the principle of the family wage which was used to deny wage equality to women was gradually abandoned in wage fixation, the assumptions of the family wage and of the breadwinner/dependant relationship have been reconstructed in the tax system. Even though women's labour force participation has increased since World War II, the sex segmentation of the labour market continues to concentrate women in a narrow range of occupations that offer reduced opportunity for security, advancement and higher earnings. The increased tendency for adult women's labour force participation to be part-time, which is related to women's child-care and household obligations, exacerbates workforce segmentation and reinforces the domestic division of labour. The undervaluation of women's caring work and physical labours in the household and the enduring tendency to regard these as non-work allows the indexation of transfers for child support to remain a non-issue, and allows social policymakers to speak of 'community and family care' as if women's work involved no costs.

However, within the apparent continuities there are contradictions with progressive potentialities. The theoretical and political work of feminists (in eventual alliance with the trade unions) achieved equal pay for work of equal value and saw the achievement of cash transfers to mothers that recognise the increased costs incurred in the rearing of children. Even though changes in primary income distribution through earnings from market work and redistribution through the tax/transfer system have increased the overall share of income to women in the period 1968–69 and 1981–82, formidable obstacles remain in the pursuit of income justice. These are the persisting sex segmentation of the occupational structure making equal pay unrealisable, the persisting household division of labour that militates against men's and women's equal participation in domestic work and market work and the low priority given by successive governments to child support.

Since the political agenda of the early feminists remains unfinished, a modest prescription for future feminist scholarship in the social sciences would include investigations of the relationship between dependency and poverty, identification of the barriers in the labour market that militate against the realisation of equal pay, continued exposure of the unequal distribution of unpaid domestic work that militates against women's access to paid work and income security and continued emphasis on the inadequacy of public expenditure for child support.

5 Individual Equity and Social Policy

MEREDITH EDWARDS

The unit of analysis in social policy is an important equity issue. Overwhelmingly, social policy analysts have taken the married couple or the wider unit of the family as the appropriate unit. This position arises from assumptions that have long been made about economic relationships between men and women within the family. I will address two sets of assumptions that appear to have influenced the traditional treatment of the income unit.

One set of assumptions relates to the dependency of women on men. A good deal of social policy is predicated upon a household unit of a male earning spouse and a dependent wife, with or without dependent children. Women are assumed to have the primary task of servicing other family members. Such policies have become increasingly inequitable and inefficient as well as simply irrelevant with the entry of significant numbers of married women into paid employment and with changes in marriage and divorce patterns.

Another assumption is the irrelevance for policy of the internal decisionmaking processes within households. It has been assumed that the income of a household is pooled and that the welfare of one member of a household (or at least of a marriage partner) can be ascertained by reference to household income. While only one spouse may have legal title to income earned, it is assumed that the married couple as a unit manages, controls and benefits from income received. The legal division of income between spouses becomes irrelevant. Lipsey, for example, has noted the implicit assumption in economic theory that 'households are consistent decision-making units behaving as if they contained only one individual'.[1] Lipsey is one of the few authors of an economic text who has warned readers not to confuse households with individuals. But Lipsey himself ignores the difficulties that arise from identifying the interests of the individual with the interests of household.[2]

The main reasons why analysts and policymakers have adopted these approaches is because of this unquestioned assumption about the ways in which income is distributed and expenditure allocation decided within households. There is still comparatively little reliable information on this subject, but below I discuss some research that casts doubt on the realism of the assumption. In the following sections I scrutinise critically the assumptions upon which much of Australia's social policy has been based. This is followed by an examination of some of the inequities of current social policy that can flow from assumptions made about the appropriate income unit. The final section examines some implications of my analysis for the future direction of Australia's social policies and explores possible changes to policy based on a concept of individual equity.

In what follows, social policy is defined narrowly; the discussion of policy concentrates on the social security system. In turn, social security is narrowly defined to include only direct cash outlays, not the provision of social services. The paper does not tackle the definition of equity; it simply adopts the usual public finance meaning of this term that assistance is concentrated on people in need and that people in the same circumstances receive the same level of payment. Much of what is said, however, applies to other areas of social policy in which the income unit adopted is broader than that of the individual. Although this paper focuses on equity considerations, there are strong economic efficiency arguments for adopting the individual as the income unit.[3, 4]

Recent Social and Demographic Changes

On the whole, until not so long ago, a basic uniformity in economic behaviour of families could be observed and, fairly confidently, a general pattern of behaviour for Australians entering marriage could be predicted. Young people tended to leave their parents' home to marry and to set up on their own. Division of labour was customary for the new family: the husband remained in paid employment and the wife spent a large part of her married life in unpaid work at home. If upon marriage a woman did not move from financial dependence on her father to dependence on her husband, she certainly did so when her first child came. Other patterns were less common and socially acceptable.

Over the past two decades, dramatic changes in the proportion of married women in paid employment make this unit only one of a variety of household types. In any one year, more married women are now in some paid employment than are not. In just twenty years, women's expectations about their labour force participation have undergone substantial change. Marriage is no longer seen as a reason for giving up paid employment; rather, the birth of the first child generally causes a woman to reassess the extent of her paid activity. A young child, or lack of child care, does inhibit women's full-time paid activity. However, it is becoming increasingly uncommon for women to be totally dependent financially on husbands and increasingly common for them to seek some employment after, even if not during, child-bearing years. While married women have continued the role of being primarily responsible for the care of children and the home, they are increasingly combining that role with at least some paid employment.

Although high unemployment levels and depressed economic activity have modified these trends, they are unlikely to be reversed; women are simply becoming relatively more important components of the total unemployed. It is reasonable to conclude that an increasing proportion of women will seek paid employment after the birth of a child, will be taxpayers and will attempt to retain a measure of economic independence.

Alongside the changes in the labour force participation of married women have occurred substantial changes in family structure and household formation. There has been a decline in the marriage rate, an increase in the average age at marriage, an increase in the variety of *de facto* marriage relationships and an increase in the rate of marital dissolution, with a consequent increase in the proportion of sole parent families, remarriages and blended families. A young woman contemplating a marriage-type relationship today will not necessarily be able to rely on the security of a legal tie, nor on the security of a partner on whom to be dependent financially for the rest of her life. Demographic, economic and social trends suggest that spouses will be relying less on each other for their financial support and will either more readily pursue their own economic independence, or be more dependent on the state.

One point is clear; an increasing number of people are living in situations that do not fit the traditional model of the nuclear family household. The meaning of the once common statement that 'the family is the fundamental economic and social unit of society' has become ambiguous.

The fact that we can no longer talk of the typical family has led to some difficult policy issues. In policy, questions are being raised about whether older adolescents should be treated as part of the family unit; whether partners in a *de facto* relationship should be accorded the same rights as formally married couples (at least where there are children); whether we need to distinguish between blended families and 'traditional' families; how absent partners should contribute to the maintenance of their children; and ways in which assistance for sole-parent families should differ from assistance provided to other family types.

Despite the rapidity and extent of recent social changes and despite some pressing questions, Australia's social policies, so far, have scarcely been adapted to meet these new social circumstances. It seems to follow that our social policies are having unintended effects on many people.

Intra-family Distribution of Income

Although there is wide support for the marital or the family unit as the basis for social policy, there is little literature on the extent to which family members pool their income and share its benefits. Sociologists have spent much time defining the concept of 'marital power' and have debated at length the methodological problems resulting from any attempt to measure it. Financial decisionmaking is an important part of marital decisionmaking. However, empirical research that has tried to discover whether the husband or the wife makes decisions or whether those decisions are joint has not sufficiently explored the issues of allocation and control of income between husband and wife.

If sociologists have had little to offer on the distribution of income within the family, economists have offered even less, because they have been trained to treat the household synonymously with the individual consumer; any change in the welfare of one member of the household is assumed to be a change in the welfare of all household members. (An exception is Lancaster.)[5] This simplification is made because economists are not primarily concerned with a behavioural analysis of what takes place within the family but rather with analysing the behaviour of the 'consumer' (household) in relation to the market place. As Galbraith says of economic textbooks:

> The separate identities of men and women are merged into the concept of a household. The inner conflicts and compromises of the household are not explored; by nearly universal consent, they are not the province of economics. Instead by a distinctly heroic simplification, the household is assumed to be identical with an individual.[6]

The available sociological literature and that about poverty has come to the following conclusions.

- The earnings of a wife are important in increasing her bargaining position within the family.

- The wife with young dependent children has a relatively weak position within the family.
- Housekeeping allowances do not automatically keep up with increases in the husband's wage or with increases in prices.
- Husbands tend to receive more personal spending money than do their wives.

These findings lead to the possibility that the standard of living of some wives—in higher-income as well as in lower-income families—can be lower than that of their husbands. More recently, the literature suggests a separateness of finances in couples in which both partners earn. The literature that does exist on the distribution of income within the family, as well as the broader literature on marital power, gives little support to the almost universal assumption in social policy literature that husbands and wives pool their incomes.

The findings of my own exploratory survey on financial arrangements among married couples were very much in accord with other empirical findings on this topic.[7] One finding was that wives played a much more prominent role than did husbands in the handling of family money and in making actual payment. On the other hand, husbands had a greater overall influence over all but minor purchasing decisions than did wives, although joint control was common. Status in the labour force did appear to influence the system of financial arrangement adopted. However, in higher-income families in which there was only one income, husbands were more likely to give wives a set housekeeping allowance. In lower-income families, the wife had a dominant role in the management of family finances. In families in which both husband and wife earned, the higher the wife's income, the more likely it was that husband and wife would keep their incomes separate. Women who did not earn had least control over the spending pattern of their family.

An analysis was made of the personal spending money of husbands and wives to help answer the question: Who benefits from family income? The finding was in accord with that in the literature—more personal spending money was normally allotted to the husband, wives frequently identifying the housekeeping money as their own.

The evidence on diversity in financial arrangements and the finding that, in some families, there was little sharing of the benefits of income suggest a need for caution in relying on the assumption that husbands and wives pool their incomes in tax transfers and other social policies. The findings, like the survey of the literature, did not provide support for the assumption. Rather, limited as the findings are, they suggest that the income source, and whether the husband or the wife receives it, could be important factors in affecting expenditure patterns within marital units.

Current Inequities

The finding of the diversity in financial arrangements reinforces the point that, whatever unit is used, an inappropriate assumption will be made about household decisionmaking for some households. Sharing is a matter of degree, so neither the individual nor a wider concept of the unit could be totally appropriate. But some assumption has to be made. There would appear to be two good equity reasons for abandoning policies resting on the assumption that husbands and wives pool income and share equally in its benefits.

The first reason is that hardships and inequities occur when one person's standard of living is assumed to depend on another's. If a policy objective is to ensure that all individuals (including children), have a minimum level of income support when they suffer an earnings disability, empirical work suggests that that objective is not necessarily achieved when individuals are forced to depend on another person. One important implication of the findings of the survey, then, is that if there is an inadequate redistribution of income in some families, there is the real possibility that any estimates of the numbers of people in poverty based on the married couple or the family as the unit will be too low.[8, 9, 10] The concept of 'individual equity' seems a relevant criterion to adopt in evaluating the effects of social policies.

The second reason for abandoning policies that assume transfers of income between husband and wife is that the economic, social and demographic changes already mentioned make it less appropriate than even twenty years ago to assume either that a woman will be financially dependent once she marries, or that the marriage relationship will be long-lasting. In the context of personal taxation, Munnell[11] explains the importance of these changes thus:

> The rationale for employing the couple as the basic unit of taxation involves a presumption that couples do pool income and jointly meet financial obligations out of a common budget. If the couple were a stable and permanent unit, this might be a legitimate assumption. In view of the dramatic increase in the likelihood of divorce, however, for many couples the long-term economic welfare of each spouse may depend more on his or her earnings than on the couple's combined income. The prospect of divorce suggests that the taxing authorities should not presume that income will be pooled.

Some examples of specific inequities can be identified as a result of using an income unit in social security policy that is wider than that of the individual. An inequity that is likely to become increasingly important occurs when one of the marriage partners becomes unemployed. The unemployed spouse is not entitled automatically to unemployment benefit because of an income test on spouse's income (so there is no compensation for the loss of the income) and the employed spouse is assumed to share equally his or her income with the unemployed spouse, irrespective of the financial arrangements the couple adopted when both had an income.

Another inequity concerns cohabiting couples. There is little evidence about the financial arrangements of couples who live together but who are not legally married. It is reasonable to assume that the income of a cohabiting couple reflects even less accurately the welfare of individuals than does the combined income of a legally married couple. Yet social policy frequently operates on the assumption that if a man and a woman live together, they will share their income.

A major source of horizontal inequity—in social policy generally and for social security payments in particular—is the level of payment made to a married couple compared to the level of payment to any other two people who live together. The distinction between married and single rates is difficult to justify. The origins of the distinction may relate to the assumed obligation of a husband to support a dependent wife. However, in determining payment relativities, the relevant issue is not which unit shares its *income* but which unit shares *expenditure* and therefore benefits from joint consumption. The unit that shares income is only relevant in determining who should be the unit in assessing eligibility for payments and benefits and which unit is the appropriate one on which to operate any income test. This paper has suggested that the answer to these questions should be, in principle, the individual.

A final inequity worth mentioning is the very high effective rate of taxation placed on social security recipients exacerbated by the aggregation of spouses' incomes for the purpose of income tests. The effective marginal tax rate can exceed 130 per cent.[12] A system that imposes higher tax rates on social security recipients than on the highest income recipients is inequitable as well as inefficient. Poverty traps can be alleviated, if not removed, if social security relies less on marital status.[13]

Future Policy Direction and Concluding Comments

The definition of the income unit for social policy has recently come under scrutiny. This is not surprising, given recent and profound economic and social changes in the nature and economic behaviour of families. I have argued the need to re-examine present social policies with a view to placing less emphasis on the married couple as a unit and greater emphasis on the resources and needs of individuals.

In taxation policy, to move to sole reliance on the individual unit

would require only the abolition of rebates based on marital status—
the dependent spouse rebate and the sole parent rebate being the
most important. To remove marital status entirely from the social
security system, given its payment structure, would be much more
complex and could cause many hardships. For example, there could
no longer be a separate payment for sole parents or for wives of pen-
sioners; in addition, there could not be a payment to beneficiaries for
their dependent spouses. A social security system that abandoned the
marital unit in determining level of payments and eligibility for payments would need mechanisms for protecting these 'losers', at least in
any transitional period.

If there were greater recognition of the costs of children in the tax
and transfer systems, emphasis on marital status could be reduced.
Three components of assistance for parents and children could be
given prominence: the family allowance payment, a young child
allowance and maintenance payments.[14]

The present family allowance payment is low in relation to the
costs of rearing children. A substantial increase in this payment
would mean that the separate additional and income-tested payments
currently paid on behalf of pensioner and beneficiary children could
be reduced or abolished. An increase in the family allowance payment could also be a means of paying children in their own right in
order to guarantee them a subsistence standard of living. A young
child allowance would compensate for the costs a parent forgoes in
earning income when a child is young, or for the costs of child care
incurred if the parent continues to earn income. The payment would
be geared to the particular stage in the life cycle of a child when it is
most difficult for one of its parents to earn an income. Maintenance
payments would be collected in such a way as to finance an additional
payment to children in sole-parent families. The principle lying behind the payment would be that a child should be assured of income
support from both its parents, irrespective of whether the parents live
together.[15] Through greater reliance on payments such as these, the
standard of living of children in all families, but particularly in sole-
parent families, could be protected in any move to a social security
system that abandoned the criterion of marital status. To move in the
direction suggested, however, would require greater state responsibility for achieving distributional equity for families as well as within
families.

An individually based social security system would need to ensure
that all individuals with an earnings disability were eligible for payments in their own right, including unemployment benefit. The big-
gest obstacle to adopting the individual as the unit in the payment
structure would appear to be an expected flood of claims from married women for unemployment benefit. If a strict work test were im-

posed, including prior work experience (as is common under social insurance schemes in Europe and elsewhere) any transition to an individually based system would impose particular hardship on single-income families if the single-income earner becomes unemployed and the spouse has no prior work experience.

It is not my purpose here to put forward detailed proposals for reform. I have attempted only to explore some of the components of social policy that would be less dependent on the criterion of marital status and would ensure greater equity between individuals. Policies have been suggested that would also provide for greater neutrality with respect to the economic behaviour of members of families. I have emphasised both the relevance to social policy of recent changes in the economic status of women and in marriage and divorce patterns, the importance of financial arrangements within families and the lack of empirical data to support the assumption that husbands and wives pool their income and share equally in the benefit of that income. The relevance of traditional equity criteria used to evaluate social policy has been challenged and has raised equity issues relevant to the choice of the income unit in social policy. Economic models such as that of Becker[16] need to be modified to accommodate the fact that married people may aim to maximise individual rather than household utility.

To support the current income unit treatment in social policy generally and in social security policy in particular requires reliance on ideological beliefs about encouraging economic dependency, particularly of women on men. The argument that social policy should place emphasis on marital status to 'support the family' may in fact mean that individuals within families are denied income support. To encourage 'family life' could mean to encourage dependency of one family member on another, could lead to greater inequities between individuals and could lead to poverty within families.

It is clear that much of Australian social policy is based on assumptions about the economic behaviour of family members that no longer accord with reality. If an objective of social policy were to encourage the traditional unit of husband and dependent wife, the fact that the assumptions do not accord with reality would be of no concern. Insofar as social policies are not designed to influence either marriage or labour force decisions intentionally, neutrality with respect to these decisions should be pursued as far as possible in developing policies. Economists do tend to make the assumption that neutrality on behavioural choices is desirable unless there is clear guidance to the contrary. The most appropriate income unit, however, ultimately depends on society's judgments about the role and position of women inside and outside the family and on the role of the state in affecting distributional equity.

6 The Gender of Bureaucracy: Reflections on Feminism and the State

HESTER EISENSTEIN

In the wake of the publication of the federal government's Green Paper on affirmative action[1], there has been a flurry of debate on equality of opportunity for women in Australia. Predictably, attacks on legislation to equalise the situation of women in the work place have been vociferous from the Right of the political spectrum. But there is also an undercurrent of unease from the Left, especially among feminists, who raise questions about the motives of the state in placing so much emphasis on affirmative action as its most publicised effort on behalf of women.[2]

The questions raised by feminists about affirmative action should, I believe, be seen in the context of a broader debate that is only now beginning to take shape about the relation of women, and more specifically of feminists, to the state. In most Western countries, the current wave of the women's movement has looked to the state for redress from a whole range of grievances, from reform of unjust laws on rape to the establishment of equal pay for work of comparable value. In Australia such a strategy has a long history, notably in the campaign for equal pay.[3] But some recent feminist literature has argued that the state is a bastion of patriarchy, and indeed (in some versions) that it is itself the patriarchy. Is it not, then, completely naive, not to say futile, for feminists to attempt to use the machinery of the state as a means to transform the situation of women?

Underlying this question is a whole series of important theoretical issues. First and most obvious is the classical debate about the nature of the state in capitalist society. In addition, there is the question of the nature of law in capitalist democracies. What are the possibilities of using the law, traditionally seen in Marxist discourse as exclusively a tool of the ruling class, as a lever to change social relationships and to move society in the direction of greater social justice? To this must be added some fundamentally feminist questions. What is the nature of male dominance in this and other societies and cultures? To what other structures is it connected? How may it be dismantled, and what would be the effects of dismantling it on the shape of the society? Further, what is the relation between the social construction of gender and the political economy of gender? That is, where are the points of connection between, on the one hand, the acquisition of 'masculinity' and 'femininity' in the family, the school, and other agencies of socialisation and on the other hand the sexual division of labour, how home and work are organised in relation to sex roles, and the reproduction of those roles in the work place?

The discussion of these fundamental matters among feminist social theorists and activists is taking place *in medias res*. Government initiatives on behalf of women are moving forward before the answers are in and, indeed, the outcomes will not be known for decades, assuming (optimistically) that the inhabitants of this planet have the wisdom to escape nuclear destruction. Yet I believe it is crucial to continue debating the issues, from a theoretical as well as a practical point of view, even if all of the pieces of the puzzle are not yet in place.

In this chapter I look at one particular area of debate, namely the question of how embedded the concept of 'masculinity' is in the structures of public life. In this discussion, I use materials from my experience as an equal employment opportunity officer in the state government of New South Wales, where legislation for affirmative action in the public sector was passed in 1980. First I review the debate among feminists over sex roles theory and its adequacy as a model for social change. Second, I examine some current feminist views about the masculine character of the state. Third, I give some evidence from the New South Wales experience. Finally, I point to some directions for further inquiry, and to some (very tentative) conclusions.

The Suspicions of Feminists: Is Sex Role Theory Enough?

It is important to understand that the debate about affirmative action and other such legal reforms takes a form different from the debate about such changes among the general public. This is perhaps one of the sources of the misunderstandings that arise in the discussion of these emotionally fraught matters.

In order to understand the feminist debate, one needs to know something about the history and the development of feminist theory over the past two decades.[4] With the publication of Betty Friedan's *The Feminine Mystique* in 1963 and with the further development of some of the same ideas in the 1970s by Kate Millett and Shulamith Firestone, the initial direction of renewed feminist theorising was dominated by a set of concepts borrowed, with modifications, from social psychology and sociology, namely, the theory of sex role socialisation.

This form of feminism argued that males and females were artificially differentiated from birth by a series of pressures from family, school, church, work place and other agencies of socialisation. Boys learned to be rational, logical and objective and to suppress the expression of their feelings, while girls learned to cultivate their emotions at the expense of their facility to reason and to calculate. This polarisation prepared one set of children—boys—for entry into public life, that is, paid labour and participation in civil society generally, while it prepared the other set—girls—for immersion in private life, that is, the unpaid labour of domesticity, child bearing and child rearing, with its welter of associated tasks and accompanying ideology of motherhood as woman's true and only vocation.

Sex role conditioning, the argument went, could be reversed or undone by appropriate intervention into the same agencies of socialisation that perpetuated it. If the curriculum taught traditional sex roles, it could be changed. If religion imposed traditional views of female passivity and male dominance, it could be reformed. Even the Bible could be rewritten to accommodate the new egalitarian ideal.[5] In short, the sex roles analysis seemed to imply that the way forward for women was to shake off their conditioning into a passive role and to learn a more androgynous mode of behaviour. In this way the inequalities of treatment that society meted out to women would be remedied and women would step easily from private into public life.

In the last ten years some feminist writers have become disillusioned with sex role theory as an explanation of women's oppression, and (concomitantly) with policies that derive from sex role theory as a remedy for it.[6,7] This disillusionment is a complex phenomenon, and there is insufficient space here to address all of its aspects. But one component is the sense that policies based on sex roles analysis appear to lead in directions that do not meet the requirements of feminists for comprehensive social change. In a discussion of non-sexist education policies, Jean Blackburn noted that the effort to develop 'non-sexist' schooling might have succeeded in beginning to diminish the curriculum-based difference between girls and boys.[8] There is some evidence that girls may be less inclined than in previous generations to shy away from learning the maths and physics they will need for entry into technology-based areas of work. But, Blackburn argued, what of the values implicit in these curricular choices? In the concern to direct girls away from an education that leaves them without skills that can earn them a living, has non-sexist education begun instead to direct them towards another set of values, in which they will value 'missile building' over 'caring for dependent others'?

In other words, Blackburn argued, the trouble with implementing a policy based on the sex roles analysis was the danger of assimilating girls, all too successfully, into an unchanged structure embodying masculine values. As she put it, 'Promoting *equality of opportunity* in a world where structures (including common schooling) are not neutral in relation to the sexes, or social classes, is very likely to result in the annexation into those structures of the minority of "successful" girls and women, and working class students, without changing the structures themselves'.[9]

Underlying this argument is what I and other writers call a 'woman-centred perspective'. That is the view that, in the wake of the division of work from home wrought by the Industrial Revolution, the enforced domesticity of women of the genteel classes also gave rise to another kind of division: the attribution of humane and nurturing values to women, who were (theoretically) removed from the hurly-burly cut-throat competition of industrial life, and who were therefore the guardians of gentleness and compassion. Recent histories of women's work in the last 200 years have shown this 'absence' of most women from the impact of industrial life to be something of a male fantasy.[10] Nonetheless the ideology of femininity has a basis in the reality of most women's experience.

Most women possess or acquire what Jean Baker Miller[11] termed the 'two-sided strengths' that derive from conditioning into the female role. As Miller noted, 'There is no question that most women have a much greater sense of the emotional components of all human activity than most men.'[12] The capacity to nurture, to act co-operatively within families and to be emotionally literate are, on the one hand, qualities that women have been virtually forced to develop as a result of a subordinate social role imposed upon them. On the other, these are deeply human qualities and their loss is indeed threatened if they have been relegated to women and if women now cross the boundary from private to public life in massive numbers.

Further Suspicions: On the 'Embeddedness' of Masculinity in Public Life

Among some critics, then, reforms based on a concept of 'equal opportunity' that seek to break down traditional sex role stereotyping in the work place may end up reinforcing the very structure of values that some feminists have been attempting to contest. Other feminist writers, however, have been expressing a different set of fears—that feminist-inspired legal reforms can never have a significant impact because the legal structure itself contains within it some essential and immutable quality of masculinity.

Catherine A. MacKinnon[13] has written what is in some ways a pessimistic theoretical account of feminist attempts to reform the law concerning rape, in the context of a much broader discussion of the relation of feminism to the state and to traditional Marxist accounts of state power. MacKinnon points out that feminists have looked to law and to the state for redress of grievances, without perhaps sufficient attention to the role of the state and its nature. 'Feminism', says MacKinnon, 'has no theory of the state', and it urgently needs one.[14] Interestingly, her view converges with that of some Australian writers. Rosemary Pringle and Ann Game, writing critically of their own earlier work, note, 'We are not alone in our failure to theorise the patriarchal state. Indeed, we believe it is one of the major gaps in feminist theory to date.'[15]

MacKinnon's very complex argument rests, in part, on the assumption that law regulates the public (male) realm, while women inhabit and are oppressed within the private realm. This is hardly a full account of social reality. But in broad outline, MacKinnon holds that

> the state is male in the feminist sense. The law sees and treats women the way men see and treat women. The liberal state coercively and authoritatively constitutes the social order in the interest of men as a gender, through its legitimizing norms, relation to society, and substantive policies.[16]

The so-called neutrality of the law, then, conceals a fundamentally masculine world view. The general impact of MacKinnon's argument is that women are foolish to look to law reform, or, more broadly, to the power of the state as presently constituted, for any form of relief from the exercise of male power over them.

A different but not incompatible argument is put by Ann Game and Rosemary Pringle.[17] *Gender at Work* is a pathbreaking attempt to put together two hitherto separated areas of inquiry—into technological change and its effects on control of the working class on the one hand, and into the sexual division of labour on the other. One of the points of this study is the enduring quality of the sexual division of labour over time and across all sectors of the economy. As they write, 'Gender is fundamental to the way in which work is organised, and work is central in the social construction of gender.'[18] Game and Pringle show how, even in a relatively new industry such as computers, the assignment of 'male' and 'female' work is central to the way in which the industry operates. They also show how fluid, over time, is the boundary between men's and women's work, a fact that demonstrates the social and political origins of the division and therefore its mutability.

Yet Game and Pringle are also pessimistic on one point at least: because of how work is organised, measures to create equal opportunity in employment can be absorbed effortlessly because they are entirely compatible with the form of male control now operating. In summary,

> Bureaucratic control ... operates through denial that there is any discrimination. It is asserted that gender is irrelevant, that women can make it on the same terms as men, that all will be rationally and fairly evaluated, according to the same criteria. This ignores ... the ways in which the whole world of work is structured around male norms.

The modern form of control—'rational' and bureaucratic—is more subtle but no less patriarchal, they argue, than earlier forms evolved under capitalism.

> It is embodied in the ideology that 'women can make it in a man's world' and that they can prove themselves at men's work as long as they retain their femininity. Women in banks with new 'equal opportunities' images have learnt that the power structure is still very much a male power structure, however rational and anonymous it may seem. We can call this 'Patriarchy without the Father' to signify that it comes from an apparently neutral source.[19]

In this passage, Game and Pringle seem to be saying that anti-discrimination legislation is not in conflict with the overall structure of masculine power. On the contrary, masculinity is apparently embedded in the very structures of the bureaucracy.

> What needs to be addressed is the significance of the ideology of equalities, embodied in, for example, anti-discrimination legislation, and equality of opportunity (EEO). Are liberal feminists' demands simply being co-opted or do they have a subversive potential in this context? Under what circumstances could EEO threaten patriarchal relations in the workplace?[20]

A crucial question, I would argue, and one to which I shall return.

It must be said that some evidence of the 'embeddedness' of masculinity comes from the mouths of men themselves, however unwittingly. Zillah Eisenstein has proposed the idea that liberal democratic theory itself embodies a concept of justice that is by definition exclusive of women.[21] She argues that liberal theory as originally devised by Locke and other writers depends on a definition of public life that excludes women from its ambit. Because it is dependent on a theoretical division between public and private spheres of life, the doctrine of the 'rights of men' is a concept that uses 'men' not generically but literally, to mean males only.

This view is apparently borne out by some recent writing from male theorists, who find concepts such as affirmative action abhorrent. H.J. McCloskey[22] argues that affirmative action (as practised in the United States) violates basic principles of social justice. His argument rests on a highly questionable definition of affirmative action as '"reverse discrimination" or "preferential selection", that is, the favouring of the less qualified black or woman against the better qualified white male'.[23]

One purpose of affirmative action is to ensure that qualified blacks and/or women are not blocked from appointment by prejudice and further, that unnecessary qualification requirements that have the effect of blocking white women or blacks of both sexes without those qualifications are removed. The intention of setting numerical targets for the appointment of members of disadvantaged groups is to remove the barriers to their appointment, and hence overall to increase the equity in the distribution of jobs society-wide, not to decrease it.[24] Overall, then, McCloskey's argument is not made on the basis of a fair assessment of what affirmative action measures seek to accomplish. However, I draw attention to one part of McCloskey's paper in particular, which I believe illustrates (no doubt unintentionally) the feminist claim that some male theorists see 'human' concerns solely in terms of masculine rights.

McCloskey concludes his argument against affirmative action with the hypothetical case of the infanticide of female children in contemporary China. 'In a democratized China', McCloskey writes,

> those who favoured strong affirmative action on behalf of females would in consistency be committed to arguing that when there are scarce medical resources, females by virtue of this discrimination to-day should always be preferred to males. So to discriminate would be to act with great injustice. It would be to deny the equal basic natural rights of all persons.[25]

This *reductio ad absurdum* has some interesting features. Clearly the denial of medical resources to men would be no doubt to deny their 'basic natural rights'. But McCloskey makes no further comment on the female infanticides. Does the killing of female babies (if it is practised) not violate our sense of natural justice? This kind of rhetorical extravagance lends credence to the view that in this, as in much other writing on the subject, 'social justice' (unmodified) may be taken to read 'social justice for men'.

Implementing Affirmative Action: A Challenge to Male Hegemony?

In the New South Wales context, affirmative action does not mean reverse discrimination or preferential selection. It means the selection of the best qualified person for the position without regard to that person's sex or ethnic/racial origin. I want to point to some elements of this programme, operating since late 1980, to argue for the view that this form of legislative intervention can, even in a very early phase, offer some challenge to what I have been calling the 'embeddedness' of masculine power. I look briefly at three areas: sexual harassment, the lifting of weights and return from maternity leave.

Parts IXA of the Anti-Discrimination Act of 1977, amended in 1980, required all state government departments and declared authorities to prepare an equal employment opportunity management plan and to lodge that plan with the Director of Equal Opportunity in Public Employment for evaluation. In December 1983, universities and colleges of advanced education were scheduled under the Act as well. An EEO plan consists of a statistical analysis of the workforce by sex, marital status and ethnicity; a review of personnel practices including recruitment, selection, promotion, training and staff development; and a set of strategies to eliminate practices found to be discriminatory. Plans include numerical or percentage targets for the recruitment and promotion of the disadvantaged groups, specifically migrants of non-English speaking background, Aborigines, women of all ethnic and racial origins, and the physically disabled. The Director's office advises and assists with the preparation of EEO management plans, and, once they have been lodged and approved, with their implementation.[26]

Most management plans include a provision for issuing a policy statement that defines sexual harassment, states that this is an unacceptable form of behaviour at work and sets forth procedures for resolving individual grievances. Sexual harassment grievances may also be taken outside the organisation to the Anti-Discrimination Board. In 1983, two cases concerning the head of a large statutory authority came before the Equal Opportunity Tribunal, accompanied by much press coverage. While the Tribunal in each case did not decide in favour of the complainants, it did rule that sexual harassment constitutes sex discrimination under the New South Wales Anti-Discrimination Act.[27]

There is room for debate about the effectiveness of the complaints procedure, particularly against powerful male public servants. But the publicity surrounding the cases has had some educative effects. In addition, the definition of sexual harassment as a form of sex discrimination and the issuing of policy statements by individual departments and declared authorities, by the Public Service Board and by unions, has the effect of beginning to change sexual harassment. Rather than a kind of victimisation that must be endured, like the weather, by women workers, sexual harassment becomes something that can be legitimately complained of as an unacceptable condition of employment, as a 'detriment', and that can, at least theoretically, be stopped. Whether it can be stopped in practice depends, I would argue, at least in part on the seriousness of the commitment to stopping it on the part of senior managers, and in part on increasing the number of senior managers who are sensitive to this issue—more likely (although not automatic) if they are women.

Another issue that arises in implementing EEO plans is that of women entering traditionally male areas of work. An obvious and often-posed question is: How will women lift the weights that men must if the legal restrictions on the amount of weight that a woman can be required to lift are removed? At an EEO seminar for administrators at TAFE, where most of the trades areas taught have been male-dominated, one of the trades teachers in the room said he had successfully used the entry of women students into his course to argue for his entitlement to the machinery for lifting heavy objects that his section had been promised many months earlier. The point he was making was that the entry of women into the area had prompted a re-examination of the assumptions being made about the expectations of male workers. With no legal limit on the weights they were lifting, regular injuries were commonplace. The integration of women could, in effect, be used as a reason for lessening the burden of the expectations of masculinity in the work place.

The third example is that of return from maternity leave. In the New South Wales Public Service, women are entitled to take one full year of leave following the birth or adoption of a baby, or two years working part-time. Our office has heard of many cases in which a woman returning from maternity leave to resume previous duties on a part-time basis has her entitlement questioned on the grounds that the nature of the work performed does not lend itself to part-time duties.

In assisting EEO co-ordinators to resolve some of these disputes within departments, it is necessary to examine in detail the actual duties being performed. Several cases have arisen of women attorneys who must make court appearances. Is it possible to organise this on a part-time basis? Thus far the answer appears to be yes, it is, if both the officer concerned and the administrator to whom she reports are willing to be flexible. But in general this kind of question raises all kinds of issues about work. What assumptions are being made about its organisation, its continuity, the shape of the working day and week? Are these rational, or are they connected to a concept of the male worker, for whom the details of daily life, including child care, are attended to by an (often fictional) non-working female partner? Needless to say, the outcome of these disputes is often profoundly affected by the personal views of senior male bureaucrats about women's proper roles.

The three areas of intervention point to three different aspects of the 'embeddedness' of masculinity: the right of men to sexual access to women against their will; the (on average) greater physical strength of men as the basis of entitlements to paid work; and the organisation of the work day to the requirements of a male bread-winner. I make no claim that the New South Wales affirmative action legislation has changed any of these features of male power, but it has helped to challenge their legitimacy.

Conclusions: Thinking About the Future

I have argued that an affirmative action programme such as that in the New South Wales government administration begins to make in-roads into some areas of male power over women, with the many other kinds of feminist intervention now taking place.

This is no doubt why such programmes are opposed so vociferous-ly in some quarters. A recent advertisement in the *Sydney Morning Herald*, placed by a group opposing the federal bill on sex discri-mination read: 'Stop Ryan! Australia's feminist dictator' (8 October 1983). No doubt from her vantage point as the only woman (not to mention feminist) in the cabinet, Senator Ryan would have re-ceived this characterisation of her powers with a wry smile. If the acceptance of equal employment opportunity measured 'effortlessly' is indeed a measure of their compatibility with the structures of mas-culine power, perhaps one can take heart from the degree of resist-ance that they are evoking. I would argue that, in this, as in all political situations, there are absolutely no guarantees about the outcome. The long term effects of these reforms will depend on what we as a society and (more narrowly) what we as the women's movement can make of them. As part of this effort, the fruitful exchange between theory and practice that has characterised the second wave of feminism in the past decades should continue, and feminists in the academy should take full advantage of their sisters' experience in the bureau-cracy and elsewhere to develop and to expand their theoretical frameworks.

In the first place, we must continue to examine changes over time in the sexual division of labour. Game and Pringle's research suggests that the boundary between male and female domains of work is flexible over time, within the development of given industries and from industry to industry; what seems to be constant is that a boundary is drawn. But we must look much more closely at which agencies draw those boundaries and at what historical moments. Equally, more attention needs to be given to the power exerted by women in the process, particularly as women are now beginning to move into positions of influence within government and the labour movement.

In the second place, we need a much closer examination of the elements in the formation of gender identity. Clare Burton suggests that the resistance to equal employment opportunity in the public sector of New South Wales may stem less from a rational assessment by men that they stand to lose out to women in the competition for a decreasing number of prestigious and high-paying jobs than from a deeply held sense that their own masculinity at work is related to the absence of women and children.[28] That is, the sexual division of labour and the exclusion of women from certain kinds of position form a fundamental layer of male self-confidence and identity. In this interpretation, opposition to work-based child care would have less to do with arguments about funding than with a masculine system of 'identity protection'. This interpretation is congruent with Nancy Chodorow's view that male gender identity is profoundly anchored in a sense of being not-female.[29]

In a similar vein, Bob Connell has argued for a notion of 'hegemonic masculinity', which is not a simple acquisition at the age of eighteen months of a sense of gender identity, but rather is created over a period of years, consciously and unconsciously built up as a response to a number of cues in the family, in school, and then finally at work.[30] Connell's is a rare instance of an attempt at honesty about the way an inheritor of male power experiences the process of stepping into that role.

Finally, we need to deglobalise our concepts. To say that 'the state is male' is to make a very compressed and dense set of assertions, which requires unpacking even to be understood, let alone argued. The 'rationality' and 'objectivity' of bureaucracy in the Weberian sense are certainly connected to the capacity for rational argument and the use of logic that have been encouraged and cultivated in male children. But the capacity for logic is not 'male'. It is a human quality. 'Masculinity' is embedded in the structures of state power at a number of different points, and in several different senses, as I indicated in my discussion of the New South Wales Public Service. The elements of the edifice of male power are many, complex and interconnected, as the recent debates about patriarchy illustrate. I would argue for more rigour in definitions and more attention to the level of reality under discussion: conceptual, psychological, economic, and so forth.

The virtue of all these approaches, I would argue, is that they incorporate the notion of the possibility of change. Part of the difficulty and the complexity of making this kind of analysis is due to the fact that we are living at a time of accelerated social change, and one of the things that is changing is our view of what sex and gender mean. I think that it is inaccurate to say that 'the state is male', but it is accurate to say that 'up to now the state has been male', if by that we mean that until recently public power has been wielded largely by men and in the interest of men (and indeed by only a small number of them). The possibility of altering that fact may now lie within our grasp. But the direction in which the change will take us is an open historical question. Carole Pateman has argued for some time that the feminist movement needs to take a look at the history of the labour movement, to get a sense of history and a sense of how a radical movement can be shaped by its encounters with capitalism and with the state. I think we need more history of feminism (which after all goes back more than a century) and more attempts to assess the impact of recent feminist reforms.

Above all, we need to keep under discussion and before us a notion of the kind of society we are seeking to create, and the role of feminism in that effort. Is it, in fact, the gender of bureaucracy that we are trying to change, or the things, ultimately, that the bureaucracy does? I think that woman-centred values are radical values: egalitarian, co-operative, peace-loving. It is still unclear how we can get from here to there, but I would argue that as feminists we have to get 'a foot in the door'[31] as a first requisite for change. Affirmative action and other 'reformist' measures on behalf of women may not be sufficient. But they are certainly necessary.

7 In Pursuit of Equality: Women and Legal Thought 1788–1984

JOCELYNNE A. SCUTT

Law is a reflection and a source of prejudice. It both enforces and suggests forms of bias.

Diane B. Schulder

Since 1788 in Australia, women's attempts to establish equal rights with men have often been made through legal processes. The effort has been undertaken on various fronts. Some women have chosen to protest individually by refusing to obey laws or by actively opposing established rules. Sometimes protest has been collective—women have taken to the streets, marching in rallies organised by women demanding the right to vote, the right to stand for parliament, for equal pay, the right to choose an abortion, and for equal social, political, legal and economic rights overall.

The fight for equality through law has most often been conducted on a piecemeal basis. Women protested against particular laws, often when personally confronted by legal obstacles to their participation in public life or by laws inhibiting their activities in the personal sphere of home and family. They rallied against laws interpreted to prevent them from studying at universities or from joining particular professions and trades. They agitated against unequal divorce laws, discriminatory laws governing child custody and for the right to own property during marriage. Success was perceived in the 1970s, with women lobbying for the passage of laws designed to be all-encompassing in the private and public spheres, such as the Sex Discrimination Act 1976 (South Australia), the Anti-Discrimination Act 1977 (New South Wales), the Equal Opportunity Act 1977 (Victoria), the Sex Discrimination Act 1984 (Commonwealth) and the Family Law Act 1975 (Commonwealth).[1]

That women should choose to do battle in the legal arena is ironic: perhaps in no other area is sexism so blatant yet so accepted. But many women continue to believe that legislative change will invariably bring about real advances for equality. This confidence in the system continues, despite an obvious failure on the part of the courts and other dominant legal authorities to follow the letter and spirit of the law in dealing with women, with 'women's issues', or with 'women's interests'. Although some men—judges, lawyers, politicians and others—in the past and today have expressed concern (sometimes real, sometimes opportunistic or feigned) about women's rights, they are few. Legal writing and thought have not generally expanded to accept equal rights for women as a legitimate mainstream issue. Theory and practice have usually avoided reference to women's rights. In the main, it is women who have sought to change the face of the law and legal thought by injecting feminist analysis into jurisprudence. A handful of women has carried out this task.

Women engaged in fighting for rights through law must examine whether the battle in fact advances women's cause. Ultimately the question is whether, in a society built for the immediate benefit of men, it is possible to reverse standard practice by using the legal process. If those in control of the system are wedded to the benefits they enjoy as a result of sex discrimination, is it realistic to suppose that they will be sympathetic to the elimination of inequality between women and men? Have we, as women, been on the right track for the past two hundred years, or have we been dupes of the capitalist patriarchy? It may well be that legislative and administrative moves within the system and attempts to develop and put into practice a feminist jurisprudence, suit the purposes of a liberal society seeking, without using too many resources, to give the illusion of equality to its female members. Is patriarchy so strong as to check our every move in a game that can lead only to checkmate?

Nineteenth-Century Fighting in Public and Private

> *The male touch signifies economic dominance ...*
> Phyllis Chesler and Emily Jane Goodman

From the time of Anglo-Saxon emigration to the Australian colonies, the rights of women were ignored. Women were seen as harridans to be strictly policed by their gaolers or as commodities to be provided to womenless men. Unlike male convicts, of whom only the most serious offenders were sentenced to transportation, female convicts were sent to New South Wales (and later to other colonies) whatever their offences. Free women were encouraged to emigrate to fill posts as servants and governesses or, equally frequently, to marry. The right of men to live in a world populated by women to suit their needs took precedence. The overwhelming concern was that of social control: the preponderance of men in the colonies was continually drawn to the attention of the British Colonial Office with the suggestion that, unless sufficient numbers of women were made available, discipline could not be maintained.[2]

The law did little to protect women's interests. Although during earlier times in Britain women of property or propertied widows were entitled to vote and hold public office in the same way as men of similar propertied standing, legal attitudes hardened during the nineteenth century and the rights of this elite group of women were removed. In 1850 the Acts Interpretation Act introduced the provision that in all laws where the masculine term was used it should be understood to include the feminine. It was generally agreed that although 'the law speaks of men only', women were governed by the laws passed by male parliaments and interpreted by male courts.

At common law it was considered a single woman possessed similar rights to property as men, and similar responsibilities for paying rates and taxes, except that for heiresses, if there were a boy in the family, he rather than she would inherit all real property (land and the like), whatever their respective ages. In English law relevant to the colonies, males and their heirs had preference over females. With married women, a restriction on rights began upon betrothal. When a woman consented to a proposal of marriage, she lost any right to give away her property without her husband's knowledge or to sell it; he could revoke any gift or disposition she made. A married woman had no right to sue or to contract for business or other purposes. She did not have legal custody of children of the marriage—that was solely the prerogative of the children's father. When he died, she did not gain a right to custody: the children's father could make provision for their guardianship after his death, excluding her, and where he made no such provision, his family could intervene to remove the children.[3]

In the public sphere, court decisions removed from women any ancient rights they might have possessed to undertake higher education, to enter professions and trades and to vote in municipal and other elections, as well as standing for public office.[4] Legal sophistry brought this about. Thus when women applied to be admitted to university on the ground that, being persons, they fell within the university regulations (which stated that any *persons* with particular standing could be admitted), the courts held them not to be persons on the basis that no women had applied for admission from the time universites were established; therefore the regulations could not apply to *them*. When women applied to be admitted to practice in various professions—for example, to be lawyers or notaries public—they were refused admission, again on the basis of 'non-personhood'. A married woman was not a person: her personhood was subsumed in that of her husband upon marriage, so she could not qualify. A single woman was also barred from entry, because if she married, despite being admitted as a barrister or solicitor, upon marriage she would automatically become a non-person. The mere possibility of marriage thus ruled her out. Furthermore, said the judges, Lord Coke had pronounced in the seventeenth century that women could not be attorneys. The words of a man considered then—and now—to be one of the world's finest common law jurists were conclusive.

Women in Australia were thus confronted with having to fight against laws specifically denying women equal rights with men, or against laws that were interpreted by courts to deny them equality. They were forced into a position of having to accept that the definition of 'person' did not include women, and thus lobbied to have Acts passed stating that women were entitled to enter into legal practice, to stand for public office, and to vote in local government, state and federal elections. The problem with this approach was that once having acknowledged that 'person' did not include women, it was necessary to change every law which was framed in 'person' terms. Thus when Mary Cecil Kitson applied for admission as a notary public in South Australia, she was refused on the basis that, although she was a lawyer, having been admitted to practice under the Female Law Practitioners Act 1911 (South Australia), the Public Notaries Act had not been changed.[5] It continued to be cast in terms of 'persons', thus excluding women. The very act of women fighting to be specifically acknowledged in legislation was used to justify their exclusion from other areas of public life and office.

Some women protested against the bias of judges sitting on the cases, but these protests were to little avail. Indeed, judges denied that they were influenced by patriarchal attitudes. They attested to being hamstrung by the way in which laws were written. Yet the argument was clearly fallacious. First, in interpreting legislation courts are bound to accept at face value what the law says. Only when the words of a statute are ambiguous should the courts look further. Thus, if a law used the word 'person', the ordinary, everyday meaning of that word should have been acknowledged; women would then not have been constrained to alter legislation by piecemeal methods and would have been freed to use their energies differently. Second, in arguing against the view that they adopted an anti-woman approach, judges fell into the trap of revealing their prejudices all too clearly. Sir James Easte Wills, another revered member of the judiciary, commented on the decision to exclude women from voting in council elections, saying:

'What was the cause of [the exclusion of women from voting rights] it is not necessary to go into: but, admitting that fickleness of judgment and liability to influence have sometimes been suggested as the ground of exclusion, I must protest its being supposed to arise in this country from any underrating of the sex either in point of intellect or worth. That would be quite inconsistent with one of the glories of our civilization—the respect and honour in which women are held. This is not a mere fancy of my own, but will be found in Selden [the respected legal historian], in the discussion of the origin of the exclusion of women from judicial and like public functions, where the author gives preference to this reason, that the exemption was founded upon motives of decorum, and was *a privilege of the sex* . . .'[6]

In the private sphere, women concentrated upon three major areas of reform: the right to own property, the right of a mother to custody of her children and the right to divorce upon the same grounds as men. Yet again, women faced a cleft-stick choice. With divorce, under ecclesiastical law, both women and men had, at least according to the written rules, equal rights to gain an approved separation. With reforms to divorce laws, however, men's rights were expanded beyond those of women. To gain a divorce, a woman had to prove not only that her husband had committed adultery, but also that it was accompanied by some aggravating circumstance—for example, that it was performed in the course of rape, that it was a bigamous coupling, incest, or involved bestiality. A man had only to prove that his wife had committed simple adultery. (This double standard was maintained in Victoria until 1959, when the Matrimonial Causes Act made divorce law uniform throughout Australia.) With custody, despite reforms gained by women, women similarly remained in a disadvantageous position. In 1854 and 1875 New South Wales adopted British Acts providing that a mother had a right, in equity, to seek the discretion of a court in awarding her access rights or custody of a child under seven years of age; the later Act raised the age to sixteen years. However, women did not thereby exercise equal rights with men in relation to their children. If a woman wished to secure her children's company, she was obliged to take a suit in equity. The father retained custody by right, unless the mother instituted such action and won. This was an important consideration for any woman who was unhappy in her marriage or who suffered abuse from her husband. If she left him prior to the reforms, she had no right to take the children with her; after the reforms, she had to leave her children behind and apply to the court. If a woman committed adultery, her children would never be placed in her custody but extramarital sexual relations did not impair the father's rights.[7] In a society where all judges were male, where each had been reared in a world in which Victorian morality held sway with its notorious double standard, even where she had not engaged in extra-marital sex, a woman was required to live up to a high standard of morality and womanly 'goodness' in order to obtain custody of her children. Thus reforms apparently granted women rights, yet served equally to confirm the particular place of women, woman's role and the double standard.

With the right to property ownership, the end result once more confirms the argument: that laws can apparently be changed to accommodate women's demands for equality, yet simultaneously ensure that women remain disadvantaged. The disadvantage may be the more increased because it becomes difficult for women to continue to assert, with clear illustrations, the discrimination they suffer. During the nineteenth century, women agitated for the passage of Married Women's Property Acts. Changes to property laws ensured that a woman gained the right to retain her earnings; previously they had automatically belonged to her husband upon marriage. Yet how many women had substantial earnings to retain? All women earned less than men, despite their equally hard work. Any property that a woman brought with her to marriage now remained hers, where previously it had belonged to her husband. Yet how many women brought property to a marriage? In the main, despite these changes and the strong rearguard action many men—particularly politicians and members of the judiciary—fought against them, women continued to be forced by economic circumstance to live in a marital relationship, dependent upon a husband for upkeep: inequalities in job opportunities, in wages and salaries, in the granting of loans for business or private purposes, in responsibilities for child care, in demands for cleaning up the day-to-day household mess meant that, whatever the law might formally state, however the politicans and reformers of the day putting the pro-woman view might talk of the need to grant women equal status, there was no danger that women would in fact take upon themselves a 'position of independence' apart from their husbands; nor that they would effectively gain equal rights.[8] Talk came cheap, but for the rare woman seeking to take up her rights under the new law, should she have any property of note, legal representation and tracking through the courts to secure those rights would in the large majority of cases be beyond her means. Those without any property earned by their own hand in paid employment or inherited in their own right certainly had equal formal legal rights with men[9], but they continued to work in the home without recognition of their contribution to the *husband's* economic standing. The illusion was thus created of the woman, possessed of equal rights and equal opportunities, who through personal failing remained subordinate to the man. 'Progressive' jurists nonetheless labelled this period of reform as the 'women's epoch'.[10]

Twentieth-Century Fighting in Public

> *To be powerless, without social, economic or legal status; to be unconfident, dependent, insecure, and vulnerable—is to be female.*
>
> Charlotte Bronte

The piecemeal approach to gaining equal legal rights for women was continued in the public sphere in the first two-thirds of the twentieth century. Although some women saw a need for blanket legislation, this was more difficult to achieve. Women fought against legislation passed to deprive them of jobs and against public service provisions requiring that on marriage women could be retained as temporary employees only. Discriminatory measures had to be overcome, such as the prohibitions against women sitting for examinations enabling them to enter the career divisions of federal and state public services, from which those on their way to powerful, authoritative, and highly paid positions are chosen.[11] In the corporate world, similar policies were pursued, not necessarily by overt laws or regulations but by tacit agreement or unconscious design. Not for women high-powered, high-status, highly paid, decisionmaking positions, nor access to positions placing them in line for promotion to such jobs: women's abilities were viewed, in the main, as marginal on the zero end of the maturity scale. 'Business' manuals for secretaries confirmed this:

> A businessman wants a girl [sic] who can make simple decisions, one who won't run to him for answers to routine questions ...

> A good secretary never nags her boss nor does she speak to him about personal matters unless he asks. She does not wear jangling bracelets or heavy make-up. And she never eats her lunch while walking in the street.

> [The boss] may have a brief chat to you each morning before beginning the day's dictation. Listen to what he has to say and reply suitably, but do not yourself prolong the conversation. It is for him to end it.[12]

These attitudes persisted into the 1970s and 1980s. Yet with the 1970s, a change in the women's movement approach to the fight for law reform meant that women's organisations, in particular WEL, the Women's Electoral Lobby, began lobbying for anti-discrimination, equal opportunity, or sex discrimination legislation to 'cover the field'. Women began to have more success in injecting into contemporary jurisprudence a perspective arising out of their feminist orientation and experience.

In 1972 the new federal Labor government was disposed towards introducing human rights and sex discrimination legislation. After ratifying the International Labour Organisation Convention No. 111 on Discrimination in Employment and Occupation, in June 1973 as an interim measure the government established federal and state committees on discrimination in employment and occupation. The committees were designed to provide an avenue of complaint for those discriminated against in the paid work place, and to reveal the extent of the problem. This was intended to serve as a basis for passing legislation to cover discrimination in all areas—work, education, accommodation, provision of goods and services—which were recognised as being interconnected.

At this point, however, difficulties arose for the government and as a result impinged upon women's fight for rights. Due to its failure to attain a majority in the Senate, the Labor government was experiencing problems with its legislative programme. Legislation outlawing discrimination on grounds of sex took a back seat while human rights legislation and legislation prohibiting racial discrimination were drafted and placed before the Parliament in 1973. WEL objected to sex discrimination being omitted from the immediate programme and began a nationwide lobbying campaign to have sex included as a ground in the legislation. It was not successful. The Race Discrimination Act became law in 1975 and was restricted to discrimination on grounds of race and ethnicity. The Human Rights Bill lapsed.

In lobbying for the inclusion of sex in the Race Discrimination Act and in thus arguing for the Bill to be held up to effect this, WEL placed itself in a position where it could be criticised for being insufficiently mindful of Aboriginal rights. In complaining about the terms of the Human Rights Bill and lobbying for its expansion, WEL made itself vulnerable to misunderstanding, misrepresentation of its aims and to criticism from those sectors of the community that so often retort to claims for women's rights that 'it is *human* rights that are important'. Yet many women who are members of WEL have actively participated in the battle against discrimination on racial grounds: before WEL was formed in 1972 they joined organisations battling for an Aboriginal rights amendment to the Constitution and for associated aims; after joining WEL they retained active membership in these organisations. Aboriginal and Islander women have been and are WEL members. WEL women have fought in many capacities for human rights. It is unfair to suggest that any Human Rights Bill is adequate if in the absence of sex discrimination legislation it fails to address women's rights as a specific issue. Further, the Race Discrimination Act does not succeed in dealing with the double discrimination of being black and female.

Women had also to contend with the jurisprudential world in which during the early 1970s concerns about discrimination and human rights had been voiced by a minority and a trickle of articles was being published in law journals, yet the dominant theme was not that of women's rights. Against this backdrop, women's concerns were made to appear trivial or an overreaction to a steady movement forward. The most apposite analogy is that which faced women at the end of the Civil War in the United States when at their protests against the framing of the Fourteenth Amendment extending equal protection of laws to black Americans in terms of *males* only, they were told, 'Stand back, ladies, it's the Negroes' hour'. Then, as later in Australia, it was not recognised that 50 per cent of that population was female, with legitimate demands equal to those of their black brothers and white male rulers.

WEL's lobbying efforts were further subverted with the dismissal of the Whitlam Labor government from office in November 1975 and its replacement by a Liberal-National Party government. Working on its earlier approaches to the then Opposition, WEL began lobbying the new government. This proved to be even more difficult, for despite numerous government statements of support for sex discrimination legislation, no concrete moves were forthcoming. Already conservatism in the fight was expressing itself not only in governmental circles but amongst women. Women employed in the Office of Women's Affairs began urging WEL to lower its sights; when WEL refused to compromise one member was directly approached by an officer of the Office of Women's Affairs and told to 'stop'. Women were thus divided by the machinations of government and the problem of bureaucratic allegiance.

The upshot of the debate was that, after seven years in power, the Liberal-National Party government concluded its term in office without fulfilling the promise of its many press releases. Even the Opposition Labor Party's Sex Discrimination Bill, entered into the Senate as a private member's Bill in 1982, failed to gain its support. However in 1984, following another election, the Sex Discrimination Act became law under the new Labor government. Ironically, it contains those provisions for which WEL had lobbied over more than ten years, with the omission of provisions dealing with affirmative action.[13] Does this signify a win for women? Taking into account past experience and the experience of women in states already operating under sex discrimination or equal opportunity laws, it may well be that this is simply the beginning of a new battle or the old battle renewed.

Today, as in the past, the law is schizophrenic in its approach. Early this century one revered judge stated

> ... I do not think so ill of our jurisprudence as to suppose that its principles are so remote from the ordinary needs of civilised society and the ordinary claims which it makes upon its members as to deny a legal remedy where there is so obviously a social wrong.[14]

This statement was made when an obvious social wrong—that of the denial to women of legal equality with men—was perpetuated almost unremittingly. It was made at a time that judges were engaged in wholly artificial decisionmaking about the rights of women to enter professions, trades and public offices, and was supported by jurisprudential writings of the day. It was maintained while women were fighting against legislation passed to take away their right to paid employment, solely on the basis of their sex or marital status. The issue therefore becomes whether, whatever the law states and however it is framed, the rights of women are capable of recognition by lawyers and courts, or whether attorneys and judges adhering to a patriarchal philosophy will make determinations that subvert the spirit (and sometimes the letter) of the legislation.

The 1983 decision in the New South Wales Anti-Discrimination Act case of O'Callaghan v Loder highlights the problem confronting women in trying to make effective the legislation passed by male-dominated parliaments and put into effect by male-dominated courts. It portends the failure of legal practice to change to accommodate new ideas and, worse, confirms that whatever legal theory feminists may develop as a counter to masculine legal thought, the penetration of feminist theory into the minds of men and courts is negligible.

Ms O'Callaghan complained to the Anti-Discrimination Board that she had been sexually harassed by her employer, Mr Loder. Her complaint stated:

> I wish to make a complaint of discrimination based on sex which is against the Anti-Discrimination Act. I am employed as a lift attendant at the Department of Main Roads and I have been sexually harassed by the Commissioner, Mr Loader [sic].[15]

In essence, Ms O'Callaghan's story was that during the latter part of 1981 and throughout 1982, she was 'subjected to unsolicited and unwelcome sexual contact by Mr Loder, who at the relevant time was either the incumbent Commissioner for Main Roads, or was acting as such. She at the time was a lift driver in the Department.' The Tribunal described what it termed 'the sexual contact':

> 'The sexual contact occurred in the Commissioner's suite and took the form of putting an arm around her, kissing her, attempting to touch her breasts and, on one occasion in September 1981, forcing her to hold his exposed penis until he ejaculated.'[16]

The Tribunal commented further that Ms O'Callaghan alleged that 'little if any direct sexual contact [occurred] after that date. However, Mr Loder continued to seek her out and to request that she join him in his suite. She says that these approaches acquired the quality of harassment, with sexual overtones, because of the sexual contact which had preceded it.'

The position of the Commissioner for Main Roads was, as the Tribunal described it, that

> Mr Loder admits that he invited Miss O'Callaghan to his suite on a number of occasions during that period. However, he says that these meetings were devoid of any sexual connotations except to the extent that he sometimes lightly kissed her as she was leaving. He therefore denies her claim.[17]

In addition to other preliminary matters of a technical kind, the issue facing the Tribunal before the complaint could be heard was whether sexual harassment was included within the terms of the Anti-Discrimination Act 1977 (New South Wales), despite not being specifically stated in the Act as being covered. Reviewing the New South Wales legislation and cases in the United Kingdom, Canada and the United States, the Tribunal decided that sexual harassment comes within the terms of the Act. It is unnecessary that detriment in the way of job loss should be suffered by a complainant for acts to be deemed 'sexual harassment' and 'sex discrimination'. According to the Tribunal, sexual harassment is unlawful under the Anti-Discrimination Act if 'submission to ... sexual advances [has] been made a condition of the continuance of the complainant's job—an exaction which the supervisor would not have sought from any male'. It is unlawful where '"conditions of employment" includes the psychological and emotional work environment—that the sexually stereotyped insults and demeaning propositions to which [a complainant] was indisputably subjected and which caused her anxiety and debilitation, illegally poisoned that environment.'[18]

The finding that the Act included sexual harassment as unlawful sex discriminatory behaviour was hailed as a breakthrough. Indeed it was. Counsel for the respondent had argued strongly against the ruling, stating among other matters that the United States and Canadian decisions should be ignored by the Tribunal. The Tribunal held that whatever those decisions had been, sexual harassment would come within the terms of the New South Wales Act, but also that in looking at the development of the law in the United States and Canada it was right to make a ruling according to the position now existing there, rather than going back to an earlier stage, where it was not indisputably considered in North America that sexual harassment was within the terms of sex discrimination legislation.

So far, the Loder case gives an illusion of an advance: the terms of an Act designed primarily to assist women gain equality in many areas, including the paid work place, are capable of being read in a manner more favourable to women than a traditional legal argument (that put by counsel for Mr Loder) would allow. This means that where sex discrimination legislation existing in other states does not specifically include sexual harassment as discrimination, there is a reasonable degree of certainty that it will be interpreted to do so, in accordance with the New South Wales determination. Yet why was sexual harassment not included in the Act as a specific ground in the first place? Such activity predates the 1960s upsurge of the women's movement concern about it by many years.[19] And even not being included in the words of the statute, how is it possible to frame an argument that where a man sexually molests a female fellow worker or employee by words or actions, this is not sexual discrimination? Finally, why was it necessary in the first place to frame and pass new laws providing for redress for women sexually harassed at work? Already legislation makes sexual molestation, wherever it occurs, a criminal offence. Already legislation exists requiring employers to provide a safe system of work. Health and safety regulations govern the paid work place. Thus, if working conditions (including harassment by a superior or fellow worker or a subordinate) lead to psychological or physical damage to a worker's health, redress should be available through existing provisions. As well, natural justice concepts govern terms and conditions of employment. Appointments, promotions and continuance as an employee of the Main Roads Department should not, accordingly, be made subject to conditions extraneous to work performance. Powers should be exercised in good faith with regard to the purpose for which they were granted. So women are faced with the nineteenth-century conundrum: should we stand fast and demand that existing laws be interpreted in accordance with the notion that women are legitimate operators in the present world? If laws were applied neutrally, that is how they would be interpreted. Or must we demand 'reforms' to laws, or 'new' laws, thus giving ground by the admission that existing laws do not cover women and women's concerns?

It is not sufficient to overcome the hurdle of jurisdiction. The second hurdle—of proving a case that comes within the guidelines of the determination that sexual harassment is sex discrimination and is unlawful—is necessary before a decision can be made that, in the particular case, sexual harassment occurred, was discriminatory and was unlawful. In the Loder case the Tribunal held that sexual harassment had not occurred, therefore there was no sex-based discrimination, there was therefore no unlawful activity within the terms of the Anti-Discrimination Act. The basis for this decision was that not only must acts amounting to sexual harassment be proven to have occurred (that is, activity of a sexual nature must have occurred to which the complainant objected), but also the objection of the complainant to the respondent's actions must have been known to the respondent before he could be held to have sexually harassed the complainant. Furthermore, the case in effect introduces into the civil arena a criminal standard of proof: the onus apparently placed upon the complainant is that of objecting so strongly to the activity that the respondent is in no doubt that his attentions are unwanted (and the judgment seems even to exclude recklessness on his part).

There was considerable evidence from both parties, and from an independent witness, that Ms O'Callaghan had visited Mr Loder's suite on a number of occasions. There was evidence from an independent witness that when the visits commenced, Ms O'Callaghan's attitude changed: she became 'uppity'. However at some time in September 1981 her demeanour altered again. She appeared extremely upset and voiced some anger against Mr Loder on several occasions in speaking with her immediate (male) supervisor, although she did not allude to any unwelcome sexual activity. On the evidence as presented, one view could be that there was sufficient evidence to make a determination that in fact Mr Loder did know, or should have known, that Ms O'Callaghan did not wish to participate with him in sexual activity. The point of the case is that obviously very few women would ever be in a position to prove sexual harassment if one of the conditions is that she must have made it obvious beyond any reasonable doubt to the respondent that the sexual activity was unwelcome. If a woman is in the position of employee to employer, as in the Loder case, and if the employer 'takes liberties' of a sexual nature with her, it is obvious that many women would be too afraid, too timid, too embarrassed or disbelieving to respond with outrage. The position of women vis-a-vis men generally is one of relative powerlessness, whatever the circumstances of their relationship. Any woman sexually harassed by a fellow employee would be in a difficult position, and an unequivocal rejection of such harassment would require considerable courage, the possession of a degree of self-esteem or socialisation not generally found in women.[20] Where the man is in the employer position, the woman's standing is even less secure. For many women (and other workers in low positions on the job hierarchy), the last person to whom she would complain is her employer in matters relating to her job. (The Tribunal itself pointed to the considerable disparity in Mr Loder's and Ms O'Callaghan's positions.) Where the employer is the sexual harasser, it is equally unlikely, or more so, that she will complain.

As it was, Ms O'Callaghan's evidence showed a considerable degree of effort on her part to indicate an unwillingness to participate in sexual activity with the Commissioner for Main Roads. The Tribunal accepted independent evidence that at the time of the so-called penis incident Ms O'Callaghan's mood 'underwent a dramatic and permanent change. While she had previously been outgoing and assertive, she became withdrawn and nervous.' Although another 'possible explanation ... was ... that it resulted from her distress when her boyfriend of seven years finally left her', the Tribunal said that the independent evidence was '... clearly capable of providing substantial support for [Ms O'Callaghan's] version of what occurred at about that time between herself and Mr Loder ... [W]e consider that [her] distress was attributable to something more than the breakdown of her relationship with her boyfriend....'

If Ms O'Callaghan's story were true, what more could she have done within the constraints of her female socialisation, her desire to retain her job, and the power position existing between her and her employer, both in employer-employee terms and male-female terms? The problem with laws is that they are most likely to be interpreted not with women in mind, but in accordance with what 'rational' men think should happen and with what safeguards should be built in for those holding powerful positions, in class terms and in patriarchal terms. Laws are not usually designed or interpreted in accordance with what rational women think should happen, nor do they accord with the daily lives of women. They are not concerned about gaining women's rights. If they were, in the sexual harassment case the law would be viewed from a different perspective—that of the woman, not the man.

Feminist analysis recognises that going to an employer's suite does not necessarily indicate a willingness to go. Numerous studies have been made of the compliance with which women act in a variety of social situations, not because women enjoy being with particular people or conversing with them, but because women have been socialised into believing it is necessary to 'please'. In view of the research, a demand could fairly be made that all men should be on notice that their attentions are not necessarily welcome, particularly in the work place. The onus could fairly be placed on the respondent in a sexual harassment case to show that he did not know that his attentions were unwelcome, not upon the complainant to show that she signified to him she did not want the attentions he was bestowing upon her.

Twentieth-Century Fighting in Private

> *There is nothing more intolerable than a wealthy woman.*
>
> Juvenal

The possibility that an overall approach might succeed in the legal battle to eliminate discrimination against women in the private sphere of the home has been longer in the making than that in the world of paid employment and other aspects of public life. Only in the late 1970s and the 1980s has the piecemeal approach been mooted as having outworn its usefulness, or being detrimental to women's interests and the demand been made for an overall revision of the economic base of marriage, so that by law women own equally throughout marriage and on divorce all property accumulated during it.[21] This may be, in part, due to the rhetoric of the partnership marriage that has found its way into general discourse and into the law books—into statutes, regulations, court decisions and legal articles.[22] The rhetoric is not always recognised to be just that. Too often, the belief is created that equal legal rights in marriage are a reality. Further, the personal nature of marriage and similar relationships might have retarded the outspoken recognition, even in feminist circles, that almost every woman (feminists included) is bound into a male-female relationship adverse to her interests and to those of other women. Almost every woman is touched by marriage and the laws and rhetoric surrounding it; gaining equality for women in the private sphere means that almost every man and every woman will be required to change their way of relating to one another.

In 1975 the Family Law Act was passed, providing that on marriage breakdown the efforts traditionally made by women in the home—as wives, housewives and mothers—should be taken into account in distributing property between ex-husbands and wife. In the past the law had little difficulty in calculating women's efforts where the party benefiting from that calculation was a husband. Thus courts often totted up the value to a man of his wife where she was killed or injured in an accident, leaving him bereft of wife, housewife, mother. They were also wont, in the past, to tot up the value where a wife had run off to live with her lover; a husband could seek damages from the man who cuckolded him or 'enticed away' his wife. Yet taking into account a woman's efforts where she was to benefit was not within the competence of the courts.

In their calculations under the new powers, however, the Family Court is tied by its existence in a world where women and men are not equal, and where unpaid work—particularly that done by women 'for love'—is not seen as equal to paid work, especially that done by a 'breadwinner' (synonymous in patriarchal terms with 'man'). The inheritance of changes supposedly wrought by the Married Women's Property Acts remains: the implication is that, since women have equal rights to build up independent wealth and to gain incomes as high as any man, if they do not it is because their efforts in paid work—their business acumen, their brawn, their persistence, their application—are not as great as those of their husbands. Women's work in the home also clouds any work done outside for money; to the court the latter becomes proportionately insignificant. Simultaneously housework, child care and child rearing and cossetting a husband are 'expected', often invisible to husbands and court (where most judges are themselves husbands!), and are not accorded equal weight with man's paid work. Despite all this, the court continues to say it is dealing with men's and women's work efforts equally or giving 'substantial weighting' to women's work at home.

The Family Law Act, in itself an advance on previous laws, conceals other problems of marriage and women's rights. The Act deals only with divorce and separation, not with an ongoing marriage. Although women are disadvantaged on divorce, they are even more disadvantaged during marriage. Women's traditional and paid work efforts may gain unequal recognition on divorce, but during marriage they gain no legal recognition at all. A woman cannot claim, while the marriage exists, that her work as wife, housewife and mother justifies her ownership of half, or indeed any, of the property bought from her husband's income. If her own money (*not* housekeeping money) buys property—including land, a house, or even cups and saucers or blankets—that property will belong to her. But how many women buy property, particularly property of a lasting nature, even if they have incomes?[23] Without a legal acknowledgement that a woman's place in a marriage partnership is equal to that of a man, and that her contribution to marriage means she has an equal right to ownership of any assets accumulated during marriage, women remain economically subordinate to their husbands.

Economic subordination is the base of women's oppression. It bolsters social and political subordination. Existing marriage and divorce laws do not address the problem, because they enable courts to place their own interpretation on rules for divorce property division, and permit individual judges to indulge their prejudices. Without substantive property and income rights, women will remain subordinate. They will remain vulnerable not only to the everyday exigencies of inequality, but also to violence in personal relationships.

Rather than taking on the question of economic subordination during marriage and lobbying for overall changes to the Marriage Act and the Family Law Act to attempt to stem judicial bias, in the 1970s women lobbied, in the various states, for laws to protect women's bodily integrity during marriage. This was a piecemeal fight: although rape in marriage was seen in the overall context of rape law reform, the context of marital exploitation was not fully explored; the 'solution' was seen in law reform terms as a simple change so that a husband could be prosecuted for raping his wife.[24] In South Australia in 1976, amendments to the Criminal Law Consolidation Act provided that, within certain limits, a husband could be prosecuted for marital rape. Subsequently, changes were made to the law in New South Wales, making it clear that a man was in no different position if he raped his wife than if he raped a stranger. In Victoria and Western Australia the most legislatures could do was provide that a man could be prosecuted for rape of his wife where the parties were living separately and apart at the time of the offence. Tasmania and the Northern Territory proposed changes akin to the New South Wales law. Queensland began making noises about reform. The Australian Capital Territory, clearly out of step, proposed altering the law so that *de facto* husbands and husbands would be immune from prosecution.

The South Australia amendment is a lesson in the way law reform can in fact disadvantage women, despite being undertaken with the utmost sincerity for improving women's position. The original South Australian proposed amendment stated that 'no person shall, by reason only of the fact that he is married to some other person' be presumed to have consented to sexual intercourse with, or to an indecent assault by, that other person (12(5) Bill No. 55, 1976). Treloar describes the circumstances that led to its being altered by the Legislative Council. '[The government] had already offended the churches, the Festival of Light, many of the legal profession and some (retired) judiciary by daring to exceed [the Mitchell Committee's] recommendation as far as the immunity of husbands went. They took up as their war-cry that unfortunate phrase from [the Mitchell Report]: that to unequivocally criminalise rape-within-marriage would be "putting a dangerous weapon into the hands of a vindictive wife".'[25]

In addition to reactionary community forces, the amendment faced hostility in parliament. 'At the time the rape reforms were implemented, the Dunstan [Labor] government had a majority of one seat in the House of Assembly. It never held its due control of the Upper House ... [The amendment to the original proposal] arose directly out of Parliamentary pressures and procedures. The bill passed the lower house with full government support; despite its being a so-called conscience vote. In the Legislative Council three former members of the Liberal Movement indicated they would cross the floor and vote with the government. The upper house, foolishly as it turned out, rose on the promise of victory when votes would be cast the following day. In the meantime, overnight, those three opposition members were jumped by the churches, and by Party "thugs" who threatened their future pre-selection ...

The government accepted [the] "compromise" because it was seen as being ultimately meaningless, because we saw it as in no way watering down the principle, or its symbolic value, which would be established in law. Needless to say, this is hardly an ideal attitude toward law-making and the writing of statutes.'

Treloar's final statement is painfully true. The amendment proposed and passed into law by the upper house provides that no person should be convicted of rape or indecent assault upon his spouse, or an attempt to commit the same

> unless the alleged offence consisted of, was preceded or accompanied by, or was associated with –
> (a) assault occasioning actual bodily harm, or threat of such an assault, upon the spouse;
> (b) an act of gross indecency, or threat of such an act, against the spouse;

   (c) an act calculated seriously and substantially to humiliate the spouse; or

   (d) threat of the commission of a criminal act against the person: (S. 12(5) Criminal Law Consolidation Act 1935 (S.A.))

Although the provision may be meaningless to some (and analysis reveals its potential for causing abject confusion), it is inherently dangerous, as well as limiting rights that prior to its passage without doubt extended to women.

By including 'indecent assault' within the qualifications, the legislature succeeded in removing a protection that married women already enjoyed at common law. The repressive attitude of the common law to sexual activity is accepted. It is reasonable to suppose that the 'consent to intercourse' envisaged by the law generally as relating to activity between married couples meant 'consent to intercourse in the missionary position', or at most consent to sexual intercourse of the vaginal–penile variety. Thus if a man were to attempt buggery on his wife, he could be held guilty of indecent assault of any acts leading up to it: at common law buggery could not be consented to, because it was an unlawful act in itself, whether between married or unmarried parties. Similarly if a man flagellated his wife, the act would qualify as indecent assault. If Section 12(5) of the Act means anything at all, it undoubtedly limits the protection of married women in limiting the circumstances under which an indecent assault by a husband on his wife will be unlawful.[26]

Subsections (b), (c) and (d) add only confusion. A clear definition of 'gross indecency' is hard to find; both court reports and textbooks are coy in describing just what acts will constitute the offence. Perhaps it means, in this case, penetration of the anus, yet this is classified in the new Act as rape if done without consent. So what does subsection (b) mean? What of (c)? Isn't any form of rape seriously and substantially humiliating? Then what does the subsection add? As for (d): if rape is a crime, whether carried out on a wife or not, then the threat to commit it falls within this subsection. Is it intended to be tautologous?

However, Subsection (a) raises serious problems. It means, in effect, that if a husband is to be prosecuted successfully for rape of his wife, he must at the same time have wounded her physically, breaking the skin or causing noticeable bruising, or causing her to bleed, or he must have threatened such an assault. Therefore the prosecution is in the position of having to show that he was armed in some way and threatened her with arms during the rape attack, or that he was a person given to such violence that any unarmed threats he made against her would invariably result in actual bodily harm.

This 'law reform' is equally disturbing because it accepts that rape by a husband is not a crime at common law. In fact, a strong case can be marshalled to show that a husband can be prosecuted for rape of his wife under the common law as it is. The basis upon which the argument is made that a husband cannot be so prosecuted is three-fold: first, a pronouncement in the seventeenth century by yet another 'revered' jurist, Mathew Hale, who stated that a man may not be guilty of the rape of his wife, because 'by their mutual matrimonial consent and contract the wife hath given up herself in this kind unto her husband, which she cannot retract'; secondly, the judgments of the House of Lords in R. *v* Clarence decided in 1888; and third, that despite sexually molesting their wives, men are not prosecuted for it (or, alternatively, that men do not in fact sexually abuse their wives).[27] Yet Hale made his statement without any authority but his own. Clarence involved a case where there was no doubt but that the wife in question had in fact consented to her husband's act of intercourse (that is, the artificial nature of 'consent' to sexual intercourse because the woman was the man's wife was not in issue). Finally, evidence that men are sexually abusive to wives today, as in the past, is readily to hand; that men are not prosecuted for bashing and battering their wives is no argument against the proposition that criminal laws clearly outlaw assault by a man on his wife. The argument is reminiscent of that accepted earlier by the courts in the public sphere that, because no woman had applied to become an attorney or a university student prior to the first woman making application, women were not qualified to be attorneys or students.

In Clarence the majority of judges who addressed the question of consent of a wife by virtue of marriage did not state that that consent could never be withdrawn. Only one judge said it was clear that in law a wife had to submit to the sexual acts her husband imposed upon her; he even went so far as to say that she had to submit, even, to physical violence. (None of the other judges accepted that extreme position, which ran directly counter to R. *v* Jackson,[28] decided three years later, which held that a man has no right to beat his wife.) The majority of judges in Clarence called for a revision of the so-called Hale rule. And in 1891 it was held in R. *v.* Jackson that a husband who in effect kidnapped his wife, taking her away to his own home after she had left him, had no right to do so. By analogy, this case supports the proposition that a man has no right to rape his wife.

At common law, a wife had a duty to remain with her husband, to live in his house and to follow him wherever he went. However, if she chose to leave him, he had no right to forcibly return her to his company. A second wifely duty at common law was that of a wife to engage in sexual intercourse with her husband at all times he chose.

By analogy, the argument should readily be accepted that if she chooses not to participate in sexual intercourse in a particular instance, he has no right to force her to do so. Thus, the danger in women mooting changes to laws relating to rape lies in the non-acceptance by the parliament of a provision stating only (as in the New South Wales case) that a husband and wife are in no different position from a stranger and his victim where the crime alleged is rape. The Victorian 'reform', for example, is even worse than the South Australian amendment, in that it has effectively written into the law the proviso that a husband can be prosecuted for rape of his wife only where they are living separately and apart. The argument can no longer be made in Victoria that at common law a wife is protected against her husband's sexual violation.

Seemingly spurred on by the success of gaining a high profile in the cause of women's rights, governments around Australia established working parties to write reports on the problem facing women victims of criminal assault at home. Invariably, these government-sponsored bodies called for law reform. Yet women should have called a halt. In fact, WEL Sydney wrote to the Premier of New South Wales pointing out that the law already provides that assault of anyone is wrong, wife or not, and the law did not need to be changed in this respect.[29] WEL's position was accepted by the Premier as correct. However, at the same time some women within the bureaucracy were unable to accept the WEL view, adopting the statements of male bureaucratic lawyers (in opposition to feminist lawyers) that legal changes were necessary. This had the effect of weakening women's position, because (just as had been the case with sex discrimination legislation at federal level under the Liberal-National government) the women's movement was seen to be divided. Unfortunately, due to the distortion created by working party reports on domestic violence and the compelling need for positive steps to be taken to alleviate the suffering of women victims, women outside the bureaucracy were sometimes equally converted to the male bureaucratic lawyers' stance. One of the problems for the women's movement in attacking male bias in the legal system is that women (like men) have been socialised into accepting male views above those of females, particularly where those males are lawyers, and even if the competing views are of feminist lawyers! By emphasising an erroneous requirement for change to laws, women were drawn into supporting the idea that the law did not make violence against women a crime. This covered up the structures and attitudes enabling police, courts and other authorities to apply the Crimes Act in accordance with sexist standards, making the law in action belie its written strictures.

Any man assaulting his wife commits a criminal act.[30] Legislation in every state and territory in Australia confirms this. Despite what is said in domestic violence task force reports, police have powers of entry on to private premises where they have an honest and reasonable belief that a serious crime is occurring or has occurred. They have power to enter where they believe a breach of the peace will recur. Police have power to arrest where a serious assault has occurred or is occurring. They have power to arrest where they observe any crime occurring. Police have power to arrest where they reasonably suspect a breach of the peace will recur. They have a duty to protect person and property from damage, whether caused by criminal means or otherwise. Yet all the evidence shows that they decline to exercise their powers where the victim is a woman and the assailant her husband, lover or boyfriend.

In response to the reports, governments in South Australia, Queensland and New South Wales introduced measures allegedly to deal with criminal assault at home by way of a 'peace complaint'. A victim of domestic violence or one who fears it should take out a peace complaint. Once she has an order of the court that the husband should forbear to beat her or should stay away from her and where she is living, the suggestion is that the wife is protected against her husband's violence. Should he return to beat or harass her, she has only (in theory) to telephone the police and they will come to her aid, arresting her husband and taking him away to lock him up, to face a magistrate as soon as reasonably possible. He must remain in the lockup for a set period—twenty-four hours—and cannot be freed on bail before that time. (De facto husbands are also included.)

Yet how effective is this 'law reform'? Studies of domestic violence show that police do not appear immediately they are called to the scene; rather, the lapse of time between receiving a call and attending often amounts to two or three hours. Sometimes police do not appear. There is no reason to believe that police will be more likely to attend more promptly because a victim says she has taken out a peace complaint. Indeed, why should the victim of criminal assault at home be required to state she has taken out a peace complaint in order to obtain police action? If she has not taken out such an order and the police arrive, experience shows that their reaction is likely to be, not to arrest the man who has committed a criminal assault on his wife, but to advise her to take out a peace complaint. If they undertake to do this, as they are empowered to do, is it really helpful to the woman victim of violence, and to all other women who suffer or may suffer domestic abuse? Effectively, the crime of assault is ignored.

Here, law reform efforts mean that men continue to believe that they are free, at least once, to 'get away with' beating their wives. Under the ordinary criminal law, if police are called to a private home because a woman is being beaten, they have a right and a duty to arrest. If they fail to do so, taking the peace complaint approach, the assailant is being 'told' his actions are not as serious as they would have been had he beaten a stranger. In the case of stranger assault, the police would arrest, not take out a peace complaint. In order to have her husband arrested, a woman will probably have to withstand at least two bouts of bashing: the first, when she calls the police and they react by taking out a peace complaint; the second, when her husband returns and she calls the police to effect his arrest. Even then, will they arrest?

In states where such 'reforms' have taken place, the police version of reality is confirmed. Women's reality is denied. Police are now supported in their proposition that laws 'had' to be changed to give them power to act. They are backed in their stance that existing criminal laws are insufficient for them to deal with cases of criminal assault by husbands on wives. Wives are denied the recognition by the legal system that the criminal acts to which they have been victim were and are in fact criminal acts. Police are now free to state erroneously (as they have) that prior to the changes in New South Wales, if officers were called to a home and arrived at the door to be greeted by a man refusing them entry, they were not entitled to enter—even if, clearly in the background stood a woman, her head bleeding, distressed, crying.[31] This equates, although with more immediately discernible dangers, with the proposition confirmed by the courts during the nineteenth and early twentieth centuries that women were not persons: then, the reality of women's very existence as human beings was denied; the reality of university authorities and professors, members of bar associations and law societies and other professional organisations was confirmed: women, not being men, were less than human and entitled to no recognition as members of faculties or professions. Now a 'law reform'—sadly, engineered in part by women—classes wives and de facto wives as non-victims of crime, despite their criminal victimisation.

As long as women remain economically vulnerable through marriage and throughout marriage as well as at divorce, they will be victims of criminal assault at home, marital rape and exploitation in its less obvious forms. Confronted with a legal system that refuses to recognise all women as equal to all men, a battle has been fought to change laws rather than to acknowledge that the problem lies in the very nature of law and in the dominant ideology of those who interpret it. Some judges in some courts may attempt to overcome their socialisation and their recognition (conscious or unconscious) of the advantages that the inequality of women gains for them in the short term, but the system does not reinforce the actions of renegades.

Conclusion

'Your laws are ineffective,' Wen declared. 'Why?
Because no system of control will work as long as most
of those administering the law against an evil have more
than a finger dipped into it themselves.'

Han Suyin

Is it unrealistic to suggest that feminist demands will be instituted in
our legal system or that, if they were, the system could accommodate
them without distortion? The problem with sex discrimination laws is
that they hold out for women the hope that, at last, women's rights
are recognised; yet in operation too frequently they deny women's
rights. In one sense they make the problem more difficult for women.
That channels allegedly lie through which women's rights may be
gained and wrongs redressed means that if a woman loses at a tribunal or in a court, or if the abrogation of her rights is simply not recognised through the operation of the law, the very existence of a statute
saying that certain activity is unlawful gives its *imprimatur* to the unacceptable actions to which she has been subjected; because it is held
not to have been unlawful, the implication is that the activity was
lawful. Thus in the Loder case the fact that the Tribunal held the
complainant not to be a victim of sexual harassment implies that not
only was she a woman who wished to engage in sexual acts with her
employer, but that she was a woman prone to bringing false complaints. The implications for her and for all women in such a result
cannot be overestimated.

The problem with recently passed domestic violence laws is that
they, too, hold out false hopes. Their negative effects can be calculated to be more far-reaching than those of any sex discrimination
law, in that they isolate one area of women's lives and men's abuses.
If a woman does not take out a peace complaint or the police do not
do so, the implication is that she is not a victim of violence at home. If
she does take out a complaint, or the police do so, the implication is
that she has not been a victim of *criminal* assault, but requires some
form of 'special protection', which ultimately fails to protect. No law
that ostensibly deals with violence against married women but
ignores the very basis of that relationship can assist. As well, no law
that confirms years of the police and courts condoning criminal
assault at home and enables it to continue can be calculated to improve women's position at home.

Women confront a legal system that professes to be attuned to the
rights of all. It professes the ideals of fairness and equality. Many
legal writers, judges and lawyers have concocted a jurisprudence that

bolsters that false notion. Yet, as some men have recognised, 'fairness' is accorded only to those (that is, men) having the means to pay, and having rights deemed worthy of protection. 'Equality' is judged according to the rule that 'some [men] are more equal than others'. It has taken women to press home the place patriarchal notions have in law.

In demanding that 'fairness' and 'equality' be redefined to include all women (and all men), women are caught in the trap of having to choose whether it is preferable to attempt to mould the system according to feminist principles or whether the legal system is impervious to feminist demands and must be ignored. Yet if we protest against reforms introduced to (ostensibly) improve women's position, we run the danger of alienating those men who have a real concern for women's rights and who ultimately have accepted the changes and a need for them. At the same time we run the risk of creating divisions within our own movement.

No law reform can be brought about without the co-operation of the men in parliament. No law reform in operation can be engineered without the involvement of male-dominated courts in interpreting the law. This may mean that in the very moment of achieving legal changes, feminist ideals have been so bastardised as to forswear feminist ideology. The group having the power to define and limit the parameters of debate has a stranglehold on victory. Or is it rather that sex discrimination legislation and proposed new marriage and divorce laws challenging distribution of wealth provide a springboard for later advances, and a too ready rejection of them as incapable of altering women's position is unwarranted? In the twentieth century, women have the cold comfort of knowing that women of the nineteenth century have been here before.

References

Introduction
1   J.S. Mill, 1970, 'The subjection of women' in *Essays on Sex Equality*, A. Rossi (ed.), Chicago, University of Chicago Press (first published 1869), page 146.
2   J. Locke, 1967, *Two Treatises of Government*, P. Laslett (ed.), Cambridge, Cambridge University Press I, § 47; II, § 82.
3   C. Pateman, 1983, 'Feminist critiques of the public/private dichotomy', in *Public and Private in Social Life*, S.I. Benn and G. Gaus (eds), London, Croom Helm; 'Women and consent', 1980, *Political Theory*, VII, 2.
4   C. Cockburn, 1983, *Brothers: Male Dominance and Technological Change*, London, Pluto Press.
5   W. Thompson, 1970, *Appeal of One Half the Human Race, Women, Against the Pretensions of the Other Half, Men, to Retain Them in Political and Thence in Civil and Domestic Slavery*, New York, Source Book Press (first published 1825).
6   H. Hartmann, 1981, 'The unhappy marriage of Marxism and feminism' in *Women and Revolution*, L. Sargent (ed.), Boston, South End Press.

Topics, Methods and Models: Feminist Challenges in Social Science
1   I am happy to acknowledge the benefit of critical comment from Kay Bussey of Macquarie University, Lila Ghent Braine of Barnard College, New York, and Carol Nagy Jacklyn of the University of Southern California.
2   E.F. Keller, 1982, 'Feminism and science' in *Signs*, 7, page 593.
3   *Ibid.*
4   M. Jehlen, 1981, 'Archimedes and the paradox of feminist criticisms' in *Signs*, 6, pages 575–601.
5   R. Bleier, 1978, 'Bias in biological and human sciences: some comments' in *Signs*, 4, pages 159–62.
6   K.E. Grady, 1981, 'Sex bias in research design' in *Psychology of Women Quarterly*, 5, pages 628–36.
7   Keller, *op. cit.*
8   M.B. Parlee, 1981, 'Appropriate control groups in feminist research' in *Psychology of Women Quarterly*, 5, pages 637–44.
9   N. Weisstein, 1971, 'Psychology constructs the female, or the fantasy life of the male psychologist' in M.H. Garsof (ed.) *Roles Women Play: Readings Towards Women's Liberation*, Belmont, California, Brooks-Cole.
10 M. Westkott, 1971, 'Feminist criticism of the social sciences' in *Harvard Educational Review*, 49, pages 422–30.
11 E. Langland and W. Gove (eds), 1981, *A Feminist Perspective in the Academy: The Difference It Makes*, Chicago, University of Chicago Press.
12 M.A. Ferber, 1982, 'Women and work: Issues of the 1980s' in *Signs*, 8, pages 273–95.

13   H. Hartmann, 1982, 'The unhappy marriage of Marxism and feminism: Towards a more progressive union' in L. Sargent (ed.), *Women and Revolution*, Boston, South End Press.

14   A. Oakley, 1974, *The Sociology of Housework*, London, Robertson.

15   E. Zaretsky, 1976, *Capitalism, The Family and Personal Life*, New York, Pluto Press.

16   G. Bottomley, 1983, 'Review of historical and sociological models of the family' in A. Burns, G. Bottomley and P. Jools (eds.), *The Family in the Modern World: Australian Perspectives*, Sydney, George Allen and Unwin.

17   L. Iragaray, 1981, 'And the one doesn't stir without the other' in *Signs*, 7, pages 589–602.

18   C. Fauré, 'Absent from history' and 'The twilight of the goddesses, or the intellectual crisis in French feminism' in *Signs*, 7, pages 71–80 and 81–86.

19   R. Hubbard, 1982, 'Have only men evolved?' in R. Hubbard, M.S. Henifin and B. Fried (eds), *Women Look at Biology Looking at Women*, Cambridge, Massachusetts, Schenkman.

20   Weisstein, *op. cit.*

21   S.A. Shields, 'Functionalism, Darwinism and the psychology of women: A study of social myth' in *American Psychologist*, 30, pages 739–54.

22   M. Guttentag and P.F. Secord, 1983, *Too Many Women? The Sex Ratio Question*, London, Sage.

23   R.R. Reuther, 1974, *Religion and Sexism: Images of Women in the Jewish and Christian Traditions*, New York, Simon and Schuster; 'The feminist critique of religious studies' in Langland and Gove (eds), *op. cit.*

24   M. Coltheart, 1975, 'Sex and learning differences' in *New Behavior*, 1, pages 54–57.

25   H.H. Lambert, 1978, 'Biology and equality: A perspective on sex differences' in *Signs*, 4, pages 97–117.

26   G. Lerner, 1979, *The Majority Finds Its Past: Placing Women in History*, New York, Oxford University Press.

27   E. Shaffer, 1980, 'Review of *The History of Sexuality: Vol. 1: An Introduction* by Michel Foucault', in *Signs*, 5, page 813.

28   A.S. Rossi, 'Life-span theories and women's lives' in *Signs*, 6, pages 4–32.

29   E. Wood, 'Women in music' in *Signs*, 6, page 293.

30   C. Baldock and B. Cass (eds), 1976, *Women, Welfare and the State*, Sydney, George Allen and Unwin.

31   E. Leacock, 1981, 'History, development and the division of labor of sex: Implications for organization' in *Signs*, 7, pages 474–91.

32   Bleier, *op. cit.*, page 161.

33   S. de Beauvoir, 1952, *The Second Sex*, New York, Knopf.

34   Reuther, *op. cit.*

35   N.S. Reinhardt, 1981, 'New directions for feminist criticism in theatre and the related arts' in Langland and Gove (eds), *op. cit.*

36   J. Berger, 1972, *Ways of Seeing*, Harmondsworth, Penguin.

37   Lerner, *op. cit.*
38   W. Leach, 1982, *True Love and Perfect Union: The Feminist Reform of Sex and Society*, New York, Basic Books.
39   Jehlen, *op. cit.*, page 576.
40   C.N. Degler, 1980, *At Odds: Women and the Family from the Revolution to the Present*, New York, Oxford University Press, page 82.
41   N.O. Keohane, 1981, 'Speakers from silence: Women and the science of politics' in Langland and Gove (eds), *op. cit.*
42   P.B. Bart, 1971, 'Sexism and social science: From the gilded cage to the iron cage, or, the perils of Pauline' in *Journal of Marriage and the Family*, 33, pages 734–745.
43   Shaffer, *op. cit.*, page 812.
44   Parlee, *op. cit.*, page 639.
45   Degler, *op. cit.*
46   J. Mitchell, 1971, *Woman's Estate*, New York, Pantheon.
47   J.S. Barnard, 1975, *Women, Wives, Mothers: Values and Options*. Chicago, Aldine Press.
48   H. Hartmann, 1971, 'The family as the locus of gender, class and political struggle: The example of housework' in *Signs*, 6, page 368.
49   Ferber, *op. cit.*
50   S.L. Harris, 1972, 'Who studies sex differences?' in *American Psychologist*, 27, pages 1077–1078.
51   W. Brienes and L. Gordon, 1983, 'The new scholarship on family violence', in *Signs*, 8, pages 490–531.
52   D.E.H. Russell and N. Howell, 1981, 'The prevalence of rape in the U.S. revisited', in *Signs*, 8, pages 688–695.
53   A. Rich, 1976, *Of Woman Born: Motherhood as Experience and Institution*, New York, Norton; 'compulsory heterosexuality and lesbian experience', 1980, in *Signs*, 5, pages 631–680.
54   Guttentag and Secord, *op. cit.*
55   M. Hill, 1973, *The Religious Order*, London, Heinemann.
56   Reuther, *op. cit.*
57   R.D. Blau, 'On the role of values in feminist scholarship' in *Signs*, 6, page 539.
58   A.J. Stewart and D.G. Winter, 1978, 'Reply to Bald and Mukhopadhyay' in *Signs*, 3, 942–943.
59   Bleier, *op. cit.*
60   F. Bentzen, 1963, 'Sex ratios in learning and behavior disorders' in *American Journal of Orthopsychiatry*, 33, pages 92–98.
61   J. Shapiro, 1982, 'Women's Studies: A note on the perils of markedness', in *Signs*, 7, page 720.
62   F.A. Pederson (ed.), 1980, *The Father-Infant Relationship: Observational Studies in the Family Setting*, New York, Praeger.
63   M.E. Lamb (ed.), 1976, *The Role of the Father in Child Development*, New York, Wiley.
64   R.D. Parke, 1979, 'Perspectives on father-infant interaction' in J.D. Osofsky (ed.), *The Handbook of Infant Development*, New York, Wiley.
65   G. Russell, 1982, *The Changing Role of Fathers*, St Lucia, Queensland,

University of Queensland Press.
66 J. Shapiro, 1981, 'Anthropology and the study of gender' in Langland and Gove (eds), *op. cit.*
67 S.L. Bem, 1983, 'Gender schema theory and its implications for child development: Raising gender-aschematic children in a gender-schematic society' in *Signs*, 8, 598–616.
68 L. Sargent (ed.), *Women and Revolution: A Discussion of the Unhappy Marriage of Marxism and Feminism*, London, South End Press.
69 S. Firestone, 1970, *The Dialectic of Sex: The Case for Feminist Revolution*, New York, Morrow.
70 D. Slive, 1983, 'Excluding women from the educational realm' in *Harvard Educational Review*, 53, pages 109–111.
71 J.R. Martin, 'A reply to Slive' in *Harvard Educational Review*, 53, pages 111–112.
72 Hartmann, *op. cit.*
73 C. Hansson and K. Liden, 1982, *Moscow Women: Thirteen Interviews*, New York, Pantheon.
74 C.A. Mackinnon, 1982, 'Feminism, Marxism, method and the state: An agenda for theory' in *Signs*, 7, pages 515–544.
75 Degler, *op. cit.*
76 *Ibid.*, page 79.
77 *Ibid.*
78 *Ibid.*, page 80.
79 *Ibid.*
80 *Ibid.*
81 Stewart and Winter, *op. cit.*, page 942.
82 M.Z. Rosaldo, 1974, 'Woman, culture and society: A theoretical overview' in M.Z. Rosaldo and L. Lamphere (eds), *Women, Culture and Society*, Stanford, Stanford University Press; 'The use and abuse of anthropology: Reflections on feminism and cross-cultural understanding', 1980, in *Signs*, 5, pages 389–417.
83 L.J. Nicholson, 1982, 'Comment on Rosaldo's "use and abuse of anthropology"' in *Signs*, 7, 732–735.
84 Mackinnon, *op. cit.*
85 J.T. Spence, 1981, 'Changing conceptions of men and women: A psychologist's perspective' in Langland and Gove (eds), *op. cit.*
86 Bem, *op. cit.*
87 M.S. Barrett, 1982, 'How the study of women has restructured the discipline of economics' in Langland and Gove (eds), *op. cit.*, page 107.
88 G. Tuchman and N. Fortin, 1980, 'Edging women out: Some suggestions about the structure of opportunities and the Victorian novel' in *Signs*, 6, page 308.
89 Editorial, 1981, *Signs*, 5, page 266.
90 S. Goldberg, *The Inevitability of Patriarchy*, New York, Morrow.
91 Lambert, *op. cit.*
92 D. Haraway, 1981, 'In the beginning was the word: The genesis of biological theory' in *Signs*, 6, pages 469–481.
93 Bleier, *op. cit.*

94   Hubbard and Lowe, *op. cit.*
95   Russell, *op. cit.*
96   C.F. Epstein, 1981, *Women in Law*, New York, Basic Books; 'Women in sociological analysis: New scholarship versus old paradigms' in Langland and Gove (eds) *op. cit.*
97   S.S. Feldman, Z.C. Biringen and S.C. Nash, 1981, 'Fluctuations of sex-related self attributions as a function of stage of family life cycle', in *Developmental Psychology*, 17, pages 97–106.
98   U. Labouvie-Vief, 1982, 'Dynamic development and mature autonomy' in *Human Development*, 25, pages 161–191.
99   J.B. Lancaster, 1975, *Primate Behaviour and the Emergence of Human Culture*, New York, Holt, Rinehart and Winston: cited by Bleier, *op. cit.*, page 161.
100   Lambert, *op. cit.*, pages 114, 115.
101   J. Habermas, 1970, *Towards a Rational Society: Student Protest, Science and Politics* (translated by J. Shapiro), Boston, Beacon Press.
102   Keohane, *op. cit.*
103   Brienes and Gordon, *op. cit.*
104   Degler, *op. cit.*, page 75.
105   Haraway, *op. cit.*, page 478.
106   Keohane, *op. cit.*, page 93.
107   *Ibid.*
108   Langland and Gove (eds), *op. cit.*
109   M. Mead, 1949, *Male and Female*, New York, Morrow, page 168.
110   Shapiro, *op. cit.*, page 123.
111   Leacock, *op. cit.*
112   Quoted in Showalter, *op. cit.*, page 411.

Women in History: Reconstructing the Past

1   J. Ackermann, 1913, *Australia from a Woman's Point of View*, London, Cassell, page vii.
2   J.S. Mill, *The Subjection of Women*, 1869, London, page 149.
3   E.H. Carr, 1968, *What is History?* Harmondsworth, Pelican, page 30.
4   G.M. Dening, 1973, 'History as a social system' in *Historical Studies*, 15, pages 673–685.
5   G. Lerner, 1979, 'The majority finds its past' in *The Majority Finds Its Past: Placing Women in History*, New York, Oxford University Press; 'The necessity of history and the professional historian', 1982, *Journal of American History*, 69, pages 7–20.
6   B. Carroll (ed.), 1976, *Liberating Women's History: Theoretical and Critical Essays*, Urbana, University of Illinois Press.
7   W. Chafe, 1978, *Women and Equality*, New York, Oxford University Press.
8   C. Degler, 1975, *Is There a History of Women?*, Oxford, Oxford University Press.
9   O. Hufton, 1971, 'Women in revolution: 1789–1796' in *Past and Present*, 53, pages 90–108; J. Kelly-Gadol, 1978, 'Did women have a Renaissance?' in R. Bridenthal and C. Koonz (eds), *Becoming Visible: Women*

in European History, Boston, Houghton Mifflin.

10 H. Smith, 1976, 'Feminism and the methodology of women's history' in Carroll (ed.), *op. cit.*

11 C. Smith-Rosenberg, 1975, 'The new woman and the new history' in *Feminist Studies*, 3, page 189.

12 N.Z. Davis, 1976, '"Women's history" in transition: The European case' in *Feminist Studies*, 3, 83–103; J. Kelly-Gadol, 1976, 'The social relations of the sexes: methodological implications of women's history' in *Signs*, 1, pages 809–823.

13 Carroll (ed.), *op. cit.*, page 34.

14 J. Mitchell, 1971, *Women's Estate*, Harmondsworth, Penguin, page 100.

15 W. Brienes, M.S. Cerullo and J. Stacey, 1978, 'Social biology, family studies and antifeminist backlash' in *Feminist Studies*, 4, pages 43–68.

16 R. Rapp, E. Ross and R. Bridenthal, 1979, 'Examining family history' in *Feminist Studies*, 5, pages 174–200.

17 E. Fox-Genovese, 1979, 'Comments on the reviews of *Woman's Body, Woman's Rights*' in *Signs*, 4, page 807.

18 J. Rigg, 1969, *In Her Own Right*, Melbourne, Nelson.

19 A. Curthoys, 1970, 'Historiography and women's liberation', *Arena*, 22, page 37.

20 A. Summers, 1975, *Damned Whores and God's Police*, Ringwood, Penguin.

21 M. Roe, 1978, 'Challenges to Australian identity' in *Quadrant*, April, pages 34–40.

22 E. Scott, 1939, *A Short History of Australia*, London, Oxford University Press.

23 W.K. Hancock, 1930, *Australia*, London, Ernest Benn.

24 *Ibid.*, page 34.

25 M. Clark. 1963, *A Short History of Australia*, Sydney, Mentor.

26 R. Ward, 1974, *The Australian Legend*, Melbourne, Oxford University Press.

27 H. McQueen, 1970, *A New Britannia*, Ringwood, Penguin.

28 P. Grimshaw, 1972, *Women's Suffrage in New Zealand*, Auckland, Auckland University Press.

29 Curthoys, *op. cit.*

30 M. Barnard Eldershaw, *My Australia*, 1939, Janolds, London, page 21.

31 M. Bayne and M. Lazarus, 1954, *The Australian Community: A Critical Approach to Citizenship*, Melbourne, Longmans Green and Co.

32 K. Tennant, 1964, *Australia: Her Story*, London, Pan.

33 H.G. Palmer and J. Macleod, 1954, *The First Hundred Years*, Melbourne, Longmans.

34 M. Kiddle, 1961, *Men of Yesterday: A Social History of the Western District of Victoria 1834–1890*. Melbourne, Melbourne University Press.

35 K. Fitzpatrick, 1975, *PLC Melbourne: The First Century 1875–1975*, Presbyterian Ladies' College, Melbourne.

36 M. Kiddle, 1950, *Caroline Chisholm*, Melbourne, Melbourne University Press.

37 M. Bayne, 1942, *Australian Women at War*, Melbourne, Left Book Club.

38 F.S.P. Eldershaw (ed.) *The Peaceful Army: A Memorial to the Pioneer Women of Australia 1788–1938*, Sydney, the Women's Executive Committee and Advisory Council of Australia's 150th Anniversary Celebrations.

39 Summers, *op. cit.*, page 35.

40 E.M. Clowes, 1971, *On the Wallaby Through Victoria*, London, Heinemann.

41 Of the following autobiographies written by women between the years 1898 and 1975, eight were written by nurses and welfare workers, eight by wives or daughters of prominent men; seven by writers, seven by pioneers; six by adventurers, e.g., fliers; five by feminists, including suffragists; four by singers, four by titled 'ladies'; three by journalists and broadcasters; two by missionaries, two by an artist or sculptor, two by parliamentarians; one by a teacher. Four were nineteenth-century reminiscences and the other seven were from women of sundry other backgrounds.

Betty Archdale, *Indiscretions of a Headmistress*, Sydney, 1972.

Clara Aspinall, *Three Years in Melbourne*, London, 1862.

Dame Zara Bate, *My Life and Harry*, Melbourne, 1967.

Mrs Mary Macleod Banks, *Memories Of Pioneer Days in Queensland*, London, 1931.

Daisy Bates, *The Passing Of The Aborigines: A Lifetime Spent Among The Natives of Australia*, London, 1938.

Jean Batten, *Solo Flight*, Sydney, 1934.

M.D. Berrington, *Stones Of Fire: A Woman's Experiences In Search Of Opal*, Melbourne, 1958.

Nancy Bird, *Born to Fly*, Sydney, 1961.

Dora Birtles, *North-West By North:* A Journal Of A Voyage, London, 1935 (Sydney to Singapore).

Beatrice Bligh, *Down To Earth*, Sydney, 1968 (describes the making of her garden).

Leigh Bonheur, *Hand Me Down: The Autobiography Of An Illegitimate Child*, Sydney, 1971.

Annie Bright, *A Soul's Pilgrimage*, Melbourne, 1907.

Mabel Brookes, *Memoirs*, Melbourne, 1974.

May Brookes, *Wild Flowers and Wanderings: Under The North Star And The Southern Cross*, Paris, 1925.

Lady Mary Anne Broome, *Colonial Memories*, London, 1904.

Dora Elizabeth Burchill, *Innamincka*, Melbourne, 1960.

—— *New Guinea Nurse*, Adelaide, 1967.

—— *Thursday Island Nurse*, Adelaide, 1972.

Caddie, a Sydney Barmaid: An Autobiography Written by Herself, London, 1953 (introduction by Dymphna Cusack.)

Ada Cambridge, *Thirty Years in Australia*, London, 1903.

Maie Casey, *Tides And Eddies*, London, 1966.

Ida Coffey, *Look Up And Laugh: Thirteen Years at the Mike*, Melbourne, 1945.

Ola Cohn, *Mostly Cats*, Melbourne, 1964.

Mrs J. Fairfax Conigrave, *My Reminiscences Of The Early Days: Per-*

sonal Incidents On A Sheep And Cattle Run In South Australia, Perth, 1938.

Mary Edgeworth David, *Passages Of Time: An Australian Woman 1890–1944*, Brisbane, 1975.

Miles Franklin, *Childhood At Brindabella: My First Ten Years*, Sydney, 1963.

Mary Elizabeth Fullerton, *Bark House Days*, Melbourne, 1921.

Lady Gwendolen M. Game, *A Few Words*, Sydney, 1934.

Marjorie Gartrell, *Dear Primitive: A Nurse Among The Aborigines*, Sydney, 1957.

F.S. George, (Sister Dora), *God in Bowden*, Adelaide, 1939.

—— *In The Service Of The King*, Adelaide, 1938.

Mrs Aeneas Gunn, *We Of The Never-Never*, London, 1908.

Joan Hammond, *A Voice, A Life: Autobiography*, London, 1970.

Alice Henry, *Memoirs of Alice Henry*, (edited with postscript by Nettie Palmer), Melbourne, 1944.

H.R. Higgins, *Cloud And Sunshine: An Autobiographical Sketch Of Miss H.R. Higgins*, edited by Rev. John Southey, Melbourne, 1934.

Rosamund and Florence Hill, *What We Saw in Australia*, London, 1875.

Ada A. Holman, *Memoirs Of A Premier's Wife*, Sydney, 1947.

—— *My Wanderyears: Some Jottings On a Year's Travel*, Sydney, 1913.

Mary Kent Hughes, *Matilda Waltzes With The Tommies*, Oxford, 1944.

Dame Agnes Hunt, *This Is My Life*, London, 1940.

E. Kenny, *My Battle And Victory*, London, 1955.

Ellen S. Kettle, *Gone Bush*, Sydney, 1967 (nursing sister in the Northern Territory).

Marjorie Lawrence, *Interrupted Melody: An Autobiography*, Sydney, 1949.

Bessie Harrison Lee, *One of Australia's Daughters: An Autobiography*, London, 1906.

Joan Lindsay, *Time Without Clocks*, Melbourne, 1962.

Rose Lindsay, *Ma And Pa: My Childhood Memories*, Sydney, 1963.

—— *Model Wife: My Life With Norman Lindsay*, Sydney, 1967.

Mrs Jessie Sinclair Litchfield, *Far-North Memories, Being An Account Of Ten Years Spent On The Diamond Drills, And Of Things That Happened In Those Days*, Sydney, 1930.

Dame Enid Lyons, *Among The Carrion Crows*, Adelaide, 1972.

—— *My Life: The Illustrated Autobiography*, Melbourne, 1950.

—— *The Old Laggis*, Melbourne, 1969.

—— *So We Take Comfort*, London, 1965.

Dame Nellie Melba, *Melodies and Memories*, London, 1925.

Robin Miller, *Flying Nurse*, Adelaide, 1971.

Lady Eliza Fraser Mitchell, *Three-Quarters Of A Century*, London, 1940.

Janet Mitchell, *Spoils Of Opportunity: An Autobiography*, London, 1938.

Mary Mitchell, *Uncharted Country: Aspects Of A Life Of Blindness*, Melbourne, 1963.

Louise Mack, *A Woman's Experiences In The Great War*, London, 1915.

Gertrude F. Moberlay, *Experiences Of A 'Dinki Di' RRC Nurse*, Sydney, 1933.
Gladys Moncrieff, *My Life Of Song*, Adelaide, 1971.
Dora B. Montefiore, *From A Victorian To A Modern*, London, 1927.
Nettie Palmer, *Fourteen Years: Extracts From A Private Journal, 1925–1939*, Melbourne, 1948.
Lady Ida Margaret Poore, *Recollections of an Admiral's Wife 1903 to 1916*, London, 1916.
Mrs Campbell Praed, *My Australian Girlhood: Sketches And Impressions Of Bush Life*, London, 1902.
Katharine Susannah Prichard, *Child of the Hurricane: An Autobiography*, Sydney, 1963.
Mrs David Randall, *Reminiscences*; edited by G.C. Morphett, Adelaide, Pioneers' Association, 1939.
Henry Handel Richardson, *Myself When Young*, London, 1948.
Mrs Ellis Rowan, *A Flower-Hunter in Queensland and New Zealand*, Sydney, 1898 (letters).
Mary Louise Skinner, *The Fifth Sparrow: An Autobiography*, Sydney, 1972 (nurse-novelist).
Patsy Adam-Smith, *Hear The Train Blow: An Australian Childhood*, Sydney, 1964.
Catherine Helen Spence, *An Autobiography*, Adelaide, 1910.
Lady Jean Spender, *Ambassador's Wife*, Sydney, 1968.
Mabel Stock, *The Log Of A Woman Wanderer*, London, 1923.
Jessie Street, *Truth or Repose*, Sydney, 1966.
Ellen Joy Todd, *Looking Back; Some Early Recollections*, Sydney, 1938 (journalist).
Mrs Elizabeth Jane Ward, *Out Of Weakness Made Strong, Being A Record Of The Life And Labours Of Mrs E.J. Ward*, Sydney, 1903.
Elizabeth Webb, *Stet*, Brisbane, 1950. (newspaper columnist).
A.S.H. Weigall, *My Little World*, Sydney, 1934 (her father was Governor of Tasmania 1887–93).
Mrs Myrtle Rose White, *No Roads Go By*, Sydney, 1932.
—— *Beyond the Western Rivers*, Sydney, 1955 (life on Lake Elder station, S.A.) 1940.

42 E.M. Irvine, 1936, *Certain Worthy Women*, Sydney, New Century Press.
43 M. Bassett, 1940, *The Governor's Lady. Mrs Philip Gidley King*, Melbourne, Oxford University Press.
44 For some examples of the many publications concerning women's involvement in societies, see *Torchbearers: The Woman's Christian Temperance Union of South Australia, 1886–1948*, Advertiser Printing Office, Adelaide, 1949; *Pioneer Pathways: Sixty Years of Citizenship*, W.C.T.U., Melbourne, 1948; *The Silver Years: Story of the Country Women's Association of New South Wales, 1922 to 1947*, F.H. Johnston for the Association, Sydney, 1947; M. Hines, *Fifty Years' History of the Girls' Friendly Society in South Australia*, Adelaide, 1929; *The First Fifty Years: History of the National Council of Women of Queensland*, Brisbane, 1959.
45 Davis, *op. cit.*, page 83.

46   F. Fraser and N. Palmer (eds), 1934, *Centenary Gift Book*, Melbourne, Robertson and Mullens.

47   L. Brown *et al.* (eds), 1936, *A Book of South Australia: Women in the First Hundred Years*, Adelaide, Rigby.

48   Eldershaw, *op. cit.*, page 61.

49   G. Davison, 1978, 'Sydney and the Bush: An urban context for the Australian legend' in *Historical Studies*, 71, pages 191–209.

50   M. Durack, 1976, *To Be Heirs Forever*, London, Constable, pages 18–19.

51   Davis, *op. cit.*, page 83.

52   M. Durack, 1959, *Kings in Grass Castles*, Melbourne, Corgi, page 113.

53   A Hasluck, 1955, *Portrait with Background: A Life of Georgiana Molloy*, Melbourne, Oxford University Press.

54   M. Bassett, 1954, *The Hentys: An Australian Colonial Tapestry*, Melbourne, Melbourne University Press.

55   V. Palmer, 1940, *National Portraits*, Melbourne, Melbourne University Press, pages v–vi.

56   Some examples of current publications by women about women are Marilyn Lake and Farley Kelly (eds), *Double Time*, Penguin, forthcoming 1985. See also Kathleen Fitzpatrick, *Solid Bluestone Foundations and Other Memories of a Melbourne Girlhood, 1908–1928*, Melbourne, 1983; Zelda D'Aprano, *The Becoming of A Woman*, privately published, Melbourne, 1977; Joyce Nicholson, *The Heartache of Motherhood*, Penguin, Ringwood, Victoria, 1983; Patricia Grimshaw and Lynne Strahan (eds), *The Half Open Door*, Sydney, Hale and Iremonger, 1982. Women's organisations continue to publish their histories. Recently branches of the Country Women's Association and the National Council of Women of Victoria have done so. And women continue to write biographies of women, including Mary Hoban, *Fifty-one Pieces of Wedding Cake: A Biography of Caroline Chisholm*, Lowden, Kilmore, 1973 (This book aims to include more details of human interest than might have been possible or advisable in a work submitted as a history thesis. It also aims to present 'Caroline's thinking expressed in her own language'); Sister Mary Xaverius O'Donahue, *Mother Vincent Whitty: Woman and Educator in a Masculine Society*, Melbourne University Press, Melbourne, 1972. Vida Goldstein's niece, Leslie Henderson wrote *The Goldstein Story*, Melbourne, 1973.

57   N. Mackenzie, 1963, *Women in Australia*, Melbourne, Angus and Robertson, page 10.

58   Summers, *op. cit.*

59   M. Dixson, 1976, *The Real Matilda*, Ringwood, Penguin.

60   B. Kingston, 1975, *My Wife, My Daughter and Poor Mary Ann*, Melbourne, Nelson.

61   E. Ryan and A. Conlon, 1975, *The Gentle Invaders: Australian Women at Work 1788–1974*, Melbourne, Nelson.

62   A. Curthoys, S. Eade and P. Spearritt (eds), 1975, *Women at Work*. Australian Study of Labour History, Canberra.

63   F. Gale (ed.), 1970, *Women's Role in Aboriginal Society*, Canberra, Australian Institute of Aboriginal Studies.

64   J. Mercer (ed.), 1975, *The Other Half: Women in Australian Society*, Ringwood, Penguin.

65   D. Modjeska, 1981, *Exiles at Home: Australian Women Writers 1925–1945*, Angus and Robertson, Sydney.

66   J. Burke, 1981, *Australian Women Artists 1840–1940*, Collingwood, Greenhouse Publications.

67   K. Alford, 1983, *Production or Reproduction? An Economic History of Women in Australia 1788–1850*, Melbourne, Oxford University Press; K. Reiger, *The Disenchantment of the Home*, 1985, OUP, Melbourne. See also J. Matthews, *Good and Mad Women*, 1984, Allen and Unwin, Sydney.

68   Recent publications in Australian women's history include Elizabeth Windschuttle (ed.), *Women, Class and History: Feminist Perspectives on Australia 1788–1978*, Fontana, Sydney, 1980; Margaret Bevege, Margaret James and Carmel Shute (eds), *Worth Her Salt: Women At Work In Australia*, Hale and Iremonger, Sydney, 1982; Sabine Willis (ed.), *Women, Faith and Fetes*, Dove Publications, Melbourne, 1977; Judy Mackinolty and Heather Radi (eds), *In Pursuit of Justice: Australian Women and the Law 1788–1879*, Hale and Iremonger, Sydney, 1979; Norma Grieve and Patricia Grimshaw (eds), *Australian Women: Feminist Perspectives*, MUP, Melbourne, 1981. Patricia Crawford (ed.), *Exploring Women's Past: Essays in Social History*, Sisters Publishing, Melbourne, 1983. Kay Daniels (ed.) *So Much Hard Work*, Fontana, Sydney, 1984.

   Recent Australian collections which include material on women are: chapters on Catherine Spence, Brettena Smyth and Louisa Lawson in Eric Fry (ed.), *Rebels and Radicals*, George Allen and Unwin, Sydney, 1983; chapters by Elizabeth Windschuttle and Judith Godden in Richard Kennedy (ed.), *Australian Welfare History: Critical Essays*, Macmillan, Melbourne, 1982; the chapter by Judy Mackinolty in her collection, *The Wasted Years?: Australia's Great Depression*, George Allen and Unwin, Sydney, 1981.

   Some primary source and bibliographical works are Beverley Kingston (ed.), *The World Moves Slowly: A Documentary History of Australian Women*, Cassell, Sydney, 1977; Ruth Teale (ed.), *Colonial Eve: Sources on Women in Australia, 1788–1914*, Oxford University Press, Melbourne, 1978; Kay Daniels and Mary Murnane (ed.), *Uphill All The Way: A Documentary History of Women In Australia*, University of Queensland Press, Brisbane, 1980, Janet Reed and Kathleen Oakes (eds), *Women in Australian Society, 1901–45*, Australian Government Publishing Service, Canberra, 1974; Kay Daniels, Mary Murnane and Anne Picot (eds), *Women in Australia: An Annotated Guide To Records*, 2 vols., Government Printing Office, Canberra, 1977. Margaret Bettinson and Anne Summers, (eds), *Her Story: Australian Women In Print 1788–1975*, Hale and Iremonger, Sydney, 1980.

69   Kelly-Gadol, *op. cit.*, 1977, page 809.

70   S.R. Johansson, 1976, 'Herstory, a history: A new field or another fad' in B. Carroll (ed.), *Liberating Women's History, Theoretical and Critical Essays*, Urbana, University of Illinois Press, page 401.

71   C. Smith-Rosenberg, F. DuBois, M. Buhle, T. Kaplan and G. Lerner,

1980, 'Politics and culture in women's history: A symposium' in *Feminist Studies*, 1, 26–64.

72 Davis, *op. cit.*, page 90.

73 Some Australian studies that address issues of family life and historical demography are Beverley Kingston, *My Wife, My Daughter and Poor Mary Ann*; papers on family history in *Australia 1888*, Nos. 9 and 10 (published by George Allen and Unwin as *Families in Colonial Australia*, edited by Patricia Grimshaw, Chris McConville and Ellen McEwen, 1985); Peter McDonald, *Marriage in Australia*, A.N.U. Press, Canberra, 1974; Margaret Anderson (Grellier), 'The Family', in C.T. Stannage (ed.), *A New History of Western Australia*, Perth, 1981 and '"Helpmeet for man": Women in mid-nineteenth century Western Australia', in Crawford (ed.), *Exploring Women's Past*, pages 87–128. For a critique of family history, see Kay Daniels, 'Women's history' in G. Osborne and F. Mandle (eds), *New History: Studying Australia Today*, George Allen and Unwin, Sydney, 1982, 32–50.

Some articles treating domestic violence and family breakdown: Judith Allen, 'The invention of the pathological family: An historical study of family violence in New South Wales', in Carol O'Donnell and Jan Craney (eds), *Family Violence In Australia*, Longman Cheshire, Melbourne, 1981, pages 1–27; also 'Octavius Beale reconsidered: Infanticide, baby farming and abortion in N.S.W. 1880–1939', in Sydney Labour History Group, *What Rough Beast? The State and Social Order in Australian History*, George Allen and Unwin, Sydney, 1982, pages 111–129; Hilary Golder, 'An exercise in unnecessary chivalry', in Mackinolty and Radi (eds), *In Pursuit of Justice* and Margaret James, 'Double standards in divorce', in *ibid*. Margaret James is editing a forthcoming volume on family breakdown in Australasia to be published by Croom Helm.

Articles that address the issue of pioneer women and women's social status are Judith Godden, 'A new look at pioneer women', *Hecate*, Vol. 5, No. 2; Marilyn Lake, 1981 '"Building themselves up with Aspros": Pioneer women re-assessed', *Hecate*, Vol. 7, No. 2, Patricia Grimshaw, 'Women and the family in Australian history', in E. Windschuttle (ed.), *Women, Class and History*, pages 37–52.

Some Australian studies that relate political and ideological issues to the family are Ann Curthoys, 'The sexual division of labour under capitalism', in Grieve and Grimshaw (eds), *Australian Women: Feminist Perspectives*, Bettina Cass and Heather Radi, in *ibid*., Ann Game and Rosemary Pringle, 'The making of the Australian family', 1979, *Intervention*, No. 12, Teresa Brennan, 1977, 'Women and work', 1977, *Journal of Australian Political Economy*, No. 1; Kerreen Reiger, 'Women's labour redefined: Child-bearing and the rearing advice in Australia, 1880–1930s,' in Bevege, James and Shute (eds), *Worth Her Salt*; Farley Kelly, 'Mrs Smyth and the body politic: Health reform and birth control in Melbourne', in *ibid*; Farley Kelly, 'Feminism and the family', in Eric Fry (ed.), *Rebels and Radicals*, pages 134–147; Rosemary Pringle, 1973, 'Octavius Beale and the ideology of the birthrate: The Royal Commissions of 1904 and 1905', *Refractory Girl*, No. 3, Winter, pages 19–28; Carol Bacchi 'Evolution, eugenics and women: The impact of scientific theories on attitudes towards women, 1870–1920', in E. Wind-schuttle, (ed.), *Women, Class and History*, pages 132–156. A recent major study of class, R.W. Connell and T.H. Irving, 1980, *Class Structure in Australian History*, Longman Cheshire, Melbourne, made only passing attempts to relate class, family and women's status.'

Some Australian studies of women's labour are Curthoys, Eade and Spearritt, (eds), *Women At Work*; Beverley Kingston, *My Wife, My Daughter and Poor Mary Ann*; Margaret Power 'Women and economic crises: the Great Depression and the present crisis', in Windschuttle (ed.), *Women, Class and History*; Ray Markey, 'Women and labour, 1880–1900', in *ibid*; Patricia Ranald, 'Feminism and class: the United Associations of Women and the Council of Action for Equal Pay in the Depression', in Bevege, James and Shute, *Worth Her Salt*; W. Nicol, 'Women and the trade union movement in New South Wales: 1890–1900', *Labour History*, No. 36, May 1979.

Some Australian studies that link public activism to familial concerns are Judith Allen, 'Breaking into the public sphere', in Mackinolty and Radi (eds), *In Pursuit of Justice*; 'The "feminisms" of the early women's movements, 1850–1920', *Refractory Girl*, No. 17, March 1979; Carol Bacchi, 'First-wave feminism: History's judgement', in Grieve and Grimshaw (eds), *Australian Women: Feminist Perspectives*; Anthea Hyslop, 'Agents and objects: Women and social reform in Melbourne', in Bevege, James and Shute (eds), *Worth Her Salt*, pages 230–243; Elizabeth Windschuttle, 'Women and the origins of colonial philanthropy', in Kennedy (ed.), *Australian Welfare History*, pages 10–31; Judith Godden, "The work for them, and the glory for us". Sydney women's philanthropy, 1880–1900', in *ibid.*, pages 84–102; Willis, (ed.), *Women: Faith and Fetes*; Marian Simms, 1979, 'Conservative feminism in Australia: A case study of feminist ideology', *Women's Studies: International Quarterly*, Autumn, pages 305–318.

Some Australian studies of deviancy are Raelene Davidson, '"As good a bloody woman as any other woman,": Prostitutes in Western Australia, 1895–1939', in Crawford (ed.), *Exploring Women's Past*; R. Evans, 'Soiled doves—Prostitution and society in colonial Queensland', *Hecate*, Vol. 1, July 1975; Hilary Golder and Judith Allen, 'Prostitution in New South Wales 1870–1932', *Refractory Girl*, Nos. 18/19, December 1979—January 1980; Mary Murnane and Kay Daniels, 'Prostitutes and purveyors of disease—Venereal disease legislation in Tasmania 1868–1945', *Hecate*, Vol. 5, 1979.

74 A. Gordon, M. Buhle and N. Dye, 1976, 'The problem of women's history' in B. Carroll (ed.), *op. cit.*

Seeing Women in the Landscape: Alternative Views of the World Around Us

1 C.O. Sauer, 1961, 'Sedentary and mobile bents in earliest societies' in S.L. Washburn (ed.), *Social Life of Early Man*, Chicago, Aldine.

2 J. Monk and S. Hanson, 1982, 'On not excluding half of the human in

human geography', *Professional Geographer* 34 No. 1, pages 11–23.

3 J. Tivers, 1978, 'How the other half lives: the geographical study of women', *Area*, 10, page 305.

4 F. Gale and J. Wundersitz, 1982, *Adelaide Aborigines: a Case Study of Urban Life 1966-1981*, Canberra, Development Studies Centre, Australian National University.

5 R. Wild, 1983, 'Black Adelaide: Review of Fay Gale and Joy Wundersitz, *Adelaide Aborigines: a Case Study of Urban Life 1966–1981*,' *Australian Book Review*, May, page 26.

6 W. Zelinsky, J. Monk and S. Hanson, 1983, 'Women and geography: a review and prospectus', *Progress in Human Geography*, 6, pages 317–366.

7 I. Manning, 1978, *The Journey to Work*, Sydney, George Allen and Unwin.

8 G.R. Wekerle, 1980, 'Women in the urban environment', *Signs*, Spring Supplement, pages S188–214.

9 Manning, *op. cit.*

10 *Ibid.*, page 141.

11 B. Holcomb, 1982, 'Women's roles in distressing and revitalizing cities', *Women and Environments*, Summer 5, pages 11–12.

12 C. Forster, 1983, 'Spatial organisation and local employment rates, metropolitan Adelaide: significant issue or spatial fetish?', *Australian Geographical Studies* Vol. 21, No. 1, pages 33–48.

13 Wekerle, *op. cit.*, page 206.

14 D. Bell, 1983, 'Consulting with women' in F. Gale (ed.), *We are Bosses Ourselves: the Status and Role of Aboriginal Women Today*, Canberra, Australian Institute of Aboriginal Studies, page 24.

15 C.H. Berndt, 1970, 'Digging sticks and spears or, the two-sex model' in F. Gale (ed.), *Women's Role in Aboriginal Society*, Canberra, Australian Institute of Aboriginal Studies.

16 C.H. Berndt, 1950, 'Women's changing ceremonies in northern Australia', *L'Homme*, 1, pages 1–87.

17 C.H. Berndt, 1960, 'Women and the "secret life"', in C.H. and R.M. Berndt (eds), *Aboriginal Man in Australia*, Sydney, Angus and Robertson.

18 J.C. Goodale, 1971, *Tiwi Wives*, Seattle, University of Washington Press.

19 D. Bell, 1982, *Aboriginal Women and the Religious Experience*, Australian Association for the Study of Religions, Bedford Park, South Australia, South Australian College of Advanced Education.

20 D. Bell, 1983, *Daughters of the Dreaming*, Melbourne, McPhee Gribble.

21 N. Ilyatjari, 1983, 'Women and land rights: the Pitjatjantjara land claims', in F. Gale (ed.), *We are Bosses Ourselves: the Status and Role of Aboriginal Women Today*, Canberra, Australian Institute of Aboriginal Studies.

22 E. McDinny and A. Isaac, 1983, 'Borroloola community and land claims', in F. Gale (ed.), *ibid.*

23 J. Jacobs, 1983, *Aboriginal Land Rights in Port Augusta*, MA thesis Department of Geography, University of Adelaide.

Rewards for Women's Work

1   M. Edwards, 1980, 'Economics of home activities', *Australian Journal of Social Issues*, Vol. 15, No. 1 (February), pages 5–16.
2   A. Oakley, 1974, *The Sociology of Housework*, Bath, Martin Robertson.
3   A. Oakley, 1976, *Housewife*, London, Penguin.
4   B. Kingston, 1975, *My Wife, My Daughter and Poor Mary Ann*, Melbourne, Nelson.
5   P. Apps, 1975, *Child Care in the Production-Consumption Economy*, Melbourne, Victorian Council of Social Service.
6   K. Alford, 1984, *Production or Reproduction? An Economic History of Women in Australia 1788–1850*, Melbourne, Oxford University Press.
7   Edwards, *op. cit.*
8   P. Apps, 1981, *A Theory of Inequality and Taxation*, Cambridge University Press.
9   M. Thornton, 1975, 'Women's labour' in A. Curthoys, S. Eade & P. Spearitt (eds), *Women at Work*, Canberra, Australian Society for the Study of Labour History, pages 96–108.
10 A. Game & R. Pringle, 1983, *Gender at Work*, Sydney, George Allen & Unwin.
11 C. Baldock, 1983, 'Public policies and the paid work of women', in C. Baldock, and B. Cass (eds), *Women, Social Welfare and the State*, Sydney, George Allen and Unwin, pages 20–53.
12 D. Deacon, 1982, 'Political arithmetic? Women and the census 1861–1891', paper presented at the Conference of the Sociological Association of Australia and New Zealand, University of New South Wales.
13 F.L. Jones, 1983, 'Is it true what they said about women? The census 1801–1911 and women in the economy', paper prepared for seminar in Department of Sociology, Australian National University.
14 D. Tait, 1983, 'Families in Australian official statistics', paper presented at Conference of the Sociological Association of Australia and New Zealand, Melbourne College of Advanced Education.
15 Deacon, *op. cit.*, page 12.
16 *Ibid.*
17 Tait, *op. cit.*
18 J. Hagan, 1981, *The History of the ACTU*, Melbourne, Longman Cheshire.
19 G. Anderson, 1939, 'Industrial tribunals and standards of living', in F.W. Eggleston (ed.), *Australian Standards of Living*, Melbourne, Melbourne University Press, pages 65–112.
20 S. Tiffin, 1982, 'In pursuit of reluctant parents', in Sydney Labour History Group, *What Rough Beast? The State and Social Order in Australian History*, Sydney, George Allen and Unwin, pages 130–150.
21 J. Roe, 1975, 'Social policy and the permanent poor', *in* E.L. Wheelwright and K. Buckley (eds), *Essay in the Political Economy of Australian Capitalism*, Vol. 1, Sydney, ANZ Book Co., pages 130–152.
22 B. Dickey, 1980, *No Charity There: A Short History of Social Welfare*

in Australia, Melbourne, Nelson.

23 A. O'Brien, 1979, 'Left in the lurch: Deserted wives in New South Wales at the turn of the century', in J. Mackinolty and H. Radi (eds), *In Pursuit of Justice: Australian Women and the Law 1788–1979*, Sydney, Hale and Iremonger, pages 96–105.

24 J. Roe, 1983, 'The end is where we start from: Women and welfare since 1901', *in* Baldock and Cass, *op. cit.*, pages 1–19.

25 H.B. Higgins, 1922, *A New Province for Law and Order*, Sydney, Workers' Educational Association.

26 P.G. Macarthy, 1967, 'Labour and the living wage 1896–1910', *Australian Journal of Politics and History*, XIII (April), pages 67–89.

27 Higgins, *op. cit.*

28 E. Ryan and A. Conlon, 1975, *The Gentle Invaders: Australian Women at Work 1788–1974*, Melbourne, Nelson.

29 Tait, *op. cit.*, page 6.

30 Commonwealth Arbitration Court, 1937, *Basic Wage Inquiry*, Melbourne, Australian Government Publishing Service.

31 Kingston, *op. cit.*

32 Ryan and Conlon, *op. cit.*

33 P. Spearitt, 1975, 'Women in Sydney factories, c. 1920–50', in Curthoys, Eade and Spearitt (eds) *op. cit.* pages 31–46.

34 Knibbs, 1911.

35 M. Ireland, 1928, *A Survey of Women in Industry*, Victoria, Canberra, Commonwealth Department of Health.

36 M. Heagney, 1935, *Are Women Taking Men's Jobs?*, Melbourne, Milton and Veitch.

37 Royal Commission on the Basic Wage, 1920, *Report*, Melbourne, Victorian Government Printer.

38 A.B. Piddington, 1921, *The Next Step: A Family Basic Income*, London, Macmillan.

39 E. Rathbone, 1924, *The Disinherited Family: A Plea for the Endowment of the Family*, London, Edward Arnold.

40 E. Rathbone, 1940, *The Case for Family Allowances*, Harmondsworth, Penguin.

41 H. Land, 1980, 'The family wage', *Feminist Review*, 6, pages 55–78.

42 J. Street, 1966, *Truth or Repose*, Sydney, Australasian Book Society.

43 Tait, *op. cit.*, page 19.

44 Royal Commission on the Basic Wage, *op. cit.*

45 Piddington, *op. cit.*

46 G. Melville, 1954, 'Fifty years of the Labor Women's Central Organising Committee', in *Golden Jubilee Souvenir of the Labor Women's Central Organising Committee, 1904–1954*, Sydney, Australian Labor Party, pages 6–8.

47 Street, *op. cit.*

48 M. Muscio and J. Curtin, 1929, *Minority Report* of the Royal Commission on Child Endowment or Family Allowances, Canberra, Government Printer.

49 Heagney, *op. cit.*

50 K. Fitzpatrick, 1943, 'Introduction', in M. Bayne (ed.) *Australian*

Women at War, Melbourne Left Book Club.

51   Royal Commission on the Basic Wage, *op. cit.*

52   New South Wales Industrial Commission, 1927, 'Standard of living—living wage', in *NSW Industrial Gazette*, No. 6, Department of Labour and Industry, Sydney, New South Wales Government Printer.

53   P. Sekuless, 1978, *Jessie Street: A Rewarding but Unrewarded Life*, St Lucia, Queensland University Press.

54   Heagney, *op. cit.*

55   Street, *op. cit.*

56   Bayne, *op. cit.*

57   Street, *op. cit.*

58   Sekuless, *op. cit.*

59   Heagney, *op. cit.*, page 106.

60   Street, *op. cit.*, page 128.

61   M. Gaudron and M. Bosworth, 1979, 'Equal pay?', in Mackinolty and Radi (eds), *op. cit.*, pages 161–69.

62   Hagan, *op. cit.*

63   *Ibid.*, page 403.

64   Industrial Arbitration Service, Current Review, 1974, *National Wage Case*, Sydney, Law Book Company, page 46.

65   R.I. Downing, 1975, *Social Reconstruction: Social Welfare and Self-Reliance*, George Judah Cohen Memorial Lecture, 1974, Sydney, Sydney University Press.

66   R.F. Henderson *et al.*, 1970, *People in Poverty: A Melbourne Survey*, Melbourne, Cheshire.

67   Gaudron and Bosworth, *op. cit.*

68   C. Larmour, 1975, 'Women's wages and the WEB', in Curthoys, Eade and Spearitt (eds) *op. cit.*, pages 47–58.

69   R. Downing, *et al.*, 1964, *Taxation in Australia: Agenda for Reform*, Melbourne, Melbourne University Press.

70   R.J.A. Harper, 1972, 'Family assistance and the redistribution of income', *Australian Journal of Social Issues*, Vol. 7, No. 3, pages 177–89.

71   Taxation Review Committee (Asprey), 1975, *Full Report*, Canberra, Australian Government Publishing Service.

72   National Population Inquiry, 1978, *Population and Australia: Recent Demographic Trends and their Implications*, Canberra, Australian Government Publishing Service.

73   C. Keens and B. Cass, 1983, 'Fiscal welfare.' Some aspects of Australian tax policy', in A. Graycar (ed.), *Retreat from the Welfare State*, Sydney, George Allen and Unwin, pages 123–48.

74   M. Edwards, 1982, 'Families and taxation: Some current issues', *Tax Matters*, newsletter of the Taxation Institute Research and Education Trust, No. 4, January, pages 1–4.

75   B. Cass, C. Keens and G. Moller, 1981, 'Family policy Halloween: Family allowances: trick or treat?', *Australian Quarterly*, Vol. 53, No. 1, Autumn, pages 56–73.

76   M. Power, 1974, 'The wages of sex', *Australian Quarterly*, 46, pages 2–14.

77   M. Power, 1975, 'Women's work is never done by men—a socio-economic model of sex-typing in occupations', *Journal of Industrial Relations*, 17(3), September, pages 225–239.

78   M. Power, 1976, 'Cast-off jobs: women, migrants, blacks may apply', *Refractory Girl*, pages 27–31.

79   M. Power, 1980, 'Women and economic crises: The Great Depression and the present', in E. Windschuttle (ed.), *Women, Class and History*, Melbourne, Fontana Collins, pages 492–513.

80   *Ibid.*, page 496.

81   Heagney, *op. cit.*

82   Power, 1980, *op. cit.*, page 501.

83   R. Broomhill, 1978, *Unemployed Workers: A Social History of the Great Depression in Adelaide*, St Lucia, University of Queensland Press.

84   P. Travers, 1983, *Unemployment and Life History: A Pilot Study*, SWRC Reports and Proceedings No. 30, Sydney, Social Welfare Research Centre, University of New South Wales.

85   M. Jahoda, P.F. Lazarsfeld and H. Zeisel, 1933 *Marienthal: The Sociography of an Unemployed Community*, Chicago, Aldine.

86   P. Stricker and P. Sheehan, 1981, *Hidden Unemployment: The Australian Experience*, Melbourne, Institute of Applied Economic and Social Research, University of Melbourne.

87   Technical Committee for the National Economic Summit Conference, 1983, *Information Paper on the Economy*, Canberra, Australian Government Publishing Service.

88   B. Cass, 1981, *Unemployment and the Family*, SWRC Reports and Proceedings No. 7, Sydney, Social Welfare Research Centre, University of New South Wales.

89   I. Bruegel, 1983, 'Women's employment, legislation and the labour market', in J. Lewis (ed.), *Women's Welfare, Women's Rights*, London, Croom Helm, pages 130–69.

90   M. Rein, 1980, 'Women and work—the incomplete revolution', *Australian Economic Review*, 3rd Quarter, pages 11–17.

91   E. Wilson, 1982, 'Women, the community and the family', in A. Walker (ed.), *Community Care: The Family, the State and Social Policy*, Oxford, Blackwell and Martin Robertson, pages 40–55.

92   D. Kinnear and A. Graycar, 1983 'Non-institutional care of elderly people', in A. Graycar (ed.), *op. cit.*, pages 74–88.

93   C. Baldock, 1983, 'Volunteer work as work: Some theoretical considerations', in Baldock, and Cass, (eds), *op. cit.*, pages 279–97.

94   Z. Eisenstein, 1982, 'The sexual policies of the new right: Understanding the crisis of liberalism for the 1980s', *Signs*, Vol. 7, No. 3 (Spring), pages 567–88.

95   R. Poole, 1983, 'Markets and motherhood: the advent of the new right', in A. Burns, G. Bottomly and P. Jools (eds), *The Family in the Modern World*, Sydney, George Allen and Unwin, pages 103–20.

96   H. Land, 1976, 'Women: supporters or supported?', in D.L. Barker and S. Allen (eds), *Sexual Divisions and Society: Process and Change*, London, Tavistock, pages 108–32.

97   K. Waerness, 1978, 'The invisible welfare state: Women's work at home', *Acta Sociologica*, Vol. 21, supplement on the Nordic Welfare State, pages 193–207.

98   Edwards, 1980, *op. cit.*

99   J. Finch and D. Groves, 1980, 'Community care and the family: A case for equal opportunities', *Journal of Social Policy*, Vol. 9 (4), pages 487–511.

100   D. Broom, 1983, 'In sickness and in health', in C. Baldock and B. Cass (eds), *op. cit.*, pages 262–78.

101   Social Welfare Policy Secretariat, 1981, *Report on Poverty Measurement*, Canberra, Australian Government Publishing Service.

102   J. Cox, 1982, 'Equivalent income distributions', *Social Security Journal* (December), pages 22–33.

103   Commission of Inquiry into Poverty, 1975, *First Main Report: Poverty in Australia*, Canberra, Australian Government Publishing Service.

104   J. Cox, 1982, Letter to author detailing data on incidence of poverty in Australia, 1978–79.

105   *Ibid.*

106   A. Harding, 1982, 'Unequal burdens: Personal income tax changes since 1975', *Current Affairs Bulletin* (July).

Individual Equity and Social Policy

1   R.G. Lipsey, 1963, *Introduction to Positive Economics*, London, Weidenfeld and Nicolson.

2   J.K. Galbraith, 1963, *Economics and the Public Purpose*, Boston, Houghton Mifflin; 1980, 'The higher economic purpose of women' in *Annals of an Abiding Liberal*, London, Andre Deutsch.

3   P. Apps, 1981, *A Theory of Inequality and Taxation*, Cambridge, Cambridge University Press.

4   M. Edwards, 1981, *Financial Arrangements Within Families*, National Women's Advisory Council, Canberra; *The Income Unit and the Australian Tax and Social Security Systems*, PhD thesis, published by Institute of Family Studies, Melbourne, 1984.

5   K. Lancaster,1975, 'The theory of household behaviour—some foundations', in *Annals of Economic and Social Measurement*, Vol. 4, No. 1.

6   J.K. Galbraith, 1980, *op. cit.*

7   M. Edwards, *op. cit.*

8   M. Young, 1976, 'Housekeeping money' in F. Williams (ed.), *Why the Poor Pay More*, Macmillan, London.

9   H. Land, 1977, 'Social security and the division of unpaid work in the home and paid employment in the labour market' in *Department of Health and Social Security Research Paper*, London, Her Majesty's Stationery Office.

10   A. Gray, 1979, 'The working class family as an economic unit', *Sociological Review Monograph No. 8*, University of Keele.

11   A.H. Munnel, 1980, 'The couple versus the individual under the federal personal income tax' in Aaron, Henry and Boskin, *The Economics of Taxation*, Washington DC, The Brookings Institution.

12 M. Edwards, 1983, *'The income unit in the social security system: Explanation and evaluation'*, 53rd ANZAAS Congress, Perth, May.
13 M. Edwards, 1983, *The Individual as the Income Unit for Social Security Policy; An Exploration*, ANZAAS Congress, Perth, May.
14 M. Edwards, 1983, ANZAAS Congress paper, *ibid.*
15 I. Garfinkel, 1982, *The Role of Child Support in Antipoverty Policy*, discussion paper, Institute for Research on Poverty, Madison, University of Wisconsin.
16 G. Becker, 1965, 'A theory of the allocation of June', *Economic Journal*, Vol. 80, No. 9.

The Gender of Bureaucracy

1 S. Ryan and G. Evans, 1984, *Affirmative Action for Women: A Policy Discussion Paper*, Canberra, Australian Government Publishing Service.
2 L. Lynch, 1984, 'Bureaucratic feminisms: Bossism and beige suits' in *Refractory Girl*, 27 (May).
3 E. Ryan and A. Conlon, 1975, *The Gentle Invaders*, Melbourne, Nelson.
4 H. Eisenstein, 1984, *Contemporary Feminist Thought*, London and Sydney, George Allen and Unwin.
5 'O God our (mother and) father', 1983 in *Time*, 24 October.
6 Eisenstein, *op. cit.*, pages 45ff.
7 S. Franzway and J. Lowe, 1978, 'Sex role theory: Political cul-de-sac? in *Refractory Girl*, 16.
8 J. Blackburn, 1984, 'Schooling and injustice for girls' in Dorothy H. Broom (ed.), *Unfinished Business: Social Justice for Women in Australia*, Sydney, George Allen and Unwin.
9 *Ibid.*, page 18.
10 M. McMurchy, M. Oliver and J. Thornley, 1983, *For Love or Money*, Ringwood, Penguin Books.
11 J.B. Miller, 1976, *Towards a New Psychology of Women*, Boston, Beacon Press.
12 *Ibid.*, page 38.
13 C.A. MacKinnon, 1982, 'Feminism, Marxism, method and the state: An agenda for theory' in *Feminist Theory: A Critique of Ideology*, Nannerl O. Keohane *et al.* (eds) Chicago, University of Chicago Press; 'Feminism, Marxism, method and the state: Toward feminist jurisprudence' in *Signs*, 1983, 8.
14 *Ibid.*, 1983, page 635.
15 R. Pringle and A. Game, 1983, 'From here to fraternity: Women and the Hawke government', *Scarlet Woman*, 17 (Spring), page 5.
16 MacKinnon, *op. cit.*, 1983, page 644.
17 A. Game and R. Pringle, 1983, *Gender at Work*, Sydney, George Allen and Unwin.
18 *Ibid.*, page 14.
19 *Ibid.*, pages 21, 22.
20 A. Game and R. Pringle, 1984, 'Production and consumption: Public

versus private' in Broom, *op. cit.*, page 76.

21 Z.R. Eisenstein, 1981, *The Radical Future of Liberal Feminism*, New York, Longman.

22 H.J. McCloskey, 1983, 'Social justice versus discrimination and affirmative action', Festival Philosophy Lecture, Wollongong University, October.

23 *Ibid.*, page 2.

24 C. Pateman, 1981, 'The concept of equity' in Patrick N. Troy (ed.), *A Just Society? Essays on Equity in Australia*, Sydney, George Allen and Unwin.

25 McCloskey, *op. cit.*, page 19.

26 Anti-Discrimination Board of New South Wales, 1982, 1983, 1984, *Annual Report*; A. Ziller, 1981, *Affirmative Action Handbook*, Sydney, Review of New South Wales Government Administration; 'Affirmative action in public employment', in G. Rowe (ed.), *Anti-Discrimination Law in Practice* (forthcoming); P. Wilenski, 1977, *Directions for Change: An Interim Report*, Sydney Review of New South Wales Government Administration; 1982, *Unfinished Agenda: A Further Report*, Sydney, Review of New South Wales Government Administration.

27 S. Tiffin, 1984, 'Against the odds: Fighting sexual harassment under anti-discrimination legislation', in *Refractory Girl*, 27.

28 C. Burton, 1983, *Documenting the Power Structure in Academic Institutions*, paper, Equal Employment Opportunity and Affirmative Action conference, 27–28 September, Macquarie University.

29 N. Chodorow, 1978, *The Reproduction of Mothering: Psychoanalysis and the Sociology of Gender*, Berkeley, University of California Press.

30 R.W. Connell, 1983, 'Men's bodies' in *Which Way Is Up? Essays on Class, Sex and Culture*, Sydney, George Allen and Unwin.

31 Pringle and Game, *op. cit.*, page 9.

In Pursuit of Equality: Women and Legal Thought 1788–1984

1 For an outline of these Acts and their operation, see for example Chris Ronalds, 1979, *Anti-Discrimination Legislation in Australia*, Butterworth, Sydney; Helen Mills, 1981, 'Equal opportunities' in *The Dunstan Decade: Social Democracy at State Level*, A. Parkin and A. Patience, (eds) Longman Cheshire, Melbourne, page 115; Anne Riches, 1979, 'The Family Law Act' in *In Pursuit of Justice: Australian Women and the Law 1788–1979*, J. Mackinolty and H. Radi (eds), 1982, George Allen and Unwin, Sydney, page 212; Jocelynne A. Scutt, 1982, 'Principle v., practice: Defining "equality" in family property division on divorce', *Australian Law Journal*, volume 57, number 3, page 143.

2 See, for example Anne Summers, 1975, *Damned Whores and God's Police*, Penguin, Ringwood, Victoria; Charlotte J. Macdonald, 1983, 'Ellen Silk and her sisters: Female emigration to the New World' in *Men's Power, Women's Resistance—The Sexual Dynamics of History*, London Feminist History Group, Pluto Press, London, page 66.

3 For a more detailed outline of discrimination against women in this area in this era, see Jocelynne A. Scutt, 1983, *Even in the Best of Homes: Violence in the Family*, Ringwood, Penguin, particularly Chapter 1; also

Jocelynne A. Scutt and Di Graham, 1984, *For Richer, For Poorer: Money, Marriage and Property Rights*, Ringwood, Penguin, particularly Chapters 3–5.

4   For discussion and analysis of the relevant cases, see Jocelynne A. Scutt, 1985, 'Sexism in Legal Language', *Australian Law Journal*, volume 59, number 3.

5   See Re Kitson (1920), S.A.L.R. 230.

6   Chorlton v. Lings (1868) 4 L.R. C.C.R. 374, pages 388–389. (Emphasis added.)

7   Reforms to the law of child custody are discussed more fully in Jocelynne A. Scutt, 1983, *Even in the Best of Homes: Violence in the Family*, Ringwood, Penguin, Chapter 1; see also Caroline Norton, 1854, reprinted 1982, *Caroline Norton's Defense: English Laws for Women in the Nineteenth Century*, Chicago, Academy.

8   See C.H. Currey, 1955, 'The law of marriage and divorce in New South Wales (1788–1858)', *Royal Australian Historical Society Journal and Proceedings*, volume 41, number 3, page 97; John Mackinolty, 1979, 'The Married Women's Property Acts' in *In Pursuit of Justice: Australian Women and the Law 1788–1979*, J. Mackinolty and H. Radi (eds), George Allen and Unwin, Sydney, page 74.

9   That is, they had a legal right to own property if they could earn money to buy it, or if a long-lost aunt or uncle suddenly died, leaving everything to an unexpectant woman.

10 See R.H. Graveson and F.R. Crane, 1957, *A Century of Family Law 1857–1957*, London, Sweet and Maxwell.

11 See Judith Mackinolty, 1979, 'To stay or to go—sacking married women teachers' in J. Mackinolty and H. Radi, *In Pursuit of Justice: Australian Women and the Law 1788–1979*, George Allen and Unwin, Sydney, page 140; generally Jocelynne A. Scutt, 1983, 'Legislating for the right to be equal: women, the law and social policy' in *Women, Social Welfare and the State*, Cora V. Baldock and Bettina Cass (eds), George Allen and Unwin, Sydney, page 223.

12 See *New South Wales Receptionist Course Manual*, Public Service Board, used as a teaching tool until withdrawn in August 1978.

13 In June 1984 the federal government published a Green Paper on *Affirmative Action* (AGPS, Canberra) proposing a voluntary pilot programme to involve private corporations, to be reviewed after eighteen months with the subsequent legislation to be based on experience gleaned from the pilot programme. At the same time, legislation went through the federal parliament introducing changes to the Public Service Act to provide for affirmative action to take place within the service (that is, in relation to government employees).

14 Lord Aikin, S.C. In McAlister v. Stevenson 48 T.L.R. 494, page 500 (the 'snail in the bottle' case, sometimes known and Donohogue v. Stevenson).

15 O'Callaghan v. Loder and the Commissioner for Main Roads, unreported Equal Opportunity Tribunal, New South Wales, Sydney 30 September 1983, page 1.

16 *Ibid*, page 3.

17 *Ibid*.

18   *Ibid.*
19   See, for example, A Guild Office Clerk in *Life as We have Known It by Co-operative Working Women*, 1977 edition, Margaret Llewelyn Davies, (ed.), London, Virago, page 76; also excerpts in Janet Horowitz Murray, 1984, *Strong-Minded Women and Other Lost Voices from 19th-Century England* Harmondsworth, Penguin, pages 327ff.
20   See, for example, Phyllis Chesler, 1972, *Women and Madness*, New York, Doubleday; Nancy Chodorow, 1978, *The Reproduction of Mothering: Psychoanalysis and the Sociology of Gender*, Berkeley, University of California Press; Vivian Gornick and Barbara K. Moran, (eds) 1972, *Woman in Sexist Society: Studies in Power and Powerlessness*, New York, Signet Books.
21   The work of the Sydney Women's Electoral Lobby Family Law Group has been to the fore in this regard. See for example *Discussion Paper on Equal Rights to Marital Assets*, 1980, Sydney WEL; Di Graham and Jocelynne A. Scutt, 1982, 'A Room of Their Own', *Womanspeak*, volume 7, Number 1 (May/June) page 8; Jocelynne A. Scutt, 1982, 'Land rights for women: Taking the offensive against the patriarchy in the fight for equal marital property rights, in *Papers from the Second National Women's Refuge Conference*, Melbourne.
22   See discussion Jocelynne A. Scutt, 1982, 'Principle v. practice: Defining "equality" in family property division on divorce', *Australian Law Journal*, volume 57, number 3, page 143.
23   See generally Jocelynne A. Scutt and Di Graham, 1984, *For Richer, For Poorer: Money, Marriage and Property Rights*, Ringwood, Penguin.
24   See generally Jocelynne A. Scutt (ed.) 1980, *Rape Law Reform*, Australian Institute of Criminology, ACT, Canberra.
25   Carol Treloar, 1980, 'The politics of rape—a politician's perspective' in *Rape Law Reform*, Jocelynne A. Scutt (ed.), Australian Institute of Criminology, Canberra, pages 191 and 193. The immediately following quotation comes from the same source on pages 195–196.
26   For a full discussion of the difficulties and dangers inherent in the provision, see Jocelynne A. Scutt, 1977, 'Consent in rape: the problem of the marriage contract', *Monash University Law Review*, volume 3, page 255.
27   For a full discussion of these issues, see Jocelynne A. Scutt, 1977, 'Consent in rape: the problem of the marriage contract', *Monash University Law Review*, volume 3, page 255; Jocelynne A. Scutt, 1982, 'To love, honour and rape with impunity: wife as victim of rape and the criminal law' in *The Victim in International Perspective*, Hans Joachim Sneider, ed., Walter de Gruyter, Berlin-New York, page 423; Jocelynne A. Scutt, 1983, *Even in the Best of Homes: Violence in the Family*, Penguin, Ringwood, Chapter 6.
28   (1891) 1 Q.B. 671.
29   WEL Sydney records.
30   See discussion of the legal position in Jocelynne A. Scutt, 1983, *Even in the Best of Homes: Violence in the Family*, Penguin, Ringwood, Chapters 5, 9 and 10.
31   This was stated by a police officer at a conference in Albury, New South Wales in 1984 which the author attended to present a paper on criminal assault at home. Sadly, the officer was female.